# Exmouth's ROLLE

## – educating students and teachers from 1870 to 2008

**Daphne Joyce Barnes-Phillips, MA (Ed), BA (Hons)**

## Copyright details

Published by: Corridor Press
19 Portland Avenue
Exmouth
Devon
EX8 2BS
England
Tel: (+44) 01395 263 494
**E-mail:** ***corridorpress@yahoo.co.uk***
**Website:** ***www.corridorpress.co.uk***



Printed and bound in Great Britain by: Imprint Digital
Seychelles Farm
Upton Pyne
Exeter
EX8 5HY
Tel: (+44) 01392 851550
E-mail: *info@imprintdigital.com*
Website: *www.imprintdigital.com*

ISBN: 978 – 1 – 897715 – 031

*Spring Gardens*

*Publications*

## Dedication

This book is dedicated
to all those who have been associated
with the Rolle campus in Exmouth
since its days as Southlands Girls' School,
through its inception as
an Emergency Teacher Training College
in the post-World War II years
to its time as a College of Education,
when it was known as Rolle College.

It is also dedicated to those
of the Polytechnic South West
and the University of Plymouth
who have more recently worked
and/or studied
on the Rolle campus
and to those who will continue
to be educated on this site
in the Rolle Centre.

More particularly, it is dedicated
to the people of Exmouth
who have helped create
Rolle's ambience,
giving it such a special feel
that all who visited it
could sense its value
to the education
of the young and not-so-young.

## Acknowledgements to:

Those who have contributed their own memories or those of deceased family members, whether by email or orally. They are mentioned on page 5 under the heading “Contributors”.

Joan Barraclough, Jackie Bryan, Jenny Budden, Edna Ireland, Deirdre Jennings and Pete & Ann Wilson, who, with their local connections, spread the word and put me in touch with many of the contributors.

Mike Cole, Sheila Davis, Linda Meikle and Margery Wonnacott who loaned me their scrapbooks and collections of Rolle memorabilia.

Geoff Perriam, a volunteer at Exmouth Museum, who directed me to the relevant material kept there.

The Staff of Devon Heritage Centre (known as Devon Record Office and West Country Studies Library until 17th September 2012) who maintain collections of letters, especially the Dartington College collection.

The Staff of Exmouth Library who maintain Street Directories and ephemera, such as Rolle College prospectuses and end-of-term Ball tickets – which have all added to my understanding of what has constituted the ROLLE Experience throughout its lifetime.

The Staff of the University of Reading Special Collections section at the Museum of English Rural Life for maintaining its annual Calendars.

Those who have submitted collections of letters (such as those of William Hale White), Street Directories or other items to the Internet; and Websites, such as *Genes Reunited* and *FreeBMD*, that have made genealogical material freely available; also the British Newspaper archive section of *Findmypast*.

As usual, it is my husband, Jim Barnes-Phillips, who has helped the most in the practical production of this book. He has designed the cover; scanned in photographs from original albums, taken others; helped with research and transcribing of oral contributions and been a great support and encouragement since I embarked upon this project.

## Contributors

Names are given as when the person was associated with the Southlands/Rolle site. Where their memories span more than one decade, the one chosen is that from which the majority of them originate.

### 1910s and 1920s

| | |
|---|---|
| David re Amos holidays | (1912) |
| Emmy Eustace re Myra | (1921–1923) |
| Betty Nottingham | (1926 letters) |

### 1930s

| | |
|---|---|
| Sela re Martin Sisters | (1923–1937) |
| Elizabeth Maycock | (1934–1942) |
| Esmé Ware | (1929–1937) |

### 1940s

| | | | |
|---|---|---|---|
| Marguerite Baker | (1946–1954) | Jeanne Boone | (1948–1950) |
| Hugh Jones re Ingrid | (1948–1989) | Freda Lovesey | (1939–1942) |
| Eileen Stafford | (1948–1950) | Sheila Stocken | (1939–1942) |

### 1950s

| | | | |
|---|---|---|---|
| Jean Halton | (1958–1960) | Romola Pascoe | (1949–1951) |
| Betty Thomas | (1951–1954) | Margery Wonnacott | (1950–1952) |

### 1960s

| | | | |
|---|---|---|---|
| Judith Atkinson | (1962–1965) | Daphne Barnes | (1963–1966) |
| M Beresford-Williams | (1960–1964) | Mike Cole | (1967–1970) |
| Chris Humphries | (1966–1969) | Linden Kilbane | (1967–1970) |
| Don Leech | (1966–1986) | Doris Spicer | (1959–1972) |

### 1970s

| | | | |
|---|---|---|---|
| Rosemary Earl | (1970–1974) | Dave Gwilliam | (1972–1975) |
| Ken Hazel | (1970–1974) | Felicity Kirton | (1971–1973) |
| Maggie Morbey | (1968–1971) | Ruth Rockett | (1967–1981) |

### 1980s

| | | | |
|---|---|---|---|
| David Keep | (1971–1989) | Keith Waddams | (1962–1988) |

### 1990s

| | | | |
|---|---|---|---|
| Nicholas Goddard | (1990–96 & 1974) | Joseph Lewis | (1996–2001) |
| Mike Newby | (1989–2004) | Debbie Winship | (1989–1992) |

### 2000s

| | | | |
|---|---|---|---|
| Andrew Bailey | (2003–06, 1969–1974) | Maureen White | (2011) |

## Table of Contents

## Photographs loaned by:

David Amos
Romola Harper
David Keep
Elizabeth Maycock
Eileen Stafford
Peter Trudgill
Daphne Barnes-Phillips
Ken & Maggie Hazel
Freda Lovesey
Paul Norris
Jill Thomas
Maureen White
Emmy Eustace
Hugh Jones
Jeanne Mallett
Betty Pascoe
Esmé Thomson
Debbie Winship

## Photographs taken by:

Daphne Barnes
John McGrouther
Rose Barnes
Mike Newby
Jim Barnes-Phillips
Janice Proctor

## Main characters associated with the site

| | | |
|---|---|---|
| Fairfield Ladies Sch. Principals 1870–1901 | Mrs Jane James<br>Miss Mary E James | 1870–1882 then joint with daughter 1882–1901 |
| Southlands School Principals 1881–1898 | Miss Mary S Chignell<br>Miss Jane E Stephens | School for girls on High School system. Jane died 1899 & Mary 1928 |
| Southlands School Principals Jan. 1899 until Dec. 1916 | Miss Jessie Vinter MA<br>Miss Fanny Vinter MA | Girton College, Cambs. Jessie died 1951 & Fanny 1958 |
| Southlands School Head Mistress | Miss Anstice Rose A Fearon | Joint with Vinters 1915 – 16 then sole 1917 – 1929 |
| Southlands School Headmistress | Miss Mary Margaret Hoyle, BA (Oxon) | January 1930 until school closed December 1942 |
| Emergency Training College Principal | Mr William F Morris BA (London), FRGS | January 1946 until retirement in 1948 |
| Exmouth Training College Principal | Miss Geraldine Mary Croft, OBE, TD, BA | September 1948 – 1951 |
| Rolle College Principal | Miss Geraldine Mary Croft, OBE, TD, BA | September 1951 til retirement in 1959, died 1962 |
| Rolle College Principal | Miss Doris E L Spicer, MA, BCom | 1 Sep. 1959 – retirement 31 Aug. 1972, died 1977 |
| Rolle College Principal | Professor Francis C A Cammaerts, MA, FCP | 1 September 1972 – retired 31 August 1981 |
| Rolle College Principal | Dr Michael Preston, MEd | 1 September 1981 – retired 31 August 1988 |
| Acting Dean of Rolle Faculty of Education | Mr Ray M Owen, MEd | 1 September 1988 – 31 December 1988 |
| Dean, Rolle Faculty of Education | Professor Michael J B Newby, BA, MA | 1 January 1989 – 31 August 1994 |
| Dean, Faculty of Arts and Education | Professor Michael J B Newby, BA, MA | 1 September 1994 – retired 31 August 2004 |
| Dean of Education | Professor Peter D John BA, MA, PhD | 1 September 2004 – 31 March 2006 |
| Acting Dean of Education | Dr Gordon Taylor, BA, PhD | 1 May 2006 – 30 June 2007 |
| Dean of Faculty of Education | Professor Michael S Totterdell | 1 July 2007 – 31 August 2008 |

## INTRODUCTION – Four acres of land in Exmouth

"Four acres of land in Sunny Exmouth; the size of two large Supermarkets or four times the floor area of Exeter Cathedral" was how an engineer, John Petty, described the proposed Rolle Centre site to me on 20th March 2012 when he had rung to check that I really had meant to give my email address as: rollecollege@yahoo.co.uk.

Less than a month later, at a Rolle Centre Open Day in the Owen Building on Saturday 14th April, someone was overheard to say that he had worked at Rolle College and, in the course of my subsequent chat to Peter Cowper, he commented that the grey building [*Eldin*] was similar to the College buildings at King Alfred's, Winchester; St. Luke's in Exeter and the Women's Training College at Salisbury. He also observed that the trees on the Rolle site are "real specimens – not your normal run-of-the-mill choice – so much thought must have gone into their planting".

Peter's part-time lecturing at Rolle in the 1980s was comparatively short but his and John's more recent observations serve to complement the memories of those who studied or worked at the site over its 60+ years. One of the latter, Mike Newby, the longest-serving Dean of the Rolle campus of the University of Plymouth, was conducting tours at the Open Day and was subsequently encouraged to give his "View from the Management" for this book.

The site mentioned above is of course not the whole of that occupied by the former Rolle College because, as David Beasley reported a month later:

> the remainder of the Rolle campus, is advertised for sale by G.V.A. Grimley on behalf of Plymouth University with the bid deadline being June 29th. Of the 6.85 acres it covered, 4.1 is for the Rolle Centre, 0.2 was two small properties, so 2.55 acres remain, including *Eldin* (and *Langstone*) and eleven separate buildings and converted villas and an array of mature trees, many of which are subject to Tree Preservation Orders. [*Exmouth Journal*, 24 May 2012]

The 6.85 acreage remained after many buildings – especially Halls of Residence and Study Bedroom Blocks outside the main site – had already been sold and/or demolished. However, since that figure takes us back to pretty well the size of the site that Southlands School covered, I considered it a good idea to start the book with details of that establishment as even less seems to have been published about its early years than about Rolle College itself.

You will all have had different experiences and memories of the site, even if you have only seen it from one of the double-decker buses that pass it and wondered what lay behind its walls. I was amazed when Jim and I retired to Exmouth in September 2009 to find that the bus stop we used on the Salterton Road was designated "Rolle College" even 'though the site had been termed Rolle Faculty of Education from 1st September 1988 then Rolle Campus of the University of Plymouth since 1992. Even to this day, bus tickets still have the destination "Rolle College" on them and, on 21st December 2012, our bus driver was heard to say on his intercom "I'm at Rolle College on my way to Brixington", so Mike Newby's observation that the Rolle name seemed to mean almost more to the people of Exmouth than to those who worked or studied there would most certainly seem to be the case, hence the title "Exmouth's ROLLE" for this book.

I hope this collection of personal reminiscences (from page 54) will help to revive memories of all that Rolle College and its forerunner, Southlands School, have meant to Exmouth over the past 145 years – during the two periods of 73 and 62 years, with a break of three years during World War II then seven years since Rolle's move to the University of Plymouth (rebranded Plymouth University in June 2011). Having retired to Exmouth during the years that the Rolle College site has been empty, I have become even more conscious of how fortunate I was to have enjoyed it almost in its prime from 1963 – 1966. I say 'almost' because I had to make use of the Open University and The University of Reading between 1972 and 1982 to obtain my BA (Hons) and MA (Ed) degrees part-time while teaching full-time as degree courses were not introduced at Rolle until 1966, after I had left.

However, I have often commented that those of my era were extremely fortunate to have our board and lodging found for us in Halls of Residence, in digs with Exmouth families or in Study Bedroom Blocks. Consequently, we felt very much part of the town as well as of Rolle College – attending local Churches and helping with activity groups as well as with specifically College ones, some of which local residents were able to join. As a result, many of us have maintained links with Exmouth and its townsfolk over several decades, returning to holiday and/or live in a town we came to love and we would like to think that future generations might again be able to do similar if this valuable site could again educate those from more land-locked parts of our country and further afield.

Daphne Barnes-Phillips

# Chapter 1: ROLLE UP

## 1870 – 1929: "The first principals of Southlands & Fairfield Schools"

### 1. Misses Mary S Chignell & Jane E Stephens and Mrs Jane James

Although very little official paperwork seems to have survived to give us an idea of what life was like at Southlands School for its staff and pupils, many advertisements and other articles have appeared in the local newspapers over the years and, from them, it has been possible to ascertain that the Misses Chignell and Stephens were the Principals of Southlands School, which was situated in Carlton Hill, Exmouth from at least 1881 until 1899.

A present-day picture of the building that was Southlands School in Carlton Hill – it is, in 2015, *The Swallows* Bed & Breakfast.

An advert on page 1 of 7th September 1881 *Exeter & Plymouth Gazette* starts:

> Southlands, Carlton Hill, Exmouth. Principals Miss Chignell (of Norwich High School [1]) & Miss Stephens. Pupils prepared for . . .

*The Devon and Exeter Gazette* of Friday 30th October 1885, tells us, on page 7, that Southlands School was a School for Girls on the High School system under their principalship but it also had a Kindergarten, superintended by a certificated teacher, and a Preparatory School for Boys:

> SCHOOL FOR GIRLS ON THE HIGH SCHOOL SYSTEM
> SOUTHLANDS, CARLTON HILL, EXMOUTH
> Principals: MISS CHIGNELL and MISS STEPHENS
> A limited number of Boarders received. Also a Kindergarten superintended by a certificated teacher.
> SOUTHLANDS PREPARATORY SCHOOL for BOYS
> Principals: MISS CHIGNELL & MISS STEPHENS

Marlborough College for Young Ladies, Larksbeare, Exeter is the next advertisement on that page, then another Exmouth School is mentioned:

> FAIRFIELD, EXMOUTH, LADIES' SCHOOL
> CONDUCTED BY MRS JAMES
> Assisted by Resident English, French and German GOVERNESSES and Visiting MASTERS
> Piano: Mr BALY, RAM
> Violin: Mr BARRE BALY
> Singing: Miss M SHARLAND
> Drawing: Mr BIRK MYER (School of Art)
> Arithmetic: Mr SALTER
> Dancing: Mr MASON
> PUPILS PREPARED for Local EXAMINATIONS
> TERMS MODERATE

Fairfield School seems to have been in existence prior to Southlands as page 298 of *Harrod's 1878 Royal County Directory of Devonshire* has this entry:

> James, Mrs Jane: ladies' boarding and day school, Fairfield

[1] Wikipedia describes Norwich High School for Girls as an independent day school for girls aged 3 to 18. Founded 1875, it is one of 29 schools of the Girls' Day School Trust and has one of the best academic records in Norfolk. Notable former pupils include Edith Cavell – the nurse executed by the Germans in 1915. Since she was born in 1865, she could well have been a pupil when Miss Chignell was at the school. The earliest headteachers were: Miss Ada Benson (1875) and Miss Wills (from 1875).

An advert on page 1 of the 27th August 1891 *Exeter and Plymouth Gazette* gives an even better idea that Fairfield School, Exmouth had already been established by 1871 as it is described as a "Ladies College for Daughters of gentlemen established upwards of 20 years, Principals Mrs & Miss James."

*Fairfield* – as seen from Rolle Road (now Douglas Avenue) prior to 1902 – before any of the later extensions were added in 1915.

Unfortunately neither of those advertisements gives us a location for Fairfield School at that time but we can establish further details about Mrs Jane James from the 1871 – 1901 census returns. She had been born in Swansea, Glamorgan, Wales around 1840 but was living at 1 North Street, Exmouth in the Civil Parish of Withycombe Raleigh in the St. Thomas, Devonshire district at the time of the 1871 census and in Devon, Littleham by 1901.

The 1871 census gives us Jane's maiden name as her younger unmarried sisters, Mary (30) and Elizabeth (24) Penrose were living with her at 1 North Street, Exmouth. Like her, they had been born in Glamorganshire, Swansea and were Schoolmistresses. The rest of that census entry names six boarder scholars at the same address – three of whom had been born in Devon, one in Cornwall and one in Somerset. Her daughter, Mary James (then 9, born in Glamorganshire in 1862) was the youngest – the others being 18, 16, 14, 12 and 10 years. Jane was already a widow aged 32. She had married William

James in the summer of 1860 in Gower but he had died by the end of 1865, possibly as early as 1863, so she would have had to earn a living and chose, or had it suggested to her, that she become Principal of a Boarding School.

By the time of the 1881 census, she, her daughter and her school are mentioned in a different Civil Parish ('though a spelling mistake or mistranscription could have led to that fact being overlooked as she was described as a widowed School Mistress, aged 40, living at "Hurfield [Fairfield], Littleham, Devonshire" in the St. Thomas Registration District and the Civil Parish of Littleham). We do not know what had happened to her sister Mary in the meantime, but Elizabeth had married John Henry R Sutton in Swansea towards the end of 1874. The all-female household in 1881 included her 19-year-old scholar daughter, Mary E James and 19 single Boarders, three of whom were described as Teachers:

| | | | |
|---|---|---|---|
| LOSLING, Maria (33) | 1848 | Teacher of French | Alsace, Strasbourg |
| FISHER, Alice (25) | 1856 | Teacher of English | Gadshill, Higham, Kent |
| HAMLYN, Louisa E (20) | 1861 | Teacher of Music | Hackney, Middlesex |

Four families seem to have produced nine of the 16 scholars – Cummings producing three and Farrant, Lang and Gardner two apiece. Whereas 9 girls had been born in Devon, two in Cornwall, two in Gloucestershire and one in Herefordshire, two were British subjects born in India. According to age:

| | |
|---|---|
| **1 x 18 year old**: | Mary CUMMING (Exeter) |
| **1 x 17 year old**: | Bertha KING (Camelford, Cornwall) |
| **4 x 16 year olds**: | Charlotte CUMMING (Exeter); Alice K FARRANT (Ottery St. Mary); Elizabeth HICHENS (Redruth, Cornwall); Ellen L WARNE (Rose, Herefordshire) |
| **1 x 15 year old**: | Sally LANG (Exeter) |
| **3 x 14 year olds**: | Lucy M ACKLAND (Exeter); Katie CUMMING (Exeter); Mary E HAWKIN (**Madras {British Subject}, India**) |
| **1 x 13 year old**: | Amy C FARRANT (Ottery St. Mary) |
| **3 x 11 year olds**: | Maude S FARRANT (Exeter); Edith E GARDNER (Bristol); Elizabeth A MUSGROVE (**British Subject, India**) |
| **2 x 9 year olds**: | Annie LANG (Exeter); Alice J GARDNER (Bristol) |

Two of the four Servants had been born in Devon – the Housekeeper, Mary A QUICKE (30) of Brandis Corner and the Cook, Ann POPE (40) of Chumleigh whereas the Housemaid, Elizabeth GREGORY (19) was born in Taunton, Somerset and Kitchen Maid, Mary J RICHARD (20) in Davidstowe, Cornwall.

We have seen from adverts and census returns that both Southlands and Fairfield Schools were in existence in 1881 and Fairfield in 1871 as well, so what evidence is there for any earlier life? Neither is listed among the seven "Academies and Schools" mentioned on page 211 of *Pigot's 1830 Directory of Devon and Cornwall* under "Exmouth with the villages of Salterton, Budleigh, Lymston and neighbourhood", nor under the twelve mentioned on page 235 of *White's 1850 History Gazetteer and Directory of Devonshire* although, in the latter list, a Penrose and North Street are both mentioned:

| | | | |
|---|---|---|---|
| * Penrose | Rev John | Louisa Terrace | |
| * Sharland | Wm | Manor Hs | North st |

Marked * take boarders. [see modern day view below]

The large white building in the centre of this present-day view down North Street is Manor House.

By the *1857 Billing's Directory and Gazetteer of the County of Devon*, the heading on page 483 was simply "Schools" and five of the eleven mentioned then were in Albion Street or The Strand. Rev Penrose was still at Louisa Terrace but William Sharland had moved to the Strand:

| | | | |
|---|---|---|---|
| Penrose | Rev J | (Classical & boarding) | Louisa ter |
| Sharland | W | (Classical) | Strand |

Although Jane and her sisters had been living in North Street in 1871, William Sharland had moved from the boarding school, Manor House, North Street as early as 1857. Rev John Penrose's surname is the same as that of Jane and her sisters, so was it through him that they came to teach in Exmouth?

According to the *Devon Heritage* website, Rev Penrose had been the third headmaster of Pencarwick Preparatory School, Exmouth and the longest-serving, following on from Rev C Glascott (1829–1834) then Rev F Wickham to 1846. At the time of the 1851 census, he was living at the school with his wife and three children and remained as headmaster until 1871 when Rev C R Carr took over until 1894 and Rev J H H Copleston [John] to 1908 when the school closed. The latter had been a pupil there during Penrose's headship.

Turning our attention from Fairfield School to Southlands School, we find that, whereas it had been described as a "School for Girls on the High School System" in 1885, it had become a "School for Ladies under the High School System" by 24th April 1891. By then, the Misses Chignell and Stephens were detailed as "Headmistresses" and, by 23rd October that year, the school was being described as "a School for Girls (the Daughters of Gentlemen)" in an advertisement on page 7 of the *Exeter & Plymouth Gazette.*

On page 3 of Wednesday 10th February 1886 *The Western Times*, we learn of the examinations sat by Southlands School pupils under the heading of *COLLEGE OF PRECEPTORS LOCAL EXAMINATIONS, CHRISTMAS 1885*:

> The Christmas examination of pupils by the College of Preceptors at the Exeter Centre was held in the first week of December last under the superintendence of the Hon. Sec. (Rev J G Danges MA). A separate examination was also held at Exeter High School for Girls. There were 116 candidates, 48 boys and 68 girls. Fourteen entered for the 1st Class, of whom 11 passed; 42 for the 2nd Class, of whom 30 passed; 60 for the 3rd Class, of whom 49 passed while 13 obtained certificates of lower class than that for which they entered. Thus of the 116 candidates examined 108 passed or 89 per cent. The total number of candidates who presented themselves for the Christmas examination throughout the country was 8,784 of whom 6,788 passed or 77 per cent and the number of candidates examined by the College of Preceptors for certificates during the year ending Christmas 1885 was 14,547.
>
> The following is a list of the successful candidates at the Exeter Centre with the schools from which they came.

BOYS were listed first then GIRLS – Class I, Class II and finally:

> Class III – E Crabb, C Lacey, K Pratt, M Pratt, Southlands School, Exmouth (Misses Chignell & Stephens)

In the Saturday 4th April 1896 *Exmouth Chatter* section of the *Exeter Flying Post*, the following appeared:

> A lady informs me that the Misses Chignell and Stephens were at home at Southlands School one day last week. A very talented lady gave an educational address, in the course of which she said that where possible every girl should receive a good education up to 20 years of age (girl not education), and should then go in for technical instruction. Portia could not have spoken more sagely. "A Daniel come to judgment!" Most heartily do I coincide. Technical education for girls over 20 (if the maiden be caught at 12, so much the better) might well take the forms of boiling potatoes, cooking plain joints, making coffee, tossing omelettes, plain sewing, darning, and rocking the cradle.

The fact that no Christian names are given for either Miss Chignell or Miss Stephens in any of the advertisements or other articles has increased the difficulty of this research. It is likely that the reason for the non-occurrence of first names could well relate to the custom of the time of referring to the eldest unmarried daughters within their families as Miss and subsequent daughters as Miss followed by their Christian name. The recording of the former's surname as Chigwell in the 1881 census has added to my problems! However, that census does show 22-year-old school teacher, Mary Chignell, as a visitor to 31-year-old Jane Stephens' home at Venice Villa, Queens Road, St. Thomas the Apostle, Devonshire where she lived with her widowed father (her mother, Ann Stephens, having died aged 62 in Exeter early in 1872):

| Name | Relation | Condition | Age | Year | Occupation | Born |
|---|---|---|---|---|---|---|
| STEPHENS James | Head | Widower | 72 | 1809 | Builder, (Master) | Exeter, Devon |
| **STEPHENS Jane E** | **Daughter** | **Single** | **31** | **1850** | | **Exeter, Devon** |
| STEPHENS Herbert J | Grand Son | Single | 12 | 1869 | Scholar | St. Thomas Devon |
| **CHIGWELL Mary S** | **Visitor** | **Single** | **22** | **1859** | **(Sc[hool]) Teacher** | **Southsea, Hampshire** |
| BERRY Eliza M | Servant | Single | 31 | 1850 | Genl Serv Dom | Huxham, Devon |

Knowing Miss Chignell's Christian name of Mary meant that it was possible to ascertain from the *FreeBMD* website that she was born in the first quarter of 1859 in Portsea, the first child of Thomas William Chignell (born 1825 in Colchester) and Martha Arter (born Coldwell in Havant in 1837). Thomas and Martha had married in 1857 in Havant and the 1861 census gives them as living in Portsea Island, Landport with two daughters – Mary and Margaret.

However, Margaret died at Havant on 30th August 1863, aged 2 years 8 months according to the Havant Dissenters Cemetery, New Lane, records compiled by Gillian M Peskett. A sister, Enid, had been born earlier that year in St. Thomas, Heavitree, Exeter, Devon and Maud and Thomas William were also born there, in 1865 and 1867 respectively, as listed in the 1871 census.

Martha herself died aged 34 in the second quarter of 1871, possibly as a result of childbirth since Henry's date of birth is also recorded in that quarter. Ten years later, when, as we have read on the previous page, Mary was visiting the Stephens' household, the 1881 census shows that her father has remarried:

| Surname | Forenames | Age | Place of birth | Location 1881 |
|---|---|---|---|---|
| Chignell | Thomas W | 56 | Colchester, Essex | East Wonford, Heavitree |
| Chignell | Jane | 37 | Havant, Hampshire | East Wonford, Heavitree |
| Chignell | Enid | 18 | Exeter, Devon | East Wonford, Heavitree |
| Chignell | Maud | 16 | Exeter, Devon | East Wonford, Heavitree |
| Chignell | Thomas W | 14 | Exeter, Devon | East Wonford, Heavitree |
| Chignell | Henry | 9 | Exeter, Devon | East Wonford, Heavitree |
| Hooper | Jessie | 22 | Cullompton, Dev. | East Wonford, Heavitree |

That census also gives Mary's father's occupation as Unitarian Minister at St. George's Chapel, Exeter – a most useful piece of information as it led to further details about her family from her father's cousin, William Hale White (22nd December 1831 – 1913). WHW, the writer and civil servant who sometimes wrote under the pseudonym of "Mark Rutherford", wrote many letters to mutual friends, Richard Colenutt and his wife, Sarah Fabian (née Clay) from 1870 – 1910. He had met the Colenutts (who had married in 1847 in Portsea) through Thomas William Chignell, whom he called "William". One of those letters – the third in the collection – was written a year or so after Martha's death and gives us a brief insight into how William and the family were coping when WHW and his wife Harriet paid them a visit:

**3**. To Mr Colenutt
Park Hill, Carshalton. 13th October 1872
My dear friend,
We got home from Exmouth last Thursday after a most difficult and tedious journey as you may suppose seeing that we had to change four times, and Mrs White, as you know, cannot walk. I thought you would like to know how I found William (1) and his affairs as I spent a good deal of time with him. He is very much better; preaches with great force; the people are exceedingly attentive and generally the world about him looks bright and cheerful. The children excepting Enid are well and happy; Miss Coldwell is an excellent housekeeper and the house is as well ordered and comfortable as any house need be. I cannot say more if I fill many pages but I know that to you and Mrs Colenutt this will be valuable. I enjoyed the time with him exceedingly and found that much had disappeared which for years and indeed always had disquieted me. I spoke for him once – not extempore, for I have not got the confidence for that, through loss of practice.
I was really sad that I could not come to Ryde. Ryde is a second home to us and I cannot bear that any lengthened time should go by without a visit. However I will and must come for a day or two before the close of the year unless the marriage disturbs your arrangements too much. Love to Mary and the children from us both and kindest regards to your wife and Mrs Gunnell.
Affectionately yours
W. Hale White
(1) CHIGNELL Thomas William.

Following the custom of the time when people tended to be known by their surnames, WHW particularly used that form of address for women – as can be seen in that letter, when he even referred to his wife as Mrs White! His comment, therefore that "Miss Coldwell is an excellent housekeeper" gives no hint that one of Martha's sisters could be looking after her young bereaved family. However, a failure to locate a record of the marriage of a Jane with TWC, led to the realisation that Jane Coldwell's year and place of birth matched the description of Jane Chignell's given in the 1881 census.

Another reference to Exmouth can be found in the nineteenth letter as it was written at 15 The Beacon sometime in 1883 though not specifically dated:

**19.** Miss Rowe's, 15 The Beacon, Exmouth
My dear friend,
I am leaving here on Friday and as I wish very much to see you and your husband and the other dear Ryde folk before I go back to work, you may expect me Monday or Tuesday next, unless I get countermanding orders from you at Carlshalton before then.

If the weather should improve and the roads are in fairish order I shall make the journey to Portsmouth on my tricycle and send a change of clothes to you in advance.
I don't know if I could achieve the whole distance in one day, but if not in one, I can do two easily. I wish Fabian could find out if it would be better to stable the steed at Portsmouth or bring it over the water. If at Portsmouth, what would be a good place? The steamboat charge might perhaps be excessive.
Best love to husband and the children –
Ever faithfully
W. Hale White

However, it is the 103rd letter sent from 5 High Wickham, Hastings in August 1898 that specifically refers to Miss Chignell and her school and makes us wish that we were able to see the reply to that letter. After asking for news of Mrs Colenutt and her husband, WHW mentions his children – Molly, Willie and Ernest – and describes an interesting day he spent in town with Mrs Lewes, the widow of George Eliot's stepson:

**103.** I sat at the desk where the novels were written, read her letters, and, what was still better worth reading, the little memorandum books in which she jotted down the things that came into her head. What a picture they gave of her strenuousness, of her keen, constant endeavour! I was driven when I came back to begin upon her again, and am glad to find that my love for her after so long an absence from her is unchanged. Mrs Lewes also showed me some letters of Charlotte Bronte to her father-in-law. This was the first time I had ever handled anything she had touched, and the paper seemed to shoot something electrical through my fingers to my brain.

He then continued:

I hear a rumour that Polly Chignell has left Exmouth but can learn no particulars. I think I told you she called here a few months ago. She seemed unsettled but I did not imagine she was going to give up her school. I have not heard from William for more than a year: in fact he has completely given up writing. Polly said he was beginning to anticipate the end of active work and dreaded it, I do not wonder.

Rounding off the letter with news of his sister Henrietta's husband's failed business venture, it is interesting that, although he referred to Mary S Chignell and also Mary Anne Chignell (who married George Vicat Cole – letters 74 and 81) as "Polly", he refers to his own daughter, Mary Theodora, as "Molly". Both "Molly" and "Polly" are recognised nicknames for Mary. It was only the previous year that initials were first given for both Polly and Jane in an entry on page 276 of *1897 Kelly's Directory of Devonshire:*

Chignell M C (Miss) & Stephens J E (Miss) ladies Boarding & day School Southlands Carlton hill

Since we cannot tell from the letter why Polly "has left Exmouth and given up her school", we have to see what other information is available. From the *FreeBMD* website, we discover that Jane Eliza Stephens died, aged 50, in Barnet in December 1899.

Having been born in Exeter and seemingly spending her entire life in Devon, it is interesting that Jane should die in Barnet. Was Polly's unsettledness due to her friend and business partner's illness throughout 1898 and 1899? Alternatively, had they chosen to leave Devon and buy a school in Barnet and Jane's death just happened to coincide with the move? An advertisement on page 4 of Friday 4th May 1900 *Western Times*, Exeter under Education states:

HOLMEWOOD SCHOOL
NORTH FINCHLEY
Principal: Miss Chignell
Assisted by highly efficient staff of
Resident and Visiting Masters and Mistresses
The School offers the advantages of London with
those of a bracing country neighbourhood.

Since North Finchley is less than two miles from Barnet, Middlesex, it would be relatively safe to assume that the Miss Chignell mentioned as having taken over Holmewood, a school established since 1885, was indeed Polly. One has to wonder why Barnet as there seems to be no previous mention of that town for either Jane or Polly or either of their families. The 1901 and 1911 censuses show that Polly remained in Barnet, along with her sister Maud, Enid having died aged 20 in 1883 and her father aged 82 on 30th December 1906, both in St Thomas, Devon.

St. George's Chapel in South Street, Exeter where Polly's father was a Unitarian minister for 44 years.

Polly's father, Thomas William Chignell (the "William" mentioned in WHW's letters) is commemorated in a stained glass window at 38 South Street, Exeter, which is now a Wetherspoons called *George's Meeting House*. The window (ground floor – third from front in photograph on page 21) depicts a full-length Spinoza and a profile roundel of Thomas Carlyle with a quotation halfway down each side. Its dedication is:

THIS WINDOW WAS ERECTED TO THE MEMORY OF THE REVD. T W CHIGNELL FOR FORTY-FOUR YEARS MINISTER OF THIS CHURCH WHO DIED DEC. 30. 1906 AGED 82 YEARS.

Built as a Unitarian Chapel and named after King George III (1760 – 1820), *George's Meeting House* closed as a chapel in 1983. It was converted to commercial use as *Global Village* by 1987 then became an Antiques Centre before opening as a Wetherspoons on 16th January 2005. However, the dedication on that window confirms that Polly's father lived in Exeter for 44 years so she would have spent all but the first three years of her early life in that area.

WHW had been unsure of what had happened to Thomas William Chignell's widow as the postscript to a short letter sent a year after his death implies:

> **168.** The Cottage, Groombridge, Tunbridge Wells. 22nd Dec. 1907
> My dear friend
> For how many years have you sent me a sweet not on this day! I looked for one today and here it is. My warmest love to you. Best wishes for the New Year from both of us. Molly sends you a kiss.
> Ever affectionately, W. Hale White
> I don't know Mrs Chignell's address. I have not heard where she went when she left Heavitree; in fact I have not heard that she did leave. When her husband died I asked her to tell me what she was going to do, but she has not written.

The 1901 census shows that T W Chignell had indeed been living at East Wonford Hill, Heavitree then when he was still a Unitarian Minister, but his widow, Jane, had joined Polly and Maud in Barnet, Middlesex by the 1911 census. Polly seems to have remained in Barnet until she died there, aged 69, in 1928, whereas her sister Maud died, aged 54, in 1919 in Farnham, Surrey.

## 2. Misses Jessie & Fanny Vinter

The few months between Polly Chignell "leaving her school" and 6th December 1898 when the *Exeter and Plymouth Gazette* detailed the Misses Vinter as principals of Southlands School from January 1899 must have seen some changes but we only know what is in the public domain:

> SOUTHLANDS, CARLTON HILL, EXMOUTH
> PRINCIPALS (**from January next**):
> The MISSES VINTER (late Scholars of Girton College, Cambridge.
> Many years experience.
> School in healthiest part of Exmouth. Good playground and field.
> Thorough Education for daughters of Gentlemen.
> Preparation, if desired, for Girton College, Westfield College &c and for Public Examinations. Physical Exercises, including games, under fully-qualified mistress. Kindergarten and Preparatory Classes for younger children. Special arrangements for delicate girls.
> Entire charge of children whose parents are abroad –
> Apply to MISS JESSIE VINTER, 16 Raleigh-terrace, Exmouth.

Whereas that advert gives the school's address as Carlton Hill, the one in 3rd June 1902 *Devon and Exeter Gazette*, gives it as Fairfield:

> SOUTHLANDS SCHOOL, FAIRFIELD, EXMOUTH.
> PRINCIPALS – MISSES VINTER
> (late Scholars of Girton College, Cambridge).
> Thorough Education for Daughters of Gentlemen.
> Excellent Resident and visiting Staff. Large House, with good gardens and playfield. For prospectus, apply to the Principals

It seems that the sisters had taken over *Fairfield College* as well by then. A map of 1888 shows how close the two Schools were to each other so it is possible that, when Mrs James wanted to sell, she approached the Vinters to see if they would be interested in buying *Fairfield* since both schools catered

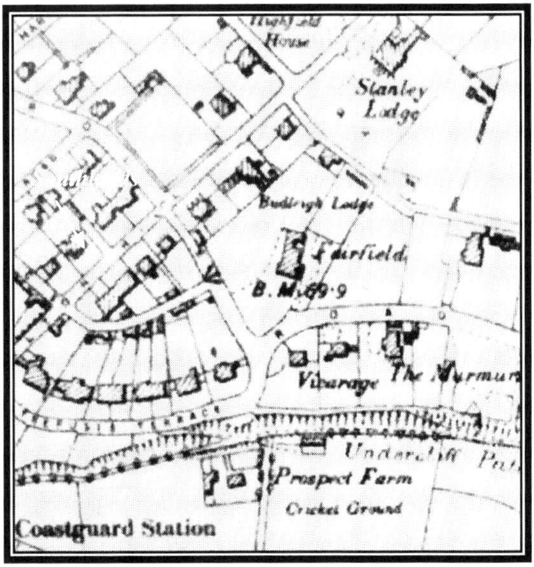


for "daughters of gentlemen". In 1900, *Exeter Flying Post* of both 6th and 8th December reported under "Town Talk's" EXMOUTH NOTES:

> The stupidity of some persons in making wild and erroneous reports has lately been in evidence. It is a great pity that the originators can not be detected and severely punished. The assertions started regarding Mrs James' school have been denied by herself and now by Dr Cock [Cook] in the newspapers. Unfortunately there always are some amongst the great unemployed who are never happy unless they are talking scandal or indulging in malicious reports, and certainly it is disgraceful that anyone without the slightest cause should endeavour to injure such a well known and first class school as that conducted by Mrs James. I only hope the steps which have been taken will prevent further misrepresentations being circulated.

Whether that incident was what induced Mrs James to want to leave Exmouth or whether she had intended retiring anyway, we do not know but an advert in the 27th July 1901 *Western Times* entitled **Fairfield Exmouth** states:

> Crews and Son have been instructed by Mrs James (who is leaving Exmouth) to sell by Auction on TUESDAY NEXT, July 30th, 1901, a portion of the genuine HOUSEHOLD GOODS and FURNITURE, china, glass, plated goods, steel-frame rosewood cottage grand pianoforte by Broadwood, Rosewood upright iron grand pianoforte by Cramer, school desks and appliances, and numerous effects, more fully described in posters. On view morning of Sale from 10 to 1 o'clock at which time the auction will commence.

By 21st October, an advert in the *Western Times* was for "maid for Southlands School, Fairfield" while Commercial section of *Kelly's Directory of Devon 1902* still gives the address as Carlton hill but does detail the sisters' initials:

> VINTER JC & FV (Misses) Ladies' School, Southlands, Carlton hill

There had been entries for both schools in the 1901 census, although J C Vinter's surname was mis-spelt and, despite being recorded as Joint Principal of School, she was the only Principal there on census night. The rest of the all-female household included three teachers, six pupils and a married general servant, Eliza Beavis of Topsham (35) and her child Gert (14). All those aged 16 or over were detailed as "Single":

Person: **VENTER, Jessie C**
Address: **1[11], Carlton Hill, Littleham, Exmouth, Devonshire**
Registration District: **St. Thomas** Piece: **2028** Folio: **32** Page: **31**

| Name | Relation | Age | Birth | Occupation | Where born |
|---|---|---|---|---|---|
| VENTER, Jessie C | Head | 35 | 1866 | Joint Principal of Sch | Bayswater, London |
| MAHIEN, Louise | Teacher | 38 | 1863 | French Mistress | France-French Subj |
| KERR, Mary Hope | Teacher | 25 | 1876 | Kindergarten Mistress | Hammersmith |
| EASTGATE, Cecil | Teacher | 25 | 1876 | Mod Lang Mistress | Yiewsley, Mid'sx |
| KIDNER, Gert | Pupil | 18 | 1883 | | Broadclyst, Devon |
| THOMAS, G P | Pupil | 16 | 1885 | | Weybridge, Devon |
| SOANES, Edith | Pupil | 16 | 1885 | | Newcross |
| PEIRSON, A | Pupil | 15 | 1886 | | Mockus |
| HANCOX, Helen | Pupil | 14 | 1887 | | Lowestoft |
| HANCOX, Dorothy | | 9 | 1892 | | Gt Finborough, Suf. |

That contrasts with the details for the all-female ***Fairfield Cottage,*** **Portland Avenue, Littleham, Exmouth** [That was how the address was recorded in the 1901 census] which had "Single" written next to all those aged 14 or above.

| Name | Relation | Age | Birth | Occupation | Where born |
|---|---|---|---|---|---|
| JAMES, Jane | Head | 62 | 1839 | Principal Of School | Swansea, Glamorgan |
| JAMES, Mary | Daughter | 35 | 1866 | Teacher | Swansea, Glamorgan |
| BOUCON, Bertha | | 23 | 1878 | Teacher | Luxembourg |
| WARNE, Jessie | | 24 | 1877 | Teacher | London |
| HAMBLY,Geraldine | Boarder | 16 | 1885 | Stu | Plymouth, Devon |
| SANDERWICK, R | Boarder | 15 | 1886 | Stu | Bristol |
| HERPACH, Zelie | Boarder | 19 | 1882 | Stu | Luxembourg |
| WESTBURY,Vere | Boarder | 16 | 1885 | Stu | Gunnislake, Cornwall |
| WREYFORD,Gwend | Boarder | 16 | 1885 | Stu | Sandford, Devonshire |
| KNOWLMAN, Amy | Boarder | 14 | 1887 | | Culmstock, Devon |
| DAVEY, May | Boarder | 14 | 1887 | | Bude, Cornwall |
| BAKER, Winnifred | Boarder | 14 | 1887 | | Bideford Devonshire |
| THOMAS, Jane | Boarder | 13 | 1888 | | Exeter, Devonshire |
| HANKIN, Marian | Boarder | 12 | 1889 | | Guildford, Surrey |

| Name | Relation | Age | Birth | Occupation | Where born |
|---|---|---|---|---|---|
| STEWART, Kath | Boarder | 12 | 1889 | | London |
| TRIGGS, Cicely | Boarder | 12 | 1889 | | Southsea, Hampshire |
| WREFORD, Kath | Boarder | 12 | 1889 | | Sandford Devonshire |
| HUTCHINGS, Henry | Servant | 19 | 1882 | House Parlourmaid | Torrington, Devon |
| MERRICK, Mary | Servant | 23 | 1878 | Cook Domestic | Oswestry, Salop |
| PERRIAM, Flor | Servant | 16 | 1885 | Kitchen Maid Dom. | Exmouth Devonshire |
| CHAPLIN, Edith | Servant | 13 | 1888 | Housemaid Dom. | Exmouth Devonshire |

The sisters would no doubt have been very happy to take on both schools because, as A V F Conridge stated on page 29 of a Rolle College Inservice B. Ed. Course dissertation of 16th December 1973:

> the evidence from Freeman's Exmouth Journal shows that by 1900 the Private Schools were still flourishing as ever with advertisements for such schools as: Exmouth College; Carlton Hill Day School for girls; Southlands preparatory school for sons/daughters of gentlemen; Ingleside High Class School for girls; Fairfield College for the daughters of Gentlemen and St. Peter's Preparatory School for the Sons of Gentlemen. Exmouth's official guide for 1902 also indicated the healthy position of private education in the following advertisement:
> "addressed to only one class of our readers . . . . they will find in Exmouth such facilities that choice between them is the only embarrassment. It is already favourably known as one of the finest places in England to which the children of Anglo-Indians coming from the sweltering clime of the East can be sent."
> (*Mates Illustrated Guide to Exmouth 1902*)

But what do we know about the new Principals? *FreeBMD* website tells us that Jessie had been born in 1866 in London, Bayswater, as had her sisters – Minnie (1862) and Fanny (1867) and her brothers – Sydney (1864) and Percy (1870) – whereas their older siblings – Harriet (1859) and Edith (1860) had been born in another area of London – St. Giles – as had their mother, Harriet Sowley Evans, who had married there in 1853. The family home was at 29 Monmouth Road, Paddington, Middlesex in 1881 when their father John Alfred Vinter's occupation was given as "Artist In Oils Lithog. The Queen Civil Service Exam Intermediate B. of Ed. Ireland." He and Harriet seem to have stayed in the same area of London between 1861 and 1891, by which time Fanny Victoria had graduated in 1890 with BA Class II in the Mathematical Tripos, being one of the first 58 women Mathematics graduates of Girton College and the first 111 of the University of Cambridge. Women had only been allowed to take the University examinations, and so be assessed in parallel with men, since 1882, so her sister, Minnie Elizabeth, who graduated in 1884 was one of the first 24 women from Girton and 36 of the University to achieve BA Class II in the Mathematical Tripos. By December 16th 1902 *Exeter & Plymouth Gazett*e, we see mention of Jessie and Fanny:

**SOUTHLANDS SCHOOL,**
**EXMOUTH**
THE LORD BISHOP OF EXETER PRESENT

> The annual distribution of prizes and certificates won by the pupils of Southlands School took place at the Town Hall, Exmouth yesterday. In response to the invites issued by the Misses Vinter (principals of the school) there was a large gathering of friends and relatives of the children . . .

At the end of the concert, Dr Ryle, Lord Bishop of Exeter, delivered a short address in which he alluded to the gratifying progress made by the school and hoped on some future occasion to have the opportunity of visiting Southlands. On the motion of the Vicar of Exmouth (the Rev E V Freeman), who spoke highly of the tone and educational value of the system followed by the Misses Vinter, a hearty vote of thanks, seconded by Mr Tucker Pain, was accorded the Bishop and Mrs Ryle for their kind attendance. At the request of the Misses Vinter, a similar compliment was paid the visitors generally by Rev F L Bazeley, and was cordially acknowledged by the Bishop. His wife, Mrs Ryle who, along with the Misses Vinter, had been given bouquets prior to the concert by the oldest and youngest pupils on behalf of the school, presented the prizes after the musical programme, which had included:

> part-songs by the senior and junior classes and recitations admirably given in English, French and German, and vocal and instrumental selections. The various items were well carried through, and reflected much credit on the young performers and on the tuition imparted by the principals of the school and their excellent staff of teachers. Little fault could be found with the quality of the class singing, which was singularly sweet and pure in tone, if slightly lacking in volume.

A total of 52 prizes were presented to nine girls in Va; two in Va (remove); seven in each of Vb and IV; five in each of VI, IV (remove) and III (remove); four in each of III and II; Amy Sherwin in I and to the following three boys:

> Preparatory: Alan Adams and Launcelot Burlton    Transition: Rex Haycroft.

There was also a published list of successes won by the school at public examinations held in connexion with London matriculation, senior Cambridge local, senior Oxford local, Joint Board of Royal Academy and Royal College of Music (pianoforte, singing, elementary, and rudiments of music) and Royal Drawing Society's annual exhibition and examinations, five divisions.

Among the 200+ attendees was Mrs S G Vinter (Jessie and Fanny's sister-in-law, wife of their elder brother, Sydney Garratt Vinter and mother of Ruth (7, who was a Southlands pupil by the time of the 1911 census). Also there, with his wife, was Mr Barre D'Bayly, a Visiting Master at *Fairfield* School in 1885 [page 12]. At the conclusion of the business the visitors were entertained at tea by the Misses Vinter. The Town Hall had been appropriately decorated:

> The Hall was pleasingly decorated for the occasion by Messrs. Crews and Son. Festoons of flags and a charming assortment of plants gave the room quite a festive appearance while arranged around the sides in an excellent position for inspection were some capital examples of work done by the pupils during the past year. This comprised preparatory and advanced brush work – that being done by the junior classes being especially praiseworthy – model and freehand drawing, shading from the cast, and plant outline. The plain and fancy needlework was particularly good, and bore witness to the careful attention bestowed on this department, while the botany specimens, the majority of which were holiday tasks, attracted a good deal of attention.

Interestingly, we realise how much in demand the Lord Bishop of Exeter was from another article also on page 9 of the same newspaper:

> **PRIZE DISTRIBUTIONS AT EXETER – EXETER SCHOOL**
> **REFERENCES TO THE PRIMATE SPEECH BY SIR JOHN KENNAWAY**
> The annual prize distribution in connection with Exeter School took place yesterday afternoon at the Barnfield Hall, Exeter and was attended by a very large number of the parents of the scholars . . .
> Mr Cunningham [head-master] said he had received letters regretting inability to be present from, among others, the Lord Bishop of Exeter and Sir Thomas Acland.

Rev Freeman was still Vicar of Exmouth when a report of another Prize Giving appeared in 15th December 1905 *Devon & Exeter Gazette*, mentioning *Fairfield* as the school house for Southlands School:

> **EXMOUTH**
> The annual distribution of prizes to the girls of Southlands School, Exmouth took place yesterday at "Fairfield", the school house. The Vicar of Exmouth (the Rev E V Freeman) presided. In the absence of the Rev Treasurer Atherton, Mrs Atherton presented the prizes. Our report will appear tomorrow.

*Kelly's Directory of Devonshire 1906* states that Southlands Preparatory School was at Carlton Hill while the Ladies' College was at Fairfield, Rolle Road as page 304 of the *Exmouth Commercial section* details:

> Vinter J C & F V (Misses) Preparatory School, Southlands, Carlton hill and ladies school, Firfield [*sic*], Rolle road

The death of Mrs Jane James "for many years the Principal of Fairfield College" was reported in 13 March 1908 *E & P G* Exmouth News. Although *Fairfield* seems to have been misspelt in 1906 Kelly's, the 1911 census shows both Jessie (45) and Fanny (43) Vinter as "Head of Household" and "Co-Principal of Private School" at "Fairfield or Southlands" in the parish of "Littleham" in the registration district of St. Thomas. Their names are followed by those of two "Assistants" – Marie Cammack and Dorothy Bannon. The household continues with the names of 29 pupils followed by their places of birth in brackets. Here they are summarised according to age:

| | |
|---|---|
| **1 x 19 year old**: | Ruth Ward (Exeter) – School Student-Teacher |
| **2 x 18 year olds**: | Barbara Stewart (Chester), Loveday Forrest (Exeter) |
| **4 x 17 year olds**: | Margaret Little (Dorking), Doris Gadsden (Hereford), Kathleen Lawson (South Kensington, London), Phyllis Young (Croydon) |
| **6 x 16 year olds**: | Jessie Forrest (Devon, Okehampton), Mary Trembett (Devon Sandford), Lalage Lee (Yorkshire), **Ruth Vinter** (Cornwall Torpoint), Phyllis Wynch (**India**), Hilda Fearnside (**India**) |
| **6 x 15 year olds**: | Ester Burd (Devon, [O]Kehampton), Margaret Hartley (Hastings), Doris Little (Dorking), Beryl Shaw (Hampstead), Enid Benstead (Herts), Ethel Gadsden (Tenby) |
| **2 x 14 year olds**: | Winifred Walsh (Yorkshire), Audrey Wynch (Cheltenham) |
| **5 x 13 year olds**: | Katherine Badgley (**India**), Dorothy Elliot & Susan Elliot (both London but different parts), Maud Dyson (**India**), Hazell Gayer (Devon, Ide, more than a mile SW of Exeter) |
| **2 x 12 year olds**: | Joan Bramwell & Margaret Branwell (both Devon Ide). |
| **One 11 year old**: | Katherine Harington (**India**) |
| **4 servants**: | Annie Fisher, Amy Harding, Annie Walters, Bessie Salter |

Five of the 29 were born in India and, of the rest, Ruth Vinter (16) is probably of most interest as she is the niece of the co-principals. Jessie and Fanny's older brother, Sydney Garratt (47 and a Medical Practitioner) and his wife Frances (née Toms) had four children and, at the time of the 1911 census, Robert Bagster William (14) and Frances Jean (7) were living with them at Udal Garth, Torpoint, with two female servants aged 22 and 20 while Edith Mary Ruth and Noel Sydney B were at Boarding School. Noel (13) was at Sherbourne Prep School, which seems to have had a similar number of boarders to Southlands but less spread of ages being only 10 – 14 years.

Interestingly, the two "Assistants" – Marie Cammack (34) "Matron Housekeeper and Sick House" and Dorothy Bannon (25) "Assistant Matron", whose names are mentioned straight after Jessie and Fanny Vinter's, are to be found together in part III of the 1940 Southlands School Magazine:

**SOUTHLANDS SCHOOL OLD GIRLS' ASSOCIATION – IN MEMORIAM**

MRS PERCY VINTER APPRECIATION BY AN OLD GIRL

One of the most cherished memories of old Southlanders now in their forties or fifties will undoubtedly be the vivid and beloved personality of "Cammie", who after an illness of three months, died on May 22nd at her home in Balcombe, Sussex

As Miss H.M. Cammack she was Matron at Southlands for eleven years. Then, in 1912, to the mingled dismay and delight of the School, she married Mr P.J. Vinter, brother of our two Head Mistresses. The wedding took place from the School in December, 1912, at Littleham Church.

No one called her anything but "Cammie". Her official position as matron, though brilliantly sustained, was entirely eclipsed by the unique personal influence, a prestige of character, which she exercised throughout the school. Somehow she seemed to have all the virtues with none of their corresponding defects. She combined firmness with charm, drive with gaiety, loyalty to her official employers (who were also her dearest friends) with a tenderness and sympathy which attracted to her the confidence – and the confidences – of everyone.

I can see her now in her immaculately starched uniform (for she was a trained nurse from Westminster Hospital) officiating at the breakfast sideboard and dispensing sausages and bacon with a characteristic mixture of cheerfulness and pleasant astringency which was our daily morning tonic.

Her common sense and her sense of humour were always active. Her utter goodness we took for granted and drew upon with the unconscious selfishness of all young things. To be with her was to be warm and comfortable.

A few bare facts of Cammie's subsequent life will interest those who knew her. In 1915 she moved with her husband to York on his appointment as Head Master of Archbishop Holgate's Grammar School, where she acted as Bursar and Chief Matron. Three years ago Mr and Mrs Vinter retired to Balcombe, where they both won the esteem and affection of the village and neighbourhood, Cammie throwing herself into the work of the local clinic for evacuees, the Nursing Association, the Mothers' Union, the Women's Institute and every good thing that came to her hand.

There are two sons. One married recently a Girtonian and holds an appointment in the Ministry of Economic Warfare. The other is a subaltern in the Royal Artillery.

G.A. BURLTON

Dorothy had predeceased Cammie as a February *Daily Telegraph* shows:

Miss Dorothy Edith Bannon, Matron in Chief L.C.C. Nursing Services, aged 54. She was responsible for the large hospital nursing services transferred to the

Council from the control of the London Boards of Guardians and the Metropolitan Asylums Board, and for the School Nursing Service in London. From 1929 she was responsible for the administration of the largest nursing service in the world, consisting of a staff of more than 13,000 nurses. She was awarded C.B.E. in 1933.

By *1914 Kelly's Directory of Devonshire*, the Vinter sisters are shown in the residential section on page 306 living at *Fairfield* whereas the school's description in the Commercial section on page 311 had changed to:

Vinter Jessie M A and Fanny M A (Misses) ladies' school, Southlands, Fairfield & Brockhurst

## 3. Miss Anstice Rose Annette Fearon

By 1915, another Principal was being mentioned in conjunction with the Misses Vinter – Miss Anstice Rose Annette Fearon (late Second Mistress of Leeds High School), according to 8 October *Exeter & Plymouth Gazette.* She had been born in Hungerford, Berkshire towards the end of 1879 and was living with the headmistress of Leeds High School, Alice Silcox (9 years her senior) and a female domestic servant at the time of the 1911 census.

However, by 1915, Anstice was recognised as owning *Fairfield* along with the Misses Vinter and a joint application for the building extensions shown below had been lodged by their architect, James Crocker on 17th August.

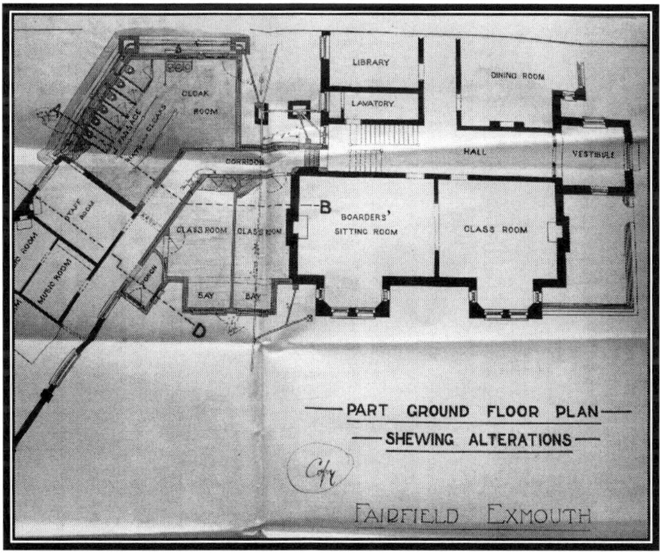


By 3rd September 1915, application for alterations to *Fairfield*, Douglas Avenue had been approved by the Exmouth Urban District Council.

James Crocker's responses are recorded in italics in the Application form that follows on page 32.

## Exmouth Urban District Council

# NEW BUILDINGS

**Form of Notice to be given on deposit of Plans and Sections at the Office of the Surveyor**

==================

***August 17th 1915***

To the Exmouth Urban District Council
Gentlemen

*I* hereby give you one month's notice that *I* intend to *make alterations* at *Fairfield Exmouth* for ***The Misses Vinter & Fearon* of *Exmouth***.
In accordance with the accompanying Plans and Sections, and the By-Laws in Force within the Urban District with respect to New Streets and Buildings.
The following particulars refer to the New Buildings:-

| | | |
|---|---|---|
| | Description of buildings | *Private Boarding School* |
| 21,22,23 | Height of building to eaves | *18' – 6"* |
| | Number of storeys | *Two* |
| 14,15,25 | State if built of brick | *Yes* |
| 22-23 | Thickness of external walls | *9" in (2) 4½" leaves tied together* |
| 22-23 | Thickness of party walls | " |
| 51 | Height of rooms | *9' 6" Ground floor – see section for first floor* |
| 11 | Is it proposed to cover the site with 6 ins. of good cement concrete ? | *yes* |
| 20 | Kind of damp course | *slate in cement* |
| 53 | Area of open space in rear of building | *a whole field* |
| 53 | Distance from such open space | " |
| 56 | All rooms to have windows equal to 1/10 of floor space, clear of sash | " |
| 57 | How is it proposed to ventilate rooms without fireplaces? | *by means of ceiling extractor* |
| 62 | Drains covering sewage will be laid in concrete, and drains under buildings will be embedded and covered in concrete | *Yes – drain under B^dg in cast iron pipe.* |
| 65 | Is ventilating pipe and air inlet provided ? | *yes* |
| 65 | Is soil pipe carried up as ventilator ? | *yes* |
| 63 | Is disconnecting chamber and access siphon provided ? | *Yes all under present system* |
| 67-80 | State if privy or water-closet, and if ventilated (as Clause 67 & 68) | *These are conformed to* |
| | One galvanized iron ashes receptacle, with proper cover, will be provided for each house | |
| 61 | Height of lowest floor above main sewer, ft, in. | *I don't know* |
| 13 | Is the lowest floor level 8.50 feet above Ordnance datum ? | *I don't know* |
| *Though not specifically stated on this form, or shown on the drawings, the said buildings will be erected and completed in all respects in strict accordance with the said Bye-Laws.* | | |

Signed ..........*James Crocker* ................

Note. – write here if Owner, Architect, *Architect to the Owners Agent or Builder.*

N.B. The Roads Committee meet on the Tuesday week previous to first Wednesday of each month, and all Plans and Particulars must be deposited at the Surveyors Office not later than the Saturday previous to the Meeting.

It was the 8th December 1915 *Devon & Exeter Gazette* which explained that the reason for the extensions to *Fairfield* in 1915 was that the purchase of *Brockhurst* in 1912 had not provided sufficient extra accommodation:

Southlands School Exmouth

-----------------

EXTENSION OF BUILDINGS

-----------------

In spite of the purchase of Brockhurst, in 1912, the accommodation at Southlands School, Exmouth, has this year proved inadequate, so a considerable extension has now been made to "Fairfield" and the premises brought up to date in every particular. The new rooms include cloak-rooms, class-rooms, and a number of extra bedrooms, all connected, with the main house and school hall by means of wide corridors, and access openings. Excellent ventilating, lighting and sanitary arrangements have been secured, and the external elevations greatly improved by the new buildings, connecting, as they do, the older parts of the premises with each other, and thus forming one continuity of treatment. The work has been carried out by Messrs Carter & Carter of Exmouth from the plans and specifications and under the personal directions of the architect, Mr James Crocker F.R.I.B.A. of Exeter.

The new two-storey extension is clearly visible in the centre of this photo with *Fairfield* House to the rear left and the Hall/Gym in the foreground to the right.

From 1917, Miss Fearon seems to have had sole charge of the school as there is no further mention of Jessie or Fanny Vinter in advertisements or other articles after 1916. It is probably appropriate therefore to include a collage of

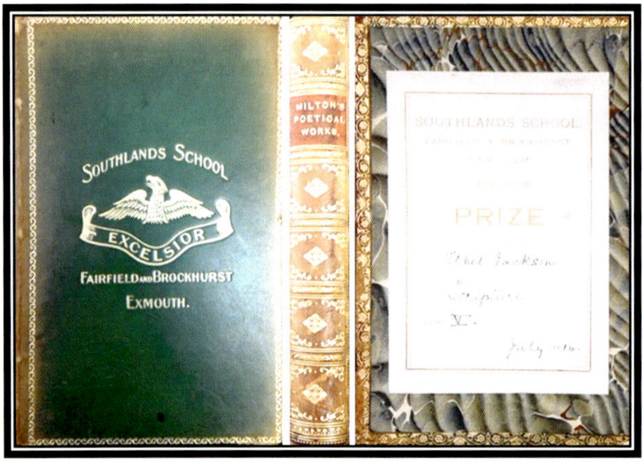


photos of a Scripture prize awarded to Ethel Jackson of form V in July 1916. On both the cover and dedication of *Miltons Poetical Works*, *Fairfield* and *Brockhurst* are printed.

Only Southlands School is mentioned on page 292 of the *1919 Kelly's Directory of Devonshire* and page 306 of the *1923 Kelly's Directory of Devonshire and Cornwall*:

Southlands School, boarding & day school for girls (Miss A R Fearon, headmistress)

By 1920, a further villa, *Eldin*, had been added to Southlands School housing stock as indicated on page 8 of Friday 25th June 1920 *The Western Times*:

FAIRY DANCING

Pleasing Outdoor Entertainment at Exmouth

The annual sale of work in aid of the Exmouth Children's Seaside Home was held in good weather at Southlands School yesterday. Besides the old school house and grounds, the lawns at Sidwell and Eldin (which have been acquired by the school authorities) were made use of, and many visitors were able to inspect Eldin for the first time. It was here that the stalls of work were arranged and managed under the supervision of the headmistress (Miss Fearon) and staff of the Southlands School, assisted by the pupils of the various Forms, each Form having a stall of its own. Willing help was also given by old pupils in the management of other stalls, which included one for flowers, fruit and vegetables, cakes and sweets, a book stall and photography. Tea was provided on the Sidwell lawn and the School Orchestra played at intervals. A dramatic and variety entertainment given by old pupils of the School formed an attraction in the hall at the School-house and on the lawn at Eldin there was some charming aesthetic dancing, in which the flower dance, the ball dance, the wish maidens and piping dance, were introduced in the fairy scene from Tennyson's "The Foresters". The scene depicts Robin Hood (who has fallen asleep in a dell in Sherwood after his day's hunting) and is found by two of the fairies of the forest. They tease him until stopped by Titania, their queen, who after listening to the charges brought against Robin and his merry men by the fairy folk, bids them rise and flee to distant haunts untrodden by man. Robin wakes to catch a last glimpse of her as she too vanishes.

In 5th December 1919 *Exeter & Plymouth Gazette* it was reported that the Rev Henry Thompson Clerk (88, and former Royal Navy Chaplain, for whom *Eldin* House had been built in Rolle Road after Architects Banks and Barry had produced details of plots of land for sale by the Rolle family of Bicton in 1865) had died there. By 16th January 1920, his executors had instructed "the important and interesting sale of pictures, old china, silver, furnishings".

In the "Fairy Dancing" article, the name *Sidwell* appears a couple of times but only *Fairfield*, *Brockhurst* and *Eldin* are shown on early maps. A comparison of later photos showed that *Sidwell* and *Brockhurst* were one and the same building 'though why the names were interchanged from 1912 to 1942 remains a mystery. Did the school rename *Brockhurst* as *Sidwell* for their purposes but the original name remained on the paperwork so, when the property was taken over for the Emergency Training College, it reverted to the name of *Brockhurst*? The Bamfield family had ***Brockhurst*** built in 1892

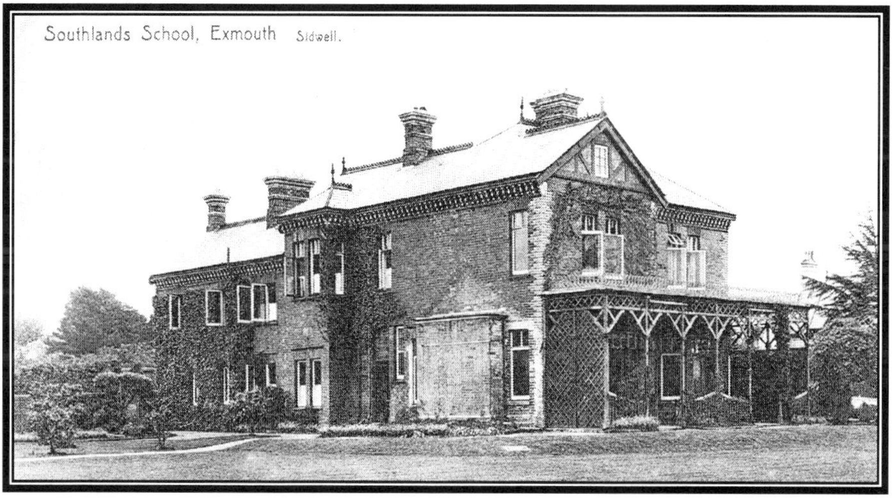


and were living there at the time of *Kelly's 1902 Directory of Devon.* Lieut. Gen. Albert Henry Bamfield JP had gained the rank of General in the service of the Indian Army while serving in the Punjab Campaign 1848/9 and been promoted to Major-General from 1889 before holding the office of Justice of the Peace for Devon. By *Kelly's 1906 Directory*, the name was shown as:

Phear Misses, Brocklehurst, Rolle road

Mum has the impression that her mother enjoyed her time at Southlands and that impression certainly seems to have been borne out by the photo album. One picture has first names only and another full names. Finally, there are some wonderful pictures of the girls putting on *As You Like it* and *A Midsummer Night's Dream*, all carefully annotated in the album but only with their character names as seen in this famous depiction (Act IV Scene I) of the latter play.

Even an article in Thursday July 26th, 1923 *Devon & Exeter Gazette*, only gives us similar information as regards the characters 'though we do glean further information about other aspects of the Shakespeare Festival from it:

SHAKESPEARE FESTIVAL
SOUTHLANDS SCHOOL
PLAYERS

Delightful performances of "A Midsummer Night's Dream" and "As You Like It" were given in the grounds of Southlands School, Exmouth, to large and appreciative audiences. The plays were presented exclusively by the pupils, the only evidence of the influence of the staff towards the success achieved being furnished by their example of complete self-effacement. This example was caught and followed by each one of the performers, and resulted in a really delightful interpretation of the plays. Perhaps the most striking feature of these brilliant comedies is the fact that completeness of dramatic effect is attained spontaneously, with the least possible reliance upon the artificial or the mechanical. The beautiful grounds supplied ideal stage and auditorium. Two garden seats and a camp table were all that were required to shift the scene from the Forest of Arden to the Palace of Theseus. These comprised the whole of the stage furniture with the notable exception of Pyramus and Thisbe's very realistic human wall. The very correct and pleasing costumes were in accord with the spirit of the whole performance.

Each added its due quota to a harmonious effect without drawing undue attention to its own individuality. The powerful footlights – an exceptionally scorching midsummer sun blazing in the faces of the performers – only emphasised the wisdom of the stage management in excluding paint and powder from the accessories of the green room. The prompter was seldom called upon, and the two performances went from start to finish without a hitch. One shrinks from individualising where the spirit of "team work" was so much in evidence. But, perhaps, Rosalind and Orlando, Helena, Puck and Mr Quince deserve special commendation for their very whole-hearted contribution to a most enjoyable and instructive entertainment. The sum of £140 6s 3d was taken and of this sum, £100 has been allocated to Exmouth Children's Seaside Home, of which the School has been one of the chief supporters for many years. The remainder will be divided among other local charities.

Rosalind and Touchstone in
"As you like it"

Southlands School comes across as quite a relaxed sort of place, especially considering the date of the photos. Was that its reputation?

A lot of my family had links to India, my father was born there as were my brothers.

Myra was married to Donald Wedderburn-Ogilvy (son of Thomas Wedderburn and Marion Agnes Koe) on 7th February 1929. Her daughter (my mother) married another Eustace. Very confusing when it comes to creating a family tree – too many cousins marrying cousins.

**1923 – 1937: "From India to Southlands for 5 sisters" by Sela Mooney**

I, Sela Mary Peters, was born in one of the houses on Carlton Hill, Exmouth in 1935. My grandparents had bought 3 Carlton Hill, in 1923 from George D McGrigor and named it "Lovedale" after a small town situated in the Nilgiri

Hills in the state of Tamil Nadu in India. It is the second last railway station on the route to Udhagamandalam (otherwise known as Ooty) from Mettupalaiyam and the highest on the entire route. It is just 5 km from Ooty. The Nilgiri Mountain Railway was extended from Coonoor to Ootacamund by the British in 1908 and, since July 2005, has been protected by UNESCO so still operates a fleet of steam locomotives, except for the stretch between Coonoor and Ooty where diesels currently operate.

My maternal great grandfather, Rev Charles Martin, had been Rector of Dartington after being Warden of Radley College. He had married Dora Frances, daughter of George Moberly, Bishop of Salisbury. Their second son, Rev John Sturges Martin was Curate of Dartington while their fourth son, Rev William Keble Martin, was Rector of Coomb-in-Teignhead, Devon so my grandfather (the fifth son and youngest of Charles' and Dora's nine children) seems to have really branched out by working in India.

My grandfather was Chief Engineer of the South Indian railway and (amongst other achievements) supervised the building of the steep line up to Coonoor (a resort that my family visited many times to escape the hot weather). Richard

Harrington Martin had married Elsie Sela Burney in Hereford in 1907 but all six of their children were born in India – five in Madras. My mother, their first child was born there in Tanjore in 1908 and named Doreen Edith Sela (so you can see where I came by my first name!). She was followed by Daphne Phyllis, who was born in Trichinopoly the following year. The only child not to have been born in Madras was Stella Dorothy [known as Stella May] who was born in Abu Road, Bombay in 1911. Coonoor, Madras was the birthplace of Rosalind Frances in 1914 and their final daughter, Stephanie Dorothy, in 1919. Their only son, Richard Harold Geoffrey, had been born in 1916 in the same place as my godmother, Aunt Daphne – Trichinopoly, Madras.

From 1923, my grandmother stayed in England and the five daughters were day pupils at Southlands but none of them distinguished themselves there! I do remember them telling me stories of their behaviour. It sounded like St. Trinian's! They were constantly playing tricks on the poor teachers. Their greatest friends were the Shelmerdine family [Joan (1912), Richard (1914), Ruth (1916) and Dinah (1920)] whose father was vicar of Holy Trinity church [from 2nd June 1931 till 2nd May 1943, when he moved to Silverton.] My grandfather left India for the last time in March 1937 then, from December 1939, he worked for the Admiralty (some of the time at Scapa Flow).

Both Aunt Stephanie and Dinah Shelmerdine feature under Old Girls' Circle 1936 in Number 45 Summer 1939 edition of Southlands School magazine:

> S. MARTIN is living at home. She had been looking after a small boy who went to Southlands in the mornings.
> D SHELMERDINE has finished a secretarial course in Exeter and is looking for a job.

Southlands was no longer in existence when I came home from India aged 11 in 1946 so I boarded at a small private School outside Tiverton called "Ingleside", which only taught to GCE "O" level so I never took "A" levels and was sent on to Domestic Science college at Lyme Regis for two years before starting nurse training. My parents reckoned I would marry and not need a career!! Well that was 60 years ago and times have changed!

My next-in-age brother, [Edgar] Richard was only 8 when our parents returned to India and he boarded at the Beacon school in Teignmouth. He and I spent many happy school holidays with our grandparents, plus unmarried Aunts Daphne and Rosalind, at "Lovedale". After serving in the WAAF during the War, Aunt Rosalind worked as secretary and personal assistant to the head at Rolle College, where her best friend "Wattie" (Miss Watson – see pages 112 & 120) was Matron. Both Rosalind and "Wattie" have been dead for 20 years or so now and no one in the family can remember the Principal that she worked for but she was an unmarried lady whom Rosalind was in awe of when she worked for her between 1950 and 1960 [Miss Croft].

I always wanted to teach but did not qualify for a grant because of my father's good income. However, I had four younger brothers [Richard plus Martin Geoffrey (born 1941), David Michael (1943) and Patrick John (1947)] going through public schools (the younger ones boarded at Winchester Lodge in Torquay) and my parents could not afford my teacher training. I therefore trained as a nurse at Barts, then married John William Case Mooney in 1958 and moved to West Africa. It was only when we ended up in Reading in 1968 when our children were 9 (Peter William Martin), 7 (John Ashley Case) and 5 (Caroline Sela) years respectively that I enrolled at Bulmershe College and got my teaching certificate in two years.

[When compiling "George Palmer School in photographs" (2004), Sela loaned me some photos taken at George Palmer Infant and Nursery Schools, Reading when she was headteacher there from 1st May 1984 until 31st December 1990. She had previously been a probationer at George Palmer Infants from 1973 – 1976. When a reprint of the book became necessary in 2014, I wanted it to be partly in colour so I contacted her to see if she had the original colour versions of those photographs so that changes could be made to the black and white version. It was then that she realised that Jim and I had moved to Exmouth and mentioned that she had been born in Carlton Hill. Further questioning elicited her family link with Southlands and Rolle.]

## 1923 – 1926: "Letters from Southlands School" by Betty Nottingham

Born at York in 1900, I was christened Evelyn Christine E. V. Nottingham but like many of my contemporaries, it was my third name by which I was known and that was shortened to Betty. After completing my degree at Cambridge University in 1922, I did a year's historical research in London before heading to the West Country towards the end of 1923. After two years of teaching history at Southlands School, Exmouth, South Devon – a boarding and day school for girls under the headmistress-ship of Miss A. R. Fearon – I felt it was time to move on, even though I enjoyed that School's ambience. I had begun to sound out ideas about my next move and, as a result, on February 11th 1926, I decided to write to Mr Leonard Elmhirst as follows:

Southlands School
Exmouth, S Devon
Feb 11th

Dear Mr Elmhirst,
I am very diffident at bothering a busy person but Mrs Elmhirst thinks that you would be able to help me with advice. I am one of the many 'adopted' nieces in whom she is good enough to take an interest, though I am not sure that that fact gives me a right to bother her real nephews. Perhaps you will forgive me.
There comes a tide in the affairs of men (& women) when some sort of an adventure must be had. I finished at Cambridge in 1922 and did a year's historical research in London and have since been teaching here. I am thrilled with teaching and love young people but will never develop into the complete genius intellectual at a select seminary for young ladies in England.
This is a very jolly school and the head has a sane and non-competitive outlook, but I want to see the world and other milieu of education. Moreover I should like more equipment for my profession. I am applying for a studentship at Teachers College, New York, which I am told has an excellent psychological department. Also foreign students are shown other schools and so on. I wonder if you know anything about it? I have to rely so much on mere hearsay. The trouble is I shall have to support myself more or less at the same time. They tell me that I ought to be able to get odd jobs but my physical endurance isn't unlimited though I'm wiry and I believe Americans work harder than English! I'd be quite prepared to take a job in any school or college in Canada or the States if it had a decent experimental attitude towards education but that's the kind of thing you can never know until you are there to see.
They tell me of Preparatory Schools which apparently aren't what they sound & I had thought of applying for a job at Havergal College Toronto, but when I saw the prospectus it looked like mid-Victorian Cheltenham but I may be quite wrong.

If you know anything about teachers college or anything else you might think suitable in Canada or USA I would be most grateful. But I do feel ashamed to take up the time of a busy person and can only apologise for so doing.
Yours sincerely,
Betty Nottingham

I was amazed to receive an immediate reply so was able to respond on 13th:

It was good of you to find time to answer my letter at once. Miss Lorsi sounds just the person to get in touch with and thank you so much for suggesting that I should come and talk things over. I'd love to and can get off any weekend that suits you. The middle of the week isn't so easy though I have Thursday afternoons once a fortnight also. I wrote to Teachers College for application which incidentally have to be in by March 1st but so far I haven't heard a thing from them. I'm not well up in the English-American postal service!
Aunt Em and Richard have told me enough of your plans – and Mrs Elmhirst's – to make me very anxious to hear more about them. Thank you both so much for taking so much trouble over me!

The plans I have referred to relate to the setting up by Leonard and Dorothy Elmhirst of educational experiments at Dartington (present-day photo – left) between 1925 and 1930. They bought Dartington Hall estate with its partly-ruined buildings in 1925 with the intention of creating a 'school for adventure', as Leonard described it to Wyatt Rawson, a former fellow undergraduate at Cambridge, who soon became involved in the project. Leonard's own schooldays had been miserable so he wanted to avoid the use of the word "school" if possible.

Dorothy's three children from her marriage to Willard Straight

– Whitney, Beatrice and Michael – had attended Lincoln School in New York, which attempted to put into practice the ideas of John Dewey, which concentrated on a child-centred "education through occupations" approach. His ideas combined with those of Rabindranath Tagore, the Bengali poet and philosopher, with whom Leonard had worked in Bengal from 1921 – 1924, formed the basis of what could be attempted at Dartington.

I used school embossed headed writing paper when I wrote on May 27th:

SOUTHLANDS SCHOOL
EXMOUTH, DEVON

Dear Mr Elmhirst,
I am really ashamed to bother you again but I have had to face such a series of battlements in attempt to get to America that I turn to you as a last hope.
To begin with I didn't get a studentship at Teachers College as they have cut down the money.
Then having decided to go in the chance of getting a job in New York to help things out I heard that my brother is ill and they fear T.B. and I don't now feel I ought to risk not having a salary. When I heard I hastily applied for a post in Montreal hoping to get to T.C. for the summer session . . . I just missed the post because I hadn't applied soon enough and it was already offered to someone else. I had first refusal if the candidate declined but she didn't! Then the American University Bureau said I oughtn't to go without a year's maintenance which I hadn't got. But I still feel quite determined. The way you could help me if you would be so kind would be to tell me how one hears of jobs either in Canada or the USA. At this stage I'm not particular what or where as long as it gives me a chance to look round. I can hear of things through the grapevine I know. I am eligible for T.C. and have a claim in a room at the International Institute if needed but I didn't know a soul in the American side and should like a little fortification before taking the plunge. A friend was going with me but now she's off to Paris instead. Forgive me for again bothering you but I'm so afraid of ending by accepting a post in England – then being too old to start abroad. I just feel I can't give up.
Exeter is very near here if ever you do happen to pass through and haven't time to write. Aunt Em told us about the daughter and with her and the School you must be well occupied.

After being interviewed on May 29th, I wrote the following on June 15th:

SOUTHLANDS SCHOOL
EXMOUTH

Dear Leonard,
Thank you so much for your kind invitation. May I come over on Saturday? Perhaps the best thing would be to meet the car at Dawlish. I should have to get

back here the same night as we are getting full up towards the end of term. Perhaps I could meet Miss Bogue then and I'm dying to see the children!
Think I be at Dawlish Station when the car comes about 1 p.m.

Having made arrangements to travel to America, I wrote on July 7th:

My Dear Mr Elmhirst,
I've fixed up to leave Liverpool on Aug 21st on the Samaria which should land me in New York about the end of August as Mrs Elmhirst suggested.
Couldn't half thank either you or Mrs Elmhirst for all your kindness to me: you made all the difference to my courage with your kindness and if Miss Bogue could possibly meet me in New York I should be more than grateful.
How is Mrs Elmhirst? I do hope she is better. I thought of her when the children were due to arrive and hoped she would be well enough to enjoy them. I just wrote her such a scrappy note after I left because I didn't think she wanted a lot of correspondence just then: but I hope she realised how amply much I am grateful to her for being so kind and taking so much trouble about me.
It must be fun having the children in the fine weather. A good many here would enjoy Witney's occupations. Your fame seems to be noised abroad. There was an article in the Daily News and some people I met at the University had been much interested. I do hope your August camp will go with a swing and give you a good start.
I heard from Aunt Em the other day – she seemed very cheerful – but had been having a bad time with the dentist.
I do hope Mrs Elmhirst is fit again now and that your building is going on apace and boys are pouring in.
With all good wishes,

As well as the influence of America and India in the persons of Dewey and Tagore, in England Baden Powell's Boy Scout Movement's combination of practicality, co-operation and service was also highly regarded by the Elmhirsts. I heard later that the school had started with ten pupils that September.

I kept in intermittent contact with Leonard Elmhirst, especially in 1929, when needing advice about visas. In April, I was living in International House, 500 Riverside Drive, New York but was at 23 Grosvenor Terrace, York in August, when I typed two letters to him about the Visa I needed before returning to New York from Liverpool on 3rd September. On 6th December 1940, I wrote from Wheaton College, Norton, Massachusetts but it's the Southlands School connections in which you'll be most interested in this book.

## 1922 – 1928: "Lady Sidmouth's grand-daughter and other pupils"

One of the pupils at Southlands when Betty Nottingham was teaching there was **Diana Elena Harris**. She died 15th March 2010 aged 92 but her memories had been recorded by Professor Andrew Quicke on 1st August 1996 and he posted them on the world-wide-web in December 2001.

Although aged only eleven when she was sent to Southlands in 1922, it was Diana's third boarding school. She had been sent to "The Study" in Wimbledon, when she was only six as her parents could not bear to have her around. She was the youngest and smallest in that school and, despite being befriended by Biddy from Newfoundland, two years her senior, was obviously very frightened. Her fear prevented her from eating so she soon became very ill. After two terms, on doctor's advice, she was taken back to her mother's family home of UpOttery Manor, in the village of UpOttery, about four miles from Honiton, by her adoring grandmother, Ethel Lady Sidmouth, who had had her under her care for the first four years of her life as her parents, wanting a son, hadn't really bonded with her – they even called her "sonny"!

Diana's grandfather Gerald, 4th Viscount Sidmouth, had died in 1915 and been succeeded by her Uncle Gerald, Marjorie's eldest brother, as 5th Viscount Sidmouth. Just two years later, Diana was sent to a family boarding school with only eleven pupils. It was run by Reverend Hudson and his wife Mary in Huntsham Rectory. Huntsham was a tiny Devon village dominated by Huntsham Court, the home of Sir Gilbert Acland-Troyte MP for Tiverton and his wife Gladys (née Quicke). Diana was happy with the Hudsons as she loved their three daughters – Mary, Frances and Anne. She even spent the holidays at the school with Mrs Hudson acting as her surrogate mother.

By the time she reached Southlands, Diana's lack of parental affection had meant that she was regarded as the naughtiest girl in the school. "Being naughty" consisted of pranks like leaving the school grounds dressed in her pyjamas. Once the headmistress asked Colonel Oscar Harris to take his daughter away but he refused, stating that "any decent school ought to be able to cope with a high-spirited girl like Diana".

Diana made life-long friends at Southlands, including Elizabeth Bernayes, (married name Wrightson) whose mother acted as a kind of surrogate mother for her. Elizabeth and Diana were confirmed together on the same day. Other friends were Eleanor Foy and Gertrude Coates (later Borrodaile).

There were no dances at Southlands, but the school drama classes were popular and they play-roled parliamentary debates. Diana's favourite subjects were gym and dance and she played lacrosse for the school. In the holidays, her home was at Broadclyst Rectory; a big house separated from the A38 by a wide field. Diana always thought the house was haunted, remembering it as having a big hall, sitting room, large dining room, study and her mother's bedroom at the top of the back stairs. There was a large garden and a grass tennis court suitable for tennis parties. A large house required a large staff to run it so the Harris family employed a cook, a maid, a batman who doubled as a groom and his wife, who helped with the cleaning. Diana frequently went riding with her father as her mother, the Honorable Marjorie (née Addington) had lost her riding nerve after India (where Diana had been born).

The Summer *1937 Southlands School Magazine (no. 43)*, gives details of her life as an Old Girl of Southlands under CIRCLE 1928:

> Mrs Quicke (née Diana Harris) has been living the itinerant life of a N.C.O.'s wife, but has now taken a house at Yelverton for seven years, principally for her small son Andrew. She went out to Malta in January, intending to stay 2½ years, but after three weeks, they were ordered home. Any O.G.s are welcome at her home, which is just off the main Yelverton – Plymouth road.

That was the first magazine under the editorship of Miss Jones, Miss Eggar having decided to spend more time on producing plays.

Younger than Diana but similarly mostly brought up by her grandparents was **Elizabeth Catherine Todd** who was born 18th January 1921 at Ootacamund – now Tamil Nadu – in the Nilgiri Hills of southern India, where her father, who was based in Madras, was a member of the Indian Civil Service. Sent to England while still a young girl, Elizabeth lived with her grandparents before being placed in the care of a retired Irish officer and his wife, who, according to her Obituary (published 17th July 2009) neglected her and her sister and applied the funds set aside for the children's care to their own wellbeing:

> Her parents eventually returned, but Elizabeth's experiences fostered a mental toughness and emotional containment that endured throughout her life. Educated at Southlands School, Exmouth, she passed her Oxford entrance exams in the

> spring of 1939 then spent that summer in France, taking a job teaching English to the daughters of a French family near Pau. But, with France mobilising and conscripts on the move, she became stranded and only got back using a third class railway ticket aboard one of the last boat-trains to England.
> With war imminent, she decided to postpone going up to Oxford and instead found a job for eight months decoding telegrams at the Office of Censors before starting a secretarial course.

Elizabeth had been Secretary of the School Committee 1937–8, and a member of the Foreign Affairs Society Committee, which had been instituted at the beginning of the Autumn Term, 1937. She was Rounders Captain, playing Back-stop in the first XI; Hockey Vice-Captain and, as Left Back, she was described as "slow and must be careful about the direction of her passes but she tackles well"; and part of the 2nd couple in the Tennis 1st VI.

Although not mentioned in her Obituary, Elizabeth's decision to postpone going up to Oxford is mentioned on page 23 of the *1940 Southlands School magazine* by Isobel Turner as she did not take up her scholarship:

> REPORT OF SCHOLARSHIP COMMITTEE
>
> A meeting of the Scholarship Committee was held before the annual general meeting of the Southlands School Old Girls' Association on April 20th. Owing to the emergency caused by Betty Todd being unable to go up to Oxford, a postal vote had to be taken from the Committee in October, 1939. By this vote, the scholarship for 1940 was awarded to Pamela Harrison, who is training at King's College of Household and Domestic Science. At the Committee it was decided that Pamela should hold the scholarship for a second year, as her training is a three year one.

From Elizabeth's Obituary, we further learn that:

> By the spring of 1941, her course completed, she was presented with the choice of working in Churchill's office or accepting an apparently more mundane – but much better paid – job at the Passport Office. Subsequently she was embarrassed to admit that the extra £2 a week won her over and she reported for work at 54 Broadway, St. James's Park where there was indeed a passport office on the ground floor. However, that proved to be merely a convenient front for what was, in fact, the main office of the Secret Intelligence Service.
> Elizabeth Todd's role was to act as third secretary to Colonel Claude Dancy, the deputy head of SIS. Such was his importance that she saw a regular procession of prominent figures passing through the office, including General de Gaulle, Lieutenant-Colonel Edward Calthrop, SIS's liaison officer with Special Operations

Executive (SOE), and the later-notorious Kim Philby. But the greatest anticipation was reserved for an envelope that would arrive each day marked ISOS, and which contained decoded information from the Enigma intercepts at Bletchley. Although possessed of remarkable qualities, Dancy was a man of his time and strongly believed that, while women might be acceptable as junior staff, they were not suited to being SIS officers. In an attempt to find some additional responsibility, Elizabeth Todd obtained a posting in Algiers where she worked for the head of the SIS's Italian section, liaised with a number of the senior Free French and immersed herself in the local culture.

From there, in October 1943, she was sent to Bari in southern Italy, a place (she recalled) of flat landscapes, grey skies, fascist sympathisers and endless troops in transit . . . .

At first Elizabeth's role was largely organisational, but it evolved to include developing cover stories for agents, working with document forgers & pinpointing drops and pickups for the Lysander pilots and Falucca crews. For this work and for some other, more covert operations, she was mentioned in despatches, something to which she never subsequently made any reference. With the Germans retreating northwards through Italy, the Bari operation moved to Rome, where she remained for the rest of the war, frequently travelling north to debrief agents or comfort the families of those missing.

In mid-1945 she finally returned to England and prepared herself to go up to St. Anne's College, Oxford, to read History. She and Brian Ashford-Russell, 14 years her senior, married in 1946. A mistake on her tutor's part meant that she had just two years instead of three in which to complete her Oxford degree. But she immersed herself in her subject and, guided by Marjorie Reeves, a mediaevalist who became one of her mentors, gained a very good second. Had she had the extra year, Marjorie Reeves thought Elizabeth Ashford-Russell would have gained a first and, on this basis, recommended her for a research degree. But by then, her husband had been offered the post of consul in Bari.

The diplomatic life on which she embarked for the next 20 years took her from Bari to Paris, then to Rome, Mexico, New York, Argentina and South Africa before finally returning to Rome. She took the opportunity to travel extensively and adventurously, particularly in Latin America, and to pursue her interests in art, architecture, drama, music or food.

For seven years after her husband retired from the Foreign Office, she became director of studies at The Cygnets, an old-fashioned finishing school in London. In 1980, when she retired from her last job as editorial assistant at the *Architectural*

*Review* in Queen Anne's Gate, she was amused to rediscover a secret tunnel that she had first walked through 40 years earlier to the neighbouring wartime premises of the SIS.
Elizabeth Ashford-Russell, who died on June 11 [2009], is survived by three daughters and a son; her husband died in 2003.

Whereas Diana had been a pupil when Miss Fearon was Head Mistress of Southlands School, Miss M M Hoyle (right) was Head Mistress when Elizabeth was a pupil, as the 4th March 1930 *Devon & Exeter Gazette* indicates:

CHILDREN'S HOME
Great Work of an Exmouth Charity

In their annual report the Committee stated that 74 children passed through the Home during 1929.
Miss Fearon and the staff and girls of Southlands School sent the Home the wonderful gift of £180, the proceeds of their summer sale and this had lifted a burden from the shoulders of the Committee, going far towards paying the heavy expenses for repairs.
They expressed regret at the retirement, from Southlands School of Miss Fearon through ill-health. She had been a great friend of the Home, not only by being a member of the Committee but also by her most generous help and interest. Egg week produced 1,037 eggs. The Chairman in moving the adoption of the report referred to the excellent structural repairs and expressed gratitude to Dr Martin and Mr F White for the advice and assistance given to the Building Committee. They were also most grateful to Southlands School for their extremely big gift, which came just at the moment when they did not know which way to look for money. The financial statement showed they were now getting into a good condition because they had been able to repay some of the money they had taken from deposit to help pay for the alterations.
Miss Hoyle was elected a new member of the Committee . . .

Although she had had to retire from Southlands School through ill-health, Miss Fearon lived a further three decades after that date as can be seen from the archives of Stoatley Rough School, Haslemere, Surrey where she was a Governor from 1935 (soon after its foundation in 1934) and Chairman of its Governors from 1945, when she bought ice-cream for everyone to celebrate V E Day [Victory in Europe]. She was 82 when the school closed in 1960 on the retirement of its founder, Dr Hilde Lion. It had been a mixed boarding school founded to cater mainly for refugee Jewish children from Nazi Europe and initially called the German-English School. According to *FreeBMD* site, she died four years later in the second quarter of 1964 in Midhurst, Sussex.

From her birth, Anstice would have been aware of many other cultures as her father was Curate of Hungerford, where she was born in 1880 but her brothers – Daniell Arthur Ogle (7 at the time of 1881 census) and Henry (3) had been born in Barnstaple, Devon and Malta, while her sister, Mabel Edith (5) had been born in Penang Straits Settlements. That made her appointments as headmistress of Southlands School with its connections to India, and governor of Stoatley Rough School, with its German connections, most appropriate.

Anstice was to keep in regular contact with Southlands School as this article from the *1937 magazine* written by Beryl Howard-Baker indicates:

> The Report on the 1936 Old Girls' Week-end has to go to press at a moment's notice, and time does not permit me to ask for details from the last Secretary – Dorothy Smith. Therefore as I was not present, I can only remind you that it was held from October 14th to 17th, and from heresay must have been as jolly a meeting as usual. There was a record number of Old Girls present, and everyone must have been overjoyed to find Miss Fearon there as well.
>
> The usual matches were held, and on Sunday afternoon talks on various subjects were given by Old Girls.
>
> On May 8th, 1937, Miss Hoyle held the London Meeting at the Women's University Club. Twenty-nine Old Girls were there, as well as Miss Fearon, Miss Gibberd . . .

It is the *1937 edition* of the magazine that is extremely useful not only for names, addresses and leaving years of 285 Old Girls (of whom 24 were members of staff) but also for addresses of former headmistresses as they held office within the Association.

Despite the changes of Head Mistresses, there had been a constant figure in the life of the school as Charles Ware had remained the School Porter for over 31 years, as Miss Fearon described in the *1938 SOUTHLANDS SCHOOL OLD GIRLS' ASSOCIATION IN MEMORIAM:*

> CHARLES WARE, School Porter at Southlands for over 31 years.
>
> Died May 4th, 1938
>
> How can I begin to write about this old, old friend of Southlands? So many memories crowd into my mind as I try to do so. Friend indeed he was. He took us all into his devoted love, gardeners, house-staff, school – we were all just Southlands to him – and we could do no wrong.
>
> How many of us can still hear his cheery greeting, his ready welcome! Did he really know all the Old Girls when they came back? He always seemed as if he

did! Did he even know the names of all the school? Or was it, as we used to say, that he knew all the girls by their shoes?

How many of us can see him collecting the post-bag (that post-bag always taken down to the Post Office at the eleventh hour with the certainty that he could always get S.S. letters taken in at the side door!), but perhaps only Miss Williams and I knew that the evening "locking up" would be hopelessly delayed because Charles was retailing to his P.O. friends our latest doings, and singing our praises!

Dear Charles! Time was of no account to him, nor indeed his own comfort or his meals. He was always on the spot, but as Miss Williams well knew, so often not quite on the *right* spot! How well I remember the day when hunting everywhere for Charles, he arrived, having happily carried the Vicar's bag down to the station – quite sure that that was what I should have wanted him to do!

He was a wonderful custodian of the school and its property, and woe betide anyone who thought they could make free with or touch any of our belongings when we were away. Miss Hoyle has a story that even Dr Armstrong was not allowed one holiday to open the music cupboard for music he had used during the term.

And then those holidays! How fully he was in possession, and how proud he was to do the honours of the school. The Headmistress was not at all a necessary adjunct for prospective parents. Miss Church reminds us of the occasion when a father wrote that there was no reason to wait to see me before entering his daughter, for a "faithful school retainer had told them all about Southlands to their complete satisfaction."

Charles was particularly proud of the school motto. Standing one day before it in the front hall, he said to me, "'Not for self, but for all,' that's the thing that Southlands stands for, isn't it?" And indeed he showed a school spirit and faithfulness beyond all reckoning.

In 1939, *MISS HOYLE'S LETTER* gives an indication of how closely she and her predecessor, Miss Fearon, had kept in touch:

My dear Southlanders,

I have spent a considerable portion of my holiday wandering round the country and have been fortunate in seeing a number of Old Girls. It is impossible not to notice what sound work they are doing in diverse directions, public and private. They have reminded me of a pair of thrushes I watched at Fiveoaks calmly bringing up and launching into the world four fat young birds despite the violent barks and threats of Peter, Miss Fearon's dog, who could look into their nest from the terrace.

It is heartening to notice how many people are considering the future and the steps to be taken to build . . .

## 1929 – 1938: "Function frocks and lacrosse" by Esmé Ware

After leaving my kindergarten school at Hatherleigh House in Exeter Road, Exmouth, I attended Southlands School as a day girl from the age of 7 to 15 as I lived in Woodbury then as indeed I do now – in the same house. That is probably why I still have a framed photograph of the whole School taken in May 1936 (see page 61) and an album of small photos of amateur dramatic productions performed by the girls.

I travelled to school by bus each day – sometimes the driver would even stop by the bridge near our house on the way back so that I did not have so far to walk home. Southlands School was situated at the top of Rolle Street in Exmouth. Its motto was "Non sibi sed toti" – "Not for one but for all". It was an expensive school, catering mainly for boarders, weekly boarders and some day girls. The boarders' parents were mostly living abroad. There were about 200 girls and three houses – Sidwell (Kindergarten), Main building and Eldin.

We had a big staff. As well as the headmistress, Miss Hoyle, there was her secretary, matron and under matrons and a gym mistress. The large teaching staff included an art mistress, French/German mistress and sports mistress. Art was taught in a huge conservatory. Each morning, we assembled in the Hall in the Main building. The pupils had to stand while the teachers came in, followed by the headmistress and her secretary, Miss Edwards, and processed to the platform. The Hall also doubled as a gym with climbing ropes (see page 73) to the ceiling; a horse accessed from a springboard and rib stalls for climbing at the bottom of the Hall.

It was in that Main Hall that we heard of the abdication of King Edward VIII and of his love for the American, Mrs Wallis Simpson. It was very emotional for us young girls as it seemed so romantic! My parents even had this photo of him when, as Prince of Wales, he had visited Woodbury on 17th May 1921, seven months before I was born.

A member of staff was at the head of each dining table for meals and maids in uniform served at all the tables. A French table was held weekly "on high", so-called because it was on a platform next to the Head Mistress. We had to speak in French throughout the meal when allocated to that table.

After lunch each day, boarders had to rest in their bedrooms and day girls had to take a cushion and blanket to rest on the floor of their house. In the afternoons, we had sports such as tennis, hockey and lacrosse. There were hard tennis courts between the road and the Main building but we had to walk to Exmouth Cricket Field for other sports. We called the walks from the school to the cricket field "Sudden death" or "Prolonged agony" on account of their steepness. Younger pupils played netball there but, as we grew older, we played hockey and lacrosse. The latter is now banned as the hard ball is considered too dangerous. We used to play friendly matches against St Peter's School as many brothers of Southlands girls were pupils there. The town itself was "out of bounds" for all pupils but, if you were feeling unwell, you were all taken for a walk along the seafront by a member of staff!

School finished at 5 o'clock but there were often special lectures or recitals arranged for the evenings or weekends. All pupils had to wear a "function frock", as we called them, which was in an attractive shade of green for

A group from the play "The Barratts of Wimpole Street"

special events, which were held in the Hall. We could choose our own design for the frocks but the colour was decreed and we had professional musicians, such as Jelly d'Aranyi [violin recital on 4th November 1936] and Moiseiwitsch [pianist on 1st December 1937] performing for us.

I joined the Old Girls' Association when I left Southlands in 1938 and, in the Number 45 Summer 1939 edition of the Southlands School magazine under Circle 1938, was:

> E. WARE has been at home. She has been riding a partially broken pony that appears to have given her a sensation the following morning which she associates with the first gym lesson of the term. She will start a domestic science course at the Maynard School, Exeter in September.

That "partially broken pony" was "Hotstuff" and he can be seen here pulling a trap with my father – Edgar Ware and myself, age 4, in 1926. Although, as that piece implies, I enjoyed riding and other country pursuits, I also enjoyed my schooldays. One school friend, though, seemed to be hardly ever at school as she was always out hunting!

Among the pupils' names that I recall from that time are: Daphne Griffin, Paddy Kingdom, June Stevenson, Mary Griffiths, Dawn Gunter, Dilys Stevenson, Joan Hamer, Margaret Innes and two who were mentioned in that same magazine: Brenda Stevenson and Margaret Wainwright. They had both been abroad – Brenda had spent a year in Paris and gained her diploma in French before taking a secretarial course at St James College in London while Margaret was having a gay time in Jerusalem in spite of the unrest in Palestine.

Sadly, the school closed due to Exmouth being bombed in the 2nd World War. I met Allan Thomson, a Canadian, while we were working at the radar station RAF Branscombe, Kings Down Tail and we married in 1944. Although we were in Devon, I do not know what happened on the Southlands School site after the school closed until a Teacher Trainer Association took it over.

### 1934 – 1942: "Elisabeth Frink and other Sweets" by Elizabeth Maycock

Although Southlands School seems to have sunk from memory, it was an important feature of Exmouth life in its day. One or two concerts were held annually in the wooden gym. Exmouth did not have much cultural entertainment in those days so, to have leading musicians performing, was quite an event. I also remember a young and nervous Cecil Day-Lewis [2] coming to read his poems to us on 6th May 1939 – long before he became Poet Laureate. His first wife, Mary [3], had been a pupil at Southlands (Circle 1920).

The School was described in a 1934 advertisement as:

> . . . beautifully situated, facing the sea in one of the highest parts of Exmouth and the buildings consist of three detached houses in contiguous grounds. The school has 12 Tennis Courts, a large Playing Field and a Bathing House. Tennis, Lacrosse, Hockey and Netball are played and the girls receive coaching in all games and in Swimming.

The Bathing House was a rented one on the seafront and swimming lessons

were in the sea but the School provided employment locally as there was quite a large domestic staff – laundry & garden workers & a handyman who looked after the Headmistress' car and occasionally attempted to give us a lesson about its mechanics! The May 1940 photo of the pupils and teaching staff taken by Panora Ltd, London WC1 around the time of Dunkirk included the domestic staff at either side – 8 female and 4 male to the far left (here) and 7 female to the far right (top of p. 58) – thus a similar total to the 19 teaching staff. Being taken

[2] Born 27 April 1904, he was Poet Laureate from 1968 until his death on 22 May 1972

[3] Constance Mary King. They married 27 December 1928, had two sons – Sean , 1931 and Nicholas, 1934 – and lived at Box Cottage, Bafford, Charlton Lane, Glos until 1939 then a thatched cottage in Mounthill Lane at Musbury in East Devon (where a bench bears the inscription: 'Mary Day Lewis 1902 – 1975') before divorcing 12 March 1951

eight months after the start of World War II, four evacuees were wearing different uniforms – two of them can be seen in the back row of the photo below. We had one in my class – Zoe van Prague. Of the 162 pupils in the photo, there were four young boys in the front row. Those 4 plus 4 adults seem to be the sum total of males as I do not recall any male teachers while I was at Southlands. The photo was taken between *School House* and *Sidwell* and I do wonder if everyone was included as the co-owners, Miss Hoyle (Headmistress, centre, wearing glasses) and Miss Williams (Matron, to her left) were aware that it might be the last school photo as they were losing money so could not continue to keep the School open. The lady with the dog is Miss Anson (biology) and next to her is Miss Stewart (French and German) with my sister Anne at her feet.

I started as a Day Girl at Southlands School, Exmouth in 1934, aged 10, so I went into Lower III. That was my first experience of school life as I did not go to school before that. We had lived on the edge of Dartmoor and my mother [4] taught me and one or two local children. One of the reasons for the family moving to Exmouth was for me to go to Southlands. It took me a term or two after starting to fit in as I had been a rather solitary child, living in the country and not meeting many other children. Most of my form had come up from *Sidwell* (right) or other kinder-gartens and seemed very sophisticated to me as they knew how to play games and enjoyed them while, at that time, I dreaded them and gym. However, in my second term, a new girl joined who came from Budleigh and she became a good friend, and my years at Southlands were mostly very happy for me and my friends.

Some Day Girls came by bus from Budleigh and some from the Lympstone direction, but most of us were within walking or biking distance and went home for lunch. Parental lifts were rarities in those days. For most of my years at the school we lived in a big house called "Mansfield" on the corner of Douglas Avenue and Cranford Avenue (now flats), so that took less than ten minutes by bike. I can't really remember how long the lunch hour was, but I don't think it was too rushed. We finished the morning at 1 p.m. and I suspect we had to be back by 2.15 in order to get to the Maer for games at 2.30.

[4] Grace Pauline Williams-White (born Bristol 1889) married 1913 in Westhampnett, Sussex, where her first three children were born – Mary (1914), Philip (1918) and myself, Elizabeth (1924)

We would return for a final lesson from 4 till 5, I think, and went home with quite a lot of prep. By the time I was a senior, I would have a quick tea and work till 7.30, stop for supper and sometimes work on a while, but I was an academic and took English Grammar and Literature (compulsory, as was Maths and French) also History, Greek and Latin so it was quite a big syllabus.

The middle school was at *Eldin* and we used to dawdle back across the garden to some lessons at *School House* in the summer as we were out of sight for some of the way! The grounds were more attractive in those days as there were considerably more lawns and flowerbeds. There were about six grass tennis courts and two hard ones facing out on to Salterton Road and another grass court between the front of *Sidwell* and Douglas Avenue – that was the one we preferred as we felt we could not be seen as easily from there!

The tennis courts facing Salterton Road can be seen in this aerial view to the left of *Fairfield* while the separate one is shown circled. (Eldin is off this photo to the right)

Beyond *Sidwell*, there was a large lawn and two big clipped bushes, which formed the stage and wings for touring theatre companies, who used to put on Shakespeare plays in the summer, with the audience seated on chairs. I remember the head gardener reporting my friends to Miss Hoyle for going under those bushes to eat their lunch – he seemed to keep a beady eye on us!

Mostly we did gym in the Gym, but occasionally in the summer, we went out to do posture exercises by the tennis courts. We took off our green tunics for this, but as our beige knickers were voluminous, we were still adequately covered! As well as the knickers, which had elastic at the legs, halfway down to our knees, we wore white blouses with a green and black striped school tie, and dark green pleated tunics to the knee. We had green berets (small) with the school badge, and dark green blazers with black binding and the school motto embroidered in black and white on the top pocket – "Non sibi sed toti" [Latin meaning "Not for oneself but for the whole"].

For the school concerts and other occasions, we had matching green tussore [5] dresses with cream collars and long sleeves, very plain. I got into trouble with Miss Hoyle because the dressmaker put a bit of embroidery on the collar of mine! In summer, we were allowed to wear our own cotton dresses.

Southlands was run, and possibly owned at one stage, by Miss Fearon who came back to visit as the former Headmistress once or twice when I was a junior. I remember her coming into one of our lessons and being surprised at how active she was.

There was mostly a good relationship between staff and pupils and, although I was absent on the day that this 1936 School photo was taken with *School House* in the background, I recorded the names of 141 pupils and 20 staff on

the back of that photo. The Head, Miss M.M. Hoyle, who taught classics and religion and used to drop in on lessons [6] – we had to read aloud to her quite a lot – is in the centre of this photo with Miss Williams (matron) 2nd to her right. Others in the close-up of the centre section of the photo (page 62) were:

[5] A strong coarse brownish Indian silk obtained from cocoons of tussore moth

[6] Possibly standing for Margaret Mary [actually Mary Margaret]. I believe she went to live in or near Stroud and taught at Stroud High School for Girls for a while

Miss Church (School secretary who travelled daily from Exeter until she was bombed out and had to stay at the School) is 2nd to Miss Hoyle's left. Between Miss Hoyle and Miss Church is Miss Lee, a very sarcastic woman, who went up country to teach in a Grammar School.

Other teachers were: Miss Jones (English); Miss Dixon (lower III, especially with those who had come up from kindergarten and also worked at *Sidwell*); Miss Freeman (maths); Miss Phipps (history); Miss Paige-Jones (geography); Miss Winter (English and junior Greek); Miss Whitcher (gym); Miss Soderling (art – there were other art teachers, but I gave it up early!); Miss Mutton (music – when my mother asked her if it was worth my learning the piano, she said 'No' – thank goodness!) and Miss Smith (needlework – I gave it up rapidly!).

I think the solitary boy had an older sister in the school and their mother did not want to have to take one child to one school and the other to another. My form are mostly to the right of the photo though Miss Hoyle made Wendy

Wall (circled) sit in the front row next to the little ones so as not to spoil the photo – she had got mud on her tunic and her mother had sent it to be cleaned so she is wearing her own dress, as we all did during the summer months!

One girl in my form lived in Dawlish Warren and came across to school by rowing boat each day. Yolan Salter's mother was Hungarian and her father had suffered from TB so the family had chosen to live in a chalet bungalow all year as the bracing fresh air was considered good for her father. I can recall an egg hunt all over the Warren as I often used to visit her family. She is the first girl after the staff on the right of the photo.

The boarders kept themselves rather apart, naturally, and it was only those in one's own form that one knew well. No account of Southlands would be complete, 'though, without mention of "the Sweets". They were the daughters of parents based in India, who only had home leave every two years. There were usually about sixteen at any one time, of varying ages and spread throughout the school. We had two in our form throughout my time.

Those girls were cared for by Miss A.G. Sweet, who had a big house in Isca Road, close to the school, called *Chypraze* [7]. [It is now called *Greenacre* and a modern-day photo of the house can be seen on the next page.] She was

[7] In 1913, the secretary of the South-Western Federation of the National Union of Women's Suffrage Societies was Miss Joan Retallack of Chypraze, Exmouth, Devon. In 1929, Miss Sweet submitted a Planning Application for Additions to be erected to Chypraze using architects Ernest E Ellis & Sons.

always known to her girls as Adgie and they mostly became very attached to her. It must have been a considerable responsibility because she had complete charge of them and communication with India was not very speedy.

She was quite independent of the school in her work, though they must have been mutually beneficial. I think the parents in India heard of her by word of mouth. There was a steady supply of girls. We went to the birthday parties for the ones we knew and I remember playing 'murder' in a scary way in the big house. We shared in their excitement when their parents were due home on leave and sometimes met them.

The most famous "Sweet" known to me was Elizabeth Frink [8]. She was younger than me, but I remember walking home with her once. We called her "Frinkie" – a rather quiet, shy girl then, but she lived quite a tumultuous life, I

[8] 14NOV1930 – 18APR1993 Dame Elisabeth Jean Frink CH, DBE, RA was born in Thurlow Suffolk, only daughter of Herbert Ralph Cuyler Frink (Indian Army Cavalry Regiment) and Jean Conway-Gordon (a Colonel's daughter) who had met and married in India. The Suffolk Painters' biography of Elisabeth Frink says "in 1941 she was evacuated to her godmother at Chypraze, near Exmouth, Devon".

think. Sadly, she died at the age of 62. She had become a sculptress with some of her early work in Coventry Cathedral, following her first major commission, a figure of St John Bosco, for the new Church of St John Bosco in Woodley, Reading, Berkshire in 1952. Here is one of her later works "Robed Figure" (1988). It can be found in the gardens in front of Reading's Abbey ruins. [9]

We also had Alice & Patty Ruttledge at school. Their father, Hugh, led the 1933 expedition up Mount Everest, though it did not reach the summit. He came to lecture to us about it afterwards and is mentioned in the Spring 1937 (no. 43) SCHOOL CALENDAR given in full here:

SPRING TERM, 1937

February 6th – Geographical Charades
" 12th and 13th – Reading of "Lady Precious Stream."
" 17th – Pianoforte Recital by John Hunt
" 27th – First performance of Films in School
March 3rd – Performance of "The Sowing of the Seed", a Missionary Play
" 4th – Hobbies Exhibition in Exmouth
" 6th – Devon Elocution Competition. Fraulein Kallas' Lecture on German Foreign Policy, in connection with the S.S.J.B.L.N.U.
" 8th – Devon Music Competition
" 13th – Paper Chase. Papers read on Brooke & Keats by members of Lit/Dra.
" 17th – **Mr Ruttledge's Lecture on "The Everest Exhibition."**
" 27th, 28th and 29th – Easter Week-end.
March 31st – School Singing Competitions.
April 3rd – Senior Coronation Celebration Party.

---

9 20 July 2007 *Western Morning News* stated: "Thirteen works by the Exmouth-educated sculptor Dame Elisabeth Frink, have been sold for nearly £1 million at an auction in London. One bronze sculpture … entitled *Running Man*, sold for £344,800 at a recent Sotheby's sale – nearly five times the £70,000 it was expected to fetch."

SUMMER TERM, 1937

| | | |
|---|---|---|
| May | 18th | – Visit to Coronation Films |
| ” | 26th | – Presentation of Coronation Souvenirs by Mrs Blackmore |
| June | 5th | – Inter-Schools Elocution Competition |
| ” | 15th | – English Classical Players’ Presentation of “Twelfth Night.” |
| ” | 18th | – School Certificate began. |
| ” | 24th | – Higher Certificate began. |

The following year, he wrote an article from the yacht *Equinox* on June 29th in Lerwick for the *1938 Southlands School magazine* (no. 44), including:

> I shall never forget a day in 1933 when Shipton and I found ourselves on steep ice on a mountain-side above the Rongbuk glacier which descends from Everest. We had only about 60 feet to climb to reach good rocks; but on the right a 2000ft slope of bare ice fell away to the glacier below. Steps were cut with an ice-axe, and we were roped together; but each of us knew that if he disobeyed the law to stand boldly upright instead of yielding to the temptation to lean inwards he would slip out of his step and pull his companion off, down that terrible slope. In one short quarter of an hour we knew ourselves and each other in a way that years of normal life could never have taught.

In that edition the Editor had commented:

> We are glad to add some old girls and a parent to the number of our writers. Such an innovation is most welcome: contact with the outside world is vital for us who live in the secluded shelter of pleasant Devon.

None of the girls’ contributions were named in any of the magazines – only their form was given – but I pencilled in the names I knew. I had a piece titled “The Churchyard” on page 17 of the 1938 magazine, when I was in form IV. The Junior Literary and Dramatic Society had been instituted in the Easter Term 1938 but there had been no matches in any sport in the Spring Term owing to a measles epidemic.

In the 1937 magazine, as well as detailed criticisms of the performances of all those who played hockey, lacrosse, tennis or rounders in the school teams, there were reports from the School Committee, Social Service, Geographical Society, The Literary and Dramatic Society, the newly-formed Art Club and the S.S.J.B.L.N.U. An interesting comment by the latter was:

> In the autumn term some of us went to hear Sir Francis Ackland make an extraordinarily good speech, and in the spring, a Nazi student from Exeter University came to speak to us on “Germany’s Foreign Policy.” We were very interested, although perhaps not converted to Herr Hitler’s ideas.

The Geographical Society threw further light on school life that year:

> A map-drawing competition was planned for the summer term, but this could not take place until near the end of term because of the preparations for the sale of work. Then, when prospective map-drawers were just beginning to chew their pens (a sign of intense concentration), preparatory to applying them to paper, a plague in the form of chickenpox descended upon the school. We were all hurriedly sent to our homes, and the competition was postponed to a later date.

That edition of the School Magazine is a really useful reference tool as it gives the contact details of all 240 members in 1937, including:

*President:*

| | |
|---|---|
| MISS HOYLE | Southlands School, Exmouth, Devon |
| | (Home), Merlebank, Donnington, Nr Newbury, Bucks |
| | [Should be Berks, but shown as Bucks in the magazine] |

*Hon. Members:*

| | |
|---|---|
| MISS F VINTER | 5 St Helen's Park Road, Hastings |
| MISS J C VINTER | 5 St Helen's Park Road, Hastings |
| MISS FEARON | Five Oaks, Haslemere, Surrey |
| MISS SKINNER | The Orchard, Mountway, Taunton |

Another interesting address was:

| | | |
|---|---|---|
| Courtenay, E (Lady Evelyn Anstey) | 1924 | Powderham Castle, Exeter |

I did board for a week while my parents were on holiday and I remember being really scared of having a bath at school as I had heard that one girl in my form was having a bath when a fireman walked in and told her she must get out straightaway as there was a fire. I think it was only a minor one but it made it into the Friday January 8th, 1937 *Devon & Exeter Gazette*:

> EXMOUTH AND PROTECTION AGAINST FIRE
>
> A letter from the headmistress of Southlands School has been received by Exmouth Council, expressing appreciation of the prompt way in which the fire brigade dealt with a fire at the school on December 2nd and of the care taken by the firemen to avoid causing any damage.

There were never more than fifteen girls in a form so there was plenty of time for discussion. We were well taught in English and History. When the war began, some parents did not wish their daughters to learn German in addition to French. Since our headmistress had read Classics at Oxford, she took the opportunity to start our form of 14-year-olds off on Greek and we enjoyed it. Interestingly, I remember Miss Hoyle visiting Russia in the 1930s.

I had a very happy time at Southlands School and am still in touch with four or five friends as well as retaining photos and six School magazines – those from 1937 to 1942. The latter of Summer 1942 is the smallest of only 25 pages and is numbered 48 which means, since the magazine was produced annually, that the first must have been produced in 1894 and no. 48 was the last one ever. In that year's letter, Miss Hoyle wrote:

September 29th, 1942

My dear School, Past and Present,

I want to quote to you a sentence from an Old Girls' letter which I have just received: "For us, Old Girls, I feel our part has grown, for it has become more and more necessary for us to build up a Southlands wherever we are by bringing to our varied activities the spirit that belongs alone to Southlands."

I quote this, for I think it illustrates our essential unity at this time. I would not have dared to write all that I have quoted, but now that one of you has said it we can claim that it rings true for us all. It is hard for everyone who loves the school that it has to close, but let us all turn to the "building up of a Southlands wherever we are." To that end I think we may rightly remember the good things we have shared over a range of years going back long before I knew the school and continuing to this day: fruitful effort, of spirit, mind and body, heart-cleansing mirth, vitalising friendship, and a daily round of worthwhile activity. And so we send out to you the magazine planned and arranged before it became clear that the school must close, judging that you would wish to see the School reflected therein, being and doing.

To all I would send my love and hopes and prayers that we may each and every one of us share in the building of the sane and lovely world for which we long, as we have shared in the life of Southlands.

If at any time you need me for anything a letter addressed to Merlebank, Donnington, Newbury will always find me.

Yours affectionately, M. M. HOYLE

["Merlebank, Donnington, Newbury" appears in the list of *Alumni Cantabrigienses* as the address of Charles Edward Hoyle in 1947. He is the youngest son of Isaac Hoyle MP and Elizabeth Smallpage and he had three brothers who were also Cambridge graduates. He married Anna Camilla Brandreth in Farnham, Surrey in 1896 and Mary Margaret Hoyle was born 18th January 1900 and baptised there in St Andrew's on 3rd March. Her brothers were also born in Farnham – Hugh Brandreth in 1901; Roger Isaac in 1902 and Randall Colvin in 1904. Her mother died age 40 when she was 12 and her father remarried when she was 15. Miss Hoyle died in Stroud in 1977.]

The Editorial Note opposite Miss Hoyle's letter states:

We regret that owing to war conditions, the Magazine size has had to be reduced.

Certainly no 48 (with news of 110 Old Girls) is less than half the size of no 43, which gave the addresses of all the Old Girls currently members of S.S.O.G.A. However, it did give an update FROM MISS FEARON on p. 12:

> Billeting has not given us much work lately, but time does not hang heavy! I have had rather an interesting bit of work the last two months – serving on the panel for interviewing the girls of 16 – 18 age. It has also meant following them up afterwards and helping them to join some organisation, if possible. I think this registration has revealed all over the country how in many cases girls of 16 – 18 have a very full day's work.
>
> Then for the last nine months I have been coaching in history a Matriculation class in our Refugee School – boys and girls who come down to me twice a week.
>
> At Easter, actually on Good Friday night – we produced Masefield's play, "Good Friday" to a packed and attentive audience in our cinema, a very happy experience for us all.
>
> I have two boy evacuees in the house – brothers of 9 and 11, but there is still room and a welcome for any Southlanders if they come this way.

and onc about MISS CHURCH on the same page:

> As most Old Girls know, Miss Church had her home at Exeter burnt out, and arrived at Southlands School with only a suitcase. She spent the Summer Term there with her two sisters, and Miss Hoyle gave a party to celebrate the fact that Miss Church had been at Southlands for 35 years. Old Girls will want to wish Miss Church all happiness for her future.

My younger sister, Anne, eventually joined me at Southlands so is in the May 1940 long photo but, as she is ten years younger, I can't remember much at all about her time at the school and she cannot recall much about how she got to *Sidwell*, which housed the Kindergarten. She does recall one occasion, probably after lunch, when she came back with me and one or both of my great friends, the Wall twins – Wendy and Elizabeth. This must have been unusual because I think we had different hours of attendance. Before the war [i.e. prior to 1939], my mother had some foreign au pairs and Anne thinks they may have taken her to School. Right from the start, when I was ten, we all went to school on our own, often meeting friends on the way.

In 1941, my family had moved up to "Hillcrest" at Littleham Cross. My grandfather had been renting "Mansfield" and, when a landmine dropped close enough to it to blow out the windows, my mother wanted to move. "Hillcrest" was quite a lot further away for my last year but I was fortunate to complete my schooling at Southlands.

Occasionally, if it was pouring with rain, my father [10] would offer me a lift if he was going out at the same time otherwise I had to go to and fro on my own I left in July 1942 and the school continued for just one more term, finally closing at the end of 1942. The war was a large factor in its closure and where some of the girls went afterwards. In 1941, there was a real threat of invasion along the south coast until Hitler decided to invade Russia instead.

[13 people had been killed when 3 bombs were dropped in the dense area of Chapel Street on 18th January, 1941 and much damage was done to property. Later that year, 4 lost their lives when 2 of the 5 bombs dropped on the centre of the town exploded on 1st March. Another serious raid took place on 28th May when 9 people were killed and houses demolished in Woodville Road. On 12th February 1942, several bombs were dropped on and around the Beacon, causing considerable damage to Holy Trinity Church and Beacon Congregational Church. Six lives were lost in Bicton Place. Miss Hoyle must have been pleased that she had closed the school at the end of 1942 as the last raid on Exmouth on 26th February 1943 was the worst in terms of fatal casualties. 8 enemy planes attacked the town at midday with high explosive bombs, cannon and machine gun fire. All eight bombs dropped exploded, demolishing a row of shops on the Strand and killing many people queuing for a bus. The death toll was 26, with 40 more being taken to hospital. The Nurses Home in Albion Hill was also demolished and a bomb struck the gasometer. Fortunately, the latter fell straight because, had it been in any way tipped, the gasometer would undoubtedly have blown up and levelled the best part of town. 3 of the planes which took part in that raid were brought down. Total number of casualties (visitors and residents) of WWII air raids was 68.]

The bombing of Exeter and casualties we had from time to time in Exmouth all influenced parents to take their girls elsewhere to seemingly safer places, despite the wording of *Exeter and Plymouth Gazette* – Friday 02 January 1942

> SOUTHLANDS SCHOOL, EXMOUTH. Inspected by the Board of Education and Recognised as Efficient. Head Mistress- MISS M. M. HOYLE. M.A., Oxon. ASSISTED by a large RESIDENT and VISITING STAFF THOROUGH EDUCATION UNIVERSITY STANDARD ~ Special attention to Modern Languages (Conversational) Large Playing Field and Gymnasium. **Visiting Pupils** may attend for Special Classes by arrangement. Preparatory and Kindergarten Classes.

---

[10] Ernest Robert Maycock (born 1883 in Torquay, Devon), was a Sub Lieut Probt R N R 414 at Albemarle, Weymouth in 1911

When Southlands closed, Anne went to the Convent of The Holy Family School in Exmouth then, at 13, after the war, she went to St Margaret's School, Exeter. Some of the other younger ones, such as Elisabeth Frink, also went to the Convent, which was a big red building – flats now – that extended beside Boarden Barn with its entrance in Montpellier Road, I think. I recall Miss Hoyle being rather cross on one occasion as, when driving in Exmouth, she had seen some untidy-looking girls and was going to stop and speak sternly to them, when she realised they were from the Convent. At least that was her explanation to our parents when she decreed that we must change from dark blue tunics into green ones!

[Elisabeth Frink recalled her wartime experiences in Exmouth when interviewed on 28th December 1992 by Sarah Kent at the British Library, just months before she died. Having said that, by the time she was nine, the War had started, she was asked "Are your memories of the War fearful?":

> Not so much, because I was cushioned largely by the school, and then I went home for holidays, and then I became a proper teenager. Well, air raids were frightening. Goodness me! I mean, we were bombed and machine-gunned in Exmouth in Devon, in broad daylight. A little crocodile of schoolgirls walking along the front, and we just had to rush up the bank, and throw ourselves down. So, of course there were aspects that were frightening.

However, in her case, Exmouth was still considered safer than Suffolk so she completed her education there, transferring to the Convent of the Holy Family at 2, Long Causeway, which was directly behind the Holy Ghost Church:

> I've skipped rather a lot. I went to a Convent School, finally, during the War, between the ages of 10 and 15/16. I went to a Convent School in Devon. Mum thought it was safer, because, you know, the bombs in Suffolk were pretty bad, because we were surrounded by aerodromes, and so we were both [her younger brother and her] sent away. And, at the Convent, there was a very nice nun, who taught me extra art.]

As I left July 1942, I went straight into war work, joining the War Office at Oxford. Many girls joined WRNS or went into nursing. We worked before we had vocational training as it was wartime. I did a residential secretarial course, then worked for a local veterinary surgeon for over 20 years. When he retired, I worked for a man who owned two garages – one in Exmouth, the other in Sidmouth, starting as an office manager and eventually becoming a director. Both jobs had long hours and I was looking after my mother as well.

## 1939 – 1942: "Boarding during wartime" by Sheila Stocken

My parents had married in Bristol in 1921 and my brother, Christopher, was born there a year later. However, my sister, Rosemary, and myself were born in Easthampstead – she in 1924 and myself five years later.

My family later moved to Devon and, although we lived in the south of the county, I boarded at Southlands School in Exmouth during the early part of World War II, starting there when I was ten. Petrol was of course in short supply during the war years [it being the first commodity to be controlled] so my journey to school entailed a train journey from Kingsbridge (which is near Salcombe) to Newton Abbott then another train from there to Star Cross where a ferry transported us across to Exmouth at the beginning of each term. There were no half-terms then though parents could visit us at mid-term. I seem to remember half-a-dozen of us travelling together at the beginning and end of term and it always seemed to be a very rough, wet crossing and our hats often drifted away! Our clothes and other belongings were sent in trunks by Passenger's Luggage in Advance so we did not have to worry about those.

Despite it being wartime with the inevitable rationing [bacon, butter and sugar were rationed from 8$^{th}$ January 1940 and almost all foods, apart from vegetables and bread, were rationed by August 1942], I do not recall our food being at all bad and there was enough of it. I was reasonably happy at the school as it seemed very outward looking and we did not feel at all restricted. We were obviously expected to conform to certain standards and I can recall Miss Hoyle vetting all books and signing them with what looked like H.H. Hoyle (but I now realise was M. M. Hoyle) at the end of each term. One concession to the war was that our dormitories were switched from upstairs to downstairs, presumably because that was considered safer. Fortunately, the school was not bombed.

Our School uniform included liberty bodices and galoshes (a type of early wellington boot made of rubber and worn over shoes). I was very sporty and can recall walking down a steep slope through woods to the lower fields where we played hockey.

Although I do not recall much about my time at Southlands, I do remember spending a night in the local hospital when I broke my arm vaulting over the horse in the gym. Apparently, I knocked over the lady who was supposed to

be catching me! Although my arm remained in plaster for weeks, the injury did not set properly. Unfortunately, all the good doctors had gone to the war, leaving only trainees, so I have had a wonky arm ever since, sticking out at a funny angle. That affected my piano playing, which I had loved up ’til then.

It must have been a very difficult decision for Miss Hoyle to close the school. A small group of us, including my particular friends – Jane Underhill and Erica Fulcher – moved to the Godolphin School at Salisbury when Southlands closed while some others, who had been day girls, went to the Maynard School in Exeter. Both schools are still functioning and I was, in fact, asked to write something for Godolphin School’s magazine not long ago.

I enjoyed my time at both Southlands and Godolphin and went on to become a School secretary.

## 1941 – 1942: "Southlands was my first school" by Freda Lovesey

I have lived in the same house in Budleigh Salterton since I was six-months-old. However, that did not stop my parents from choosing a private school in Exmouth for my education. I attended Southlands School for two years from the age of six. I don't know why I didn't start before but I do remember my mother travelling on the bus with me from Budleigh Salterton to Exmouth and back again each day, so she had to make, not only those two bus journeys, but also the two return journeys, so four per day.

The bus stopped in Salterton Road and we'd then walk along Fairfield Road to an entrance near the house which is still there – *Eldin*. That was one of only three buildings on the large site, as I recall. The rest was beautiful grounds, mostly gardens. There was a wall between *Eldin* and School House

to separate the Kindergarten from the older girls but we were taken through a sliding door into the Hall for dinner. As you can imagine, a sliding door made quite an impact on me at that age!

I can remember us girls wearing panama hats during the summer months and berets during the winter. A photograph was taken of the Infants section of the School when I was in Miss Robinson's Class. I am the fourth from the right in the back row and it is interesting to see that the younger pupils are all in their coats so perhaps it was close to "home time" for them.

As would be expected, the headmistress, Miss Hoyle, is seated centrally in the photograph. She went on to Stroud Girls' School after Southlands closed.

My teachers at Southlands School were:

1. Miss Grey (2nd from right, middle row) was short, tubby and wore glasses. She took the 1st Year Class of younger Infants (basically the Reception Class, who are seated cross-legged at the front). We worked on tables in her class in what must have been the drawing room of the big house as it had windows down to the floor and a big bay window.

2. Miss Robinson (3rd from right, middle row) had short hair. She took us 2nd Year pupils, who are standing behind her. Her classroom was at the end of the hall-way, longways across and had proper desks–wooden ones with inkwells.

On *Eldin's* ground floor, in the hallway between the classrooms, there was a glass case – like a museum exhibit – in which items of interest brought in by the children were displayed. I remember Pop sending a whole coconut from Nigeria, and, after it had been sawn in half, the shell was put on display there. He also sent cotton bolls. Above the display cabinet there were Honours Boards but I was too young to appreciate whose names were there and why.

To the left of *Eldin* was a large tree, on which us girls loved playing, sitting on its branches and swinging from them. There was a pathway to the right of

the old house and, at lunchtime, we had to walk outside to a sliding door then turn right into the building [*Sidwell*] which housed the Dining Room. School House [*Fairfield*] was to the left and Douglas Avenue was behind all that.

I was not supposed to know where Pop was going during wartime. There was a 14 mile restriction on petrol at that time, so we would travel from Budleigh to Yettington then Yettington to Exeter to see him off. On one occasion, I overheard him say, "Liverpool" at the station. Pop travelled on the Elder Dempster Line on the Appa or Accra ship – both named after places in Nigeria.

Upstairs in *Eldin* were bedrooms but, of course, I didn't get chance to see them as I was a Day Girl. However, a page of four photographs, which may well have been supplied loose in the school prospectus, shows that several girls shared a room with screens to give them some privacy and they had the usual jug and bowl for washing as hot water would have been brought to them in the jug (photo opposite). I don't seem to have the whole prospectus so perhaps that single sheet was sent to Pop while he was on his travels.

The School closed early in the War — possibly in 1942 when I was seven. I imagine that parents did not want to leave their children there during the War as Exeter was likely to be a target for bombing raids. Most of the parents were working abroad, like my father. In fact that was why my parents had chosen the school for me so that I could eventually board there if necessary.

Pop was an engineer working on a coal transporter then was an accountant for the Nigerian railway. He worked in Nigeria for over twenty years until Mum eventually got fed up with the travelling and issued him with an ultimatum! There was no work for him in that line locally so he then specialised in surgical footwear and instruments.

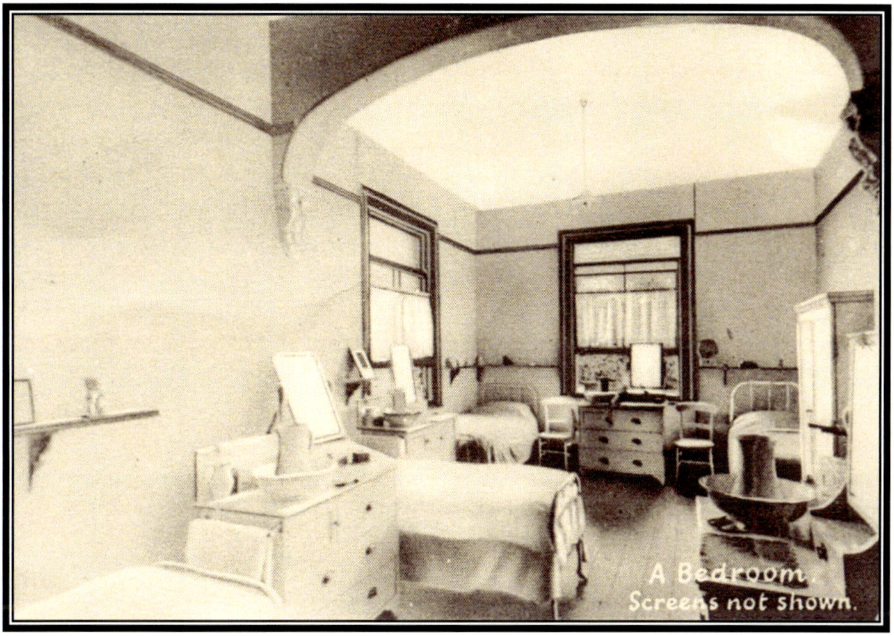
A Bedroom. Screens not shown.

When Southlands School closed, I transferred to another private school in Exmouth, which I hated. It almost gave me a breakdown so I ended up at St. Peter's in Budleigh Salterton. The Emergency Training College, which was to replace Southlands, did not start up on the site until after the War.

[By December 1942, the furnishings and equipment of Southlands School were being advertised for sale by Auction. Crews & Son of 4 Rolle Street and Strand, Exmouth placed an advert in *Devon and Exeter Gazette* on 11$^{th}$:

> SOUTHLANDS SCHOOL, "FAIRFIELD" & "BROCKHURST", ROLLE ROAD, EXMOUTH. The School Premises having been requisitioned, CREWS & SON have been favoured with instructions from Miss M. M. Hoyle, M.A., to SELL, by Auction, on THURSDAY and FRIDAY NEXT, 17th and 18th December, FURNISHINGS & EQUIPMENT

A full list of items was then detailed, which started:

THE COSTLY AND VALUABLE AGA COOKER and Equipment TO COOK FOR ONE HUNDRED AND FIFTY PERSONS; about 50 White-enamelled Combination Dressing Chests, with drawers; Cupboards, Mirror and Marble or Tiled Panels, Chests of Drawers, Woven Wire, Coiled Spring, Plycene and Diamond-mesh Iron Combination Bedsteads, Hair and Wool Mattresses, Feather Bolsters, Pillows, Blankets, Linen, Bedspreads, numerous 2ft. 6in. to 6ft. Mahogany Grained and Enamelled Wardrobes, Presses, and Cupboards of all sizes.

Pam Hayman recalled that, as a pupil at Exmouth Grammar School during WWII, three girls transferred there when Southlands closed while others went to The Maynards School in Exeter (despite *Exeter Memories* Website saying that Maynards was hit by three bombs which fell at 02.17 on 4th May 1942). She thought the Southlands site was used for Forces personnel during the remainder of the war – mostly Americans, as her husband Percy remembered them calling out to him as he rode past as a delivery boy. After D Day, there were Polish soldiers wearing blue uniforms with white shirts and red ties. They had been in the Middle East and Italy before that. However, Elizabeth Maycock thought that Jewish children had been housed there for part of the war and, Wikipedia states that "about 120 Kindertransport children grew up during the war years in hostels at Exmouth, Dawlish and South Devon, which were centres for study of secular and Jewish subjects". The hostels were large family mansions made available by their owners and helped by the British Government and Jewish social and charitable organizations. Some members of the Habonim (a Jewish youth movement) participated with the older children in helping to farm and grow agricultural produce to aid the war effort. German, Polish, Czech, Yiddish, Hebrew and English were spoken.]

Amazingly, I was to be reminded of my first school, Southlands, when I followed in Mum's footsteps and trained for teaching at Southlands Teacher Training College in London. Situated at Wimbledon Parkside in 1955, the all-female College run by the Methodist Church, had been at Battersea when Mum trained there and it is now in Richmond. Not only was I reminded of Exmouth by the similar name but I also did a week's course at Rolle College from there. I stayed in *Dunsinane* [11] then – in the large room on the first floor. I had been looking forward to seeing my first school again at that time, but found that I couldn't really relate to anything as I remembered it from my schooldays – so many changes had taken place.

---

[11] Freda may have been one of the earliest with Dunsinane connections as, in 1947, Mr and Mrs G Nichol Thomson and Miss B Nichol Thomson were still living there, their phone number being 2030

## Chapter 2: EnROLLEing

### 1946–54: "How Mr Morris progressed my career" by Marguerite Baker

I left Exmouth Grammar School aged 16 in 1941 and changed employment several times before joining National Provincial Bank in Rolle Street (now NatWest) but that was all to change when my father, Harold C. Baker, who was a builder, was in conversation with Mr Morris. He was the newly-appointed Principal of what was to be known as Exmouth Emergency Training College (later Rolle College). My father was busy converting houses near the proposed College for accommodation for the expected influx of men and women seeking careers in Education. Many had missed out on any profession due to conscription to the forces in World War II. They had been selected to take the one year course to become much-needed teachers.

Mr. Morris mentioned he was desperately in need of secretarial staff to open the office before the students arrived in February 1946. My father said that his eldest daughter would enjoy such a challenging post and Mr. Morris said, "Tell her to apply."

Although I was only in my early twenties and there were 90 applicants, I was offered the job of Assistant Secretary to the already-appointed Secretary, Miss Graham. Just as Dad thought, I was to really enjoy that post which, among other duties, involved finding schools and accommodation for students when they were on School Practice. At one point I helped organise an educational trip to Paris and, in the end, was asked if I would accompany the students!

As well as giving me those experiences after his chance conversation with my father, Mr Morris was to be instrumental in steering me towards a teaching career. He lived on the site so was around a lot and often commented that he thought I would make a good teacher because I was so enthusiastic. That led to my training at Weymouth Emergency Training College for a year then specialising in P.E. and History for teaching teenagers, which I loved. After teaching in England for about three years, I moved to Canada to teach in 1959. My future husband was a Canadian so we are still living there together as I approach my 91st birthday. As you can see, I owe a lot to Mr Morris.

I remember many students and staff from my years at Exmouth College including Miss Bowden, the Deputy Principal and Professor Floyd, who I believe married another member of the staff.

## 1946 – 1948: "Southlands and Rolle's Geographical links"

Prior to Marguerite's working at the College, there had been articles in the Devon newspapers detailing the progress of the implementation of the Government's plans for Emergency Training Colleges to cope with the raising of the school leaving age which had had to be deferred when war intervened.

At a Devon Education Committee meeting at Exeter on 26th April 1945, it had been agreed in principle that Southlands School, Exmouth, should be acquisitioned for use as an emergency training centre for teachers. According to *Western Morning News* of Friday April 27th, 1945:

> The Ministry were particularly anxious to proceed with the proposed Exmouth centre, and were looking for the co-operation of the committee in getting it open as soon as possible during that year. There was a clear need, not only for future county college purposes at Exmouth, but also for a permanent county training centre for courses of all kinds, both for teachers, youth leaders, and others.
> Sir John Daw (chairman of the County Council) told the committee a very big question was involved. Southlands was formerly a school and was requisitioned by the Government, who were still in occupation. They were fine premises, suitable as a training centre under the Government's scheme, and for later developments of the committee's work, but they were leasehold, and he understood Lord Clinton was against selling the freehold, although no definite refusal had been given.
> Sir John thought the committee ought to adopt the scheme, because it would be useless putting the new Education Act into operation if the teachers were not available to implement it.

By Monday 27th August 1945, *Western Morning News* was reporting:-

> DEVON SCHEMES Plans To Be Considered By County Council:
> . . . The Council will also consider proposals of the Ministry of Education for the administration of Southlands, Exmouth, as an emergency training college for teachers, and correspondence with the Ministry on the scheme for the establishment divisional administration.

During the College's Opening Ceremony on 15th June 1946, Devon Education Committee's chairman, Mr B. G. Lampard-Vachell, presided and stated that, by then, the college already had 223 students who, for their teaching practice, visited some 100 schools throughout Devon and Cornwall. The Right Honourable Ellen Wilkinson M.P., who formally opened the already-established Training College for Teachers, said that she felt the Teachers' Emergency Training scheme was both a great experiment and also a gamble:

The Ministry were taking a great risk in training so large a number of teachers in so short a time, but this had to be done, because raising the school-leaving age meant that by September 1948, there would be 350,000 extra children in the schools requiring at least a further 13,000 teachers. Some 16,000 applications for entry to the colleges had been received and they were still coming in at the rate of about 1,000 per week. At Exmouth it had been a double experiment, the college being the first mixed college.

Mr W. F. Morris; B. G. Lampard-Vachell; Right Honourable Ellen Wilkinson M.P. [Minister of Education from July '45 until her death in Feb '47] and Sir John Shelley (Chair Devon CC) at the opening of the Exmouth Teacher Training College on the Southlands School site on 15th June, 1946 as featured in 17 June *Western Morning News.*

The only reference to the Principal appeared towards the end of the article where "A vote of thanks to the chairman was proposed by Miss F. M. Pugh (Torquay) and seconded by Mr W. F. Morris (Principal)".

So what do we know about the first Principal? Since he had been described as a geographer from the University of Reading, I was able to ascertain that the latest information they had for him was an entry in the 1944 – 1945 Calendar:

> Geography: Sessional Assistant Lecturer, **W. F. Morris**, BA, London; Associate of University College Reading.

That terminology was repeated in each University of Reading Calendar back to 1921 – 1922, when he was first mentioned in the Faculty of Science:

| | |
|---|---|
| Geography – Lecturer: | THE REV. E. C. SPICER, M.A., New College, Oxford; M.A., Trinity College, Melbourne; Associate of University College, Reading; (Tutor). |
| Sessional Lecturer: | THE REV. A. J. POTTER, Scholae Cancellarrii, Lincoln; F.R.G.S. |
| Sessional Assistant: | **W. F. MORRIS**, B.A., London; Associate of University College, Reading. |

However, the word "Lecturer" was not added to "Sessional Assistant" until 1926 – when the University was granted its Royal Charter on 17th March. Until then, it had been known as University College, Reading from 1892, when it was founded as an extension college by Christ Church (a college of the University of Oxford), and the Schools of Art and Science, established in Reading in 1860 and 1870, were transferred to it by Reading Town Council. Receiving its first treasury grant in 1901, the University was given the site that is now known as the "London Road Campus" three years later by the Palmer family (of Huntley & Palmer's biscuits fame). W. F. Morris will have been aware that the college was unsuccessful when it first applied for a Royal Charter in 1920 but its second petition in 1925, did succeed and so it became the only new University created in England between the two World Wars.

Unfortunately, as Sarah Lodge reported to me in an email on 25th January 2013, "There are no further details or a note of his first name; everything was very formal in those days and first names were not usually used".

The same seems to have applied with his writings as Volume 45 issue 3 of the *Scottish Geographical Magazine* lists under *1929 New Books*:

> EDUCATIONAL
> *Operative Geographies; British Isles.* By W.F. Morris, B.A. London: Cassell and Co. Ltd., 1928. Price 1s.
> This little book of 40 pages, much of whose space is occupied with maps and diagrams, gives a brief account of the geography of the British Isles suitable for the upper and middle classes of the Elementary School. Questions and exercises are to be found at the end of each section. This is the second of a new series of eight volumes designed to cover the geography of the world.

However, a 1933 document did throw extra light on W. F. Morris' status and the reason why he may eventually have been appointed Principal of Exmouth Training College. The first page of the 30-page document was entitled:

> **THE CASE FOR THE IMPROVEMENT OF SPELLING**
> CORRESPONDENCE WITH THE PRESIDENT OF BOARD OF EDUCATION
> Simplified Spelling Society, Wallsend-upon-Tyne
> Made in Great Britain at the Pitman Press, Bath. 1933.
> **ENGLISH SPELLING AND THE BOARD OF EDUCATION.**

On page 4, we learn more about the Memorial:

> I also enclose a copy of the Memorial requesting the appointment of a Committee, which has up to the present been signed by nearly 800 Members of the governing

and teaching staffs of the British Universities, and the Memorial signed by nearly 200 Members of Parliament of the House of Commons. The Memorials are also supported by the following Organisations, viz.:- The National Union of Teachers, The National Association of Schoolmasters, The Incorporated Association of Assistant Masters in Secondary Schools, The Modern Language Association, The Association of Women University Teachers, and The National Union of Women Teachers. The Right Reverend Bishops of Coventry, Leicester, Sheffield, Bristol, Monmouth, and Salisbury also support the Memorials.

Then, on page 10, the **APPENDIX** starts:

LISTS OF SIGNATURES TO MEMORIALS REFERRED TO IN THE CORRESPONDENCE TO THE PRESIDENT OF BOARD OF EDUCATION.

SIR,
The undersigned, who are interested in Education, and in the question of simplifying English Spelling; in view of the growing need of an international language for use in international Conferences and Meetings and in publications of world-wide interest; and in view of the increasing conviction in Sweden, Germany, and other Countries, that the English language, which is already used by nearly two hundred million of our world's population, can best supply that need, but that its inconsistent and difficult spelling is a hindrance; respectfully submit, for your consideration; the request that you will appoint a representative Committee, to consider whether English Spelling can be and should be simplified, and if so, what improvements should be recommended, for optional or general use.

33 names from the UNIVERSITY OF READING appear on pages 20/21, including those of the Vice-Chancellor, T Franklin Sibly and his Deputy, W. G. De Burgh, but only 15 have followed the V.C.'s example and provided their Christian names. 12 of the signatories are Professors and all the others are Lecturers (including E.W. Gilbert, B.Litt., M.A. and A.A. Millers, M.Sc. who are both lecturers in Geography) apart from the Assistant Registrar, E. Smith and Mr Morris who is mentioned last, being described as:

W. F. Morris, B.A., Assistant Lecturer in Department of Geography, and Headmaster of Demonstration School

No doubt both interests were stated for Mr Morris because this was an Educational Memorial. I have been unable to find any mention of his latter role anywhere else but it is that aspect that would seem to explain how he came to be chosen as Principal of Exmouth Training College as Demonstration Schools worked in conjunction with Teacher Training Colleges, demonstrating educational principles after the educational benefactor, Julia Salis Schwabe (1819 – 1896), proposed the establishment of a teacher training college with a demonstration school in England. She was a strong proponent of the Friedrich Froebel system of education, where the first learning experiences of the very young are seen as of crucial importance to a child's development and, therefore, to the health of society as a whole. As a result, a Froebel Education College was established in Britain in 1892 and a Froebel Demonstration School opened in Colet Gardens in 1894 with six pupils under the headmistress-ship of Esther Lawrence. When the school moved to Clarence Lane, Roehampton, southwest London in 1946, it took the name of the house on the site and became Ibstock Place School, an independent co-educational day school connected with the Froebel Institute and the demonstration of its particular educational principles.

I did find more evidence of Morris' particular interest in Geography as, in the January 1938 Preface of the book "Geography in the Middle Ages", published that year by George H. T. Kimble, Lecturer in Geography in The University of Reading, his contribution is acknowledged on page v of 272:

> In preparing this work I have enjoyed the help of many friends whose scholarship I have sought to put to good account. In particular I should like to name Professor E. G. R. Taylor and Mr W. F. Morris, who read the manuscript and made many constructive criticisms . . . and the members of the University Library staff for numerous incidental courtesies . . . Lastly, my thanks are due to the University of Reading for a generous grant allocated to me for this work.

Interestingly, the Southlands School magazines 1937 – 1942 show that a former pupil, Joan Campbell, was also lecturing in the Geography Department of the University of Reading while W. F. Morris was there. Her involvement was first mentioned in the Old Girls' section of the 1940 magazine (no. 46):

> JOAN CAMPBELL has a temporary post as lecturer in geography in the University of Reading, owing to a member of the staff having been called up. The work is interesting and consists chiefly of trying to show greater knowledge than you possess.

The following year (Summer of 1941, no. 47) also under CIRCLE 1935 is:

> J. CAMPBELL is still lecturing in geography at Reading University, and is beginning to feel more at home. At the end of the summer term she took it upon herself to organise a series of field classes, and might have been seen leading a string of students on bicycles through the countryside round Reading – not work, but much enjoyed by all.

By the no. 48, Summer of 1942 magazine, under CIRCLE 1935, is:

> J. CAMPBELL has been re-appointed as lecturer in the Geographical Dept., Reading University. This year she has introduced the Tutorial System on the Oxford lines with the honours students, and this seems to have been much appreciated. During the summer vacation she is helping to conduct a party of students round the Lake District.

That is the last entry from that source as Southlands School ceased at the end of 1942. However, the three editions prior to 1940 show that Joan had been a distinguished scholar. In the Summer of 1937 magazine (no. 43) she appears in the REPORT OF SCHOLARSHIP COMMITTEE:

> How lovely it would be, if in this report next year I could write that we had raised all the rest of the £800 needed for the first scholarship and that we were starting on another.
>
> A very interesting letter was read from Joan Campbell, the present holder of the scholarship; she seems to be making the best of her time at Oxford.

In the same edition, under CIRCLE 1935 (presumably for those who left Southlands that year, we find that she is its Circle Secretary (as denoted by *):

> * Joan Campbell has just finished her second year at Oxford. The Easter vac. was spent on a geographical expedition to France and the summer one will be spent interviewing water engineers, 'bus conductors, farmers and borough surveyors, as she is writing her Regional description. In the intervals Joan plays golf.

It is the Summer 1938 magazine (no. 44) that gives us more idea of her academic ability as, under EXAMINATION SUCCESSES, we read of her 1st Class Honours. Degree in the Geography Finals at the University of Oxford, while D. Coxhead obtained 2nd Class Hons. in the same examination and D. Mason was awarded Pass Inter Arts. by the University of London.

In the Summer of 1939 magazine (no. 45) under CIRCLE 1935 is:

> JOAN CAMPBELL is at present in London being coached for the Home Civil Service exam., which she takes in July. She spent the first three months of this year staying with a family in Paris and trying to learn to speak French.

We cannot tell whether the start of World War II on 3rd September 1939 affected her choice in any way – all we know is that it obviously gave her chance to lecture in Geography at the University of Reading and University Calendars imply that she would have been in a fair amount of contact with

W. F. Morris as only four Academic Staff are listed in the Geography Department under the Faculty of Letters on page 32 of the 1940 – 41 Calendar:

> **Geography** – Lecturer in charge: A. A. MILLER, D.Sc.,
> University of London, University College;
> (Censor of Discipline, and Tutor).
> Lecturer: **JOAN E. M. CAMPBELL** B.A.,
> Oxford (Society of Home Students).
> G. H. T. KIMBLE, M.A., London; University
> of London, King's College; (Tutor).
> Sessional Assistant Lecturer: **W. F. MORRIS**, B.A.,
> London; Associate of University College, Reading.

W. F. Morris is the only member of the Department who is not detailed as a Tutor and that would tie up with the fact that the others would have been lecturing full-time whereas his lecturing was on a part-time basis to fit in with his headship of a Demonstration School. The composition of the department remained the same until the 1943 – 1944 Calendar except that there was an additional member – Dulcie J. Edmonds (Mrs) from 1942 – 1943 onwards. Joan is last mentioned in 1943 – 1944 and W. F. Morris in 1944 – 1945. The *FreeBMD* website shows that Joan E. M. Campbell married Peter C. S. Bradley in Reading in the summer of 1945 and that she (Joan E. M. Bradley) died aged 42 in Plymouth in the spring of 1961.

It has not been possible to ascertain whether Joan and W. F. Morris were aware of the link between themselves and the Southlands site as Joan may well have left before he was appointed to the principalship of Exmouth Training College. It was only after he had taken up his post of Principal there that the University of Reading purchased what was to become its main campus – Whiteknights Park – in 1947. Both he and Joan had worked on the London Road campus and Joan had lived very close to it initially – at 38 Redlands Road then at 49 London Road. It was only in her third and fourth years that she moved further afield to 72 Shinfield Road, possibly to be nearer Peter who may well have been living with his parents at 118.

The *Street Directory and Gazetteer for Exmouth 1947* states on page 123:

> TEACHERS' TRAINING COLLEGE
>
> One of the first Teachers' Training Colleges set up by the Ministry of Education, to increase the number of available teachers, necessary under the new Education Acts, was opened at Southlands School, Exmouth, by the then Minister of Education,

The Right Honourable Ellen Wilkinson, M.P., on June 15th, 1946.
There are some 200 students, and the Principal is Mr W. F. Morris.
Administration Offices, Fairfield, Rolle Road, Exmouth. Tel. 2303.
Students live for the most part in halls at Ryll Court, Albion Hill; St. Hilarian, Portland Avenue; Ferniehurst, Douglas Avenue; Brockhurst, Rolle Road; Coonoor Lodge, Salterton Road.

Other entries for Douglas Avenue in that same Street Directory show that Mr W. F. Morris was a Fellow of the Royal Geographical Society:

Exmouth Training College Principal, Mr W. F. Morris B.A., F.R.G.S. 2303

and describe *Ferniehurst* as a Training College Hostel for Men tel: 2670, just before Isca Road, where Miss A M V Sweet is shown as still living at *Chypraze* with Miss D Coxon and their phone number is 3360.

Although W. F. Morris is no longer shown as Principal in the *1948-49 Street Directory and Gazetteer for Exmouth*, he and his wife, Eleanor Laura (née Reeves, whom he married in Wokingham towards the end of 1914), were still living in Exmouth at 19 Beacon with another couple and two widows and they were still there in 1950 – 1951:

| | | |
|---|---|---|
| BEACON – 19 | Mrs W Carlyon-Keirle | Mrs M C Field |
| | Mr & Mrs W F Morris | Lt-Col & Mrs W Grigor |

Since they had lived at 3 Melrose Avenue, Reading throughout his 25 years in the Geography Department of the University of Reading, that must have been quite a change for both of them, 'though, having lived in Reading for 66 years before moving to Exmouth, I can understand how they would have found it relatively easy to adapt to the pace of life here.

It was the discovery that he had lived at 3 Melrose Avenue, Reading that enabled me to ascertain his name as William from the 1921 *Smith's Directory of Reading* and as William Frederick from the 1944 *Kelly's* one. That then led to finding him, aged 24 in the 1911 census, living at 14 Norris Road, Reading with his mother, Sarah C. Morris, a 49-year-old widow and his older sister, Alice D (28). Like him, Alice Dora was an Elementary School Teacher employed by Reading Borough Education Committee. They had been born in Yarmouth, Norfolk as had their parents – Frederick Arthur Morris and Sarah Craggy Sowells, who had married there in 1881. However, their father had died in Wokingham aged 39 towards the end of 1900 and, in the 1901 census,

Alice (already a school teacher at 18), William (14) and their 12-year-old brother, Charles Edward, are shown as still living there with their mother (38) and two boarders, Sidney & Walter Wright, both plumbers born Lambeth, London and a visitor, Joseph Philips, a machine fitter born in Somerset. This may sound crowded but in 2005 the house was detailed as having 7 bedrooms.

While Principal of Exmouth Training College, W. F. Morris received occasional mention in the local press, 'though not always with the same initials! Following the annual meeting of Exmouth Youth Committee on 28th October, the 1st November 1946 *Western Times* reported under the title: BEWARE OF "BODY SNATCHING", Capt. J. Walton Turner's *Advice to Youth Organization* when he deplored the training given by some youth organizations on Sundays. Mr Morris' thoughts about *Bewildered World* were

> Speaking on the conditions under which youth organisations carried out their work, Mr W. R. Morris (principal, Exmouth Training College) said the children of 14 leaving school now went out into a debilitated, anxious and bewildered world. Most of their education had been received under extreme tension and in schools that had become caricatures of themselves owing to shortages of teachers, apparatus and writing materials.
>
> Mr Morris added that today's children were better than those of years ago. They were more easy to control, better mannered, healthier and more intelligent. It was the duty of youth organisations to instill a sense of responsibility into boys now leaving school and to help them readjust themselves in a bewildered generation.

From the 4th June 1948 *Western Times* in an article headed "WOMEN ONLY When Exmouth Training College Reopens", we learn that:

> When Exmouth Emergency Training College for Teachers reopens in August it will be as an establishment for women only. First batch of students will be on an emergency course for one year, and in September this year, the first lot of 3-year students will join them, thus, when the emergency students complete their year's course, the emergency scheme will come to an end as far as Exmouth is concerned. In the recent session, 247 students have undergone the strenuous course, packing a three-year University course into only twelve months, and since the college opened 464 students have passed through.

However, that writer seems to have been misinformed about the future length of the course as it would not be until 1960 that a 3-year course would come into existence (as confirmed by Miss Spicer on page 120) and the *1948 – 49 Street Directory and Gazetteer for Exmouth* mentions a 2 year one on p. 137.

## Chapter 3: ROLLE CALL

### 1948 – 1950: "Exmouth Training College" by Eileen Stafford

In 2012, I was looking up something about the new McCarthy & Stone development in Douglas Avenue when I found a note about Rolle College. Well, I started as a student there in 1948 and was billeted in that wonderful old house, *Eldin.* There were sixteen of us living in lovely old *Eldin*, eight were ex-service girls and the remaining eight, of which I was one, were young innocent (!) eighteen-year-olds straight out of school.

Ex-Army girls on Eldin's south-facing balcony. They were doing the one-year emergency training course to help ease the shortage of teachers after the war.

The information on *Google* says that the Emergency Training College opened in 1949, but that's wrong because I definitely started in September 1948 and half the students then were women who had been in the Forces and were doing the one-year emergency training as there was a shortage of teachers after the war [12]. The main building wasn't built then and we were all housed in various large villas all around the town. Our year students were the first to start the 2-year course. I have a vast number of memories of those wonderful years I spent at Exmouth, and I expect you don't know that *Eldin* is haunted!

Ready to leave *Eldin* for our 1st school practice – a week in Torquay just before Xmas 1948 – I am third from left.

The irony is that, as I am now 81, I thought it might be nice to end my days back in Exmouth, hence my interest in the new McCarthy & Stone apartments going up right opposite *Eldin*, a house I loved, and which gave me so many wonderful memories. I'm not sure whether I could manage however, as the 18-year-old girl I was then would be more and more present in my mind. Imagine the headline in the paper "81-year-old returns to the town she loved aged 18!!"

I now live in Bovey Tracey, have been a teacher for many years, have written seven published novels, was married for 47 years and have two grown-up children, one of whom has followed in my footsteps and is teaching Infants. [Since writing this in April 2012, Eileen has had another novel published and converted two of her novels to Kindle e-books.]

[12] Butler's Education Act of 1944 raised the school leaving age to 15 in 1947. The Fleming Committee, set up in 1943 to consider how to meet post-war requirements for teachers, had drawn up a scheme which was piloted at Goldsmith's College in September 1944. The first emergency Training College opened in 1945 and, by December 1947, 55 such Colleges were in operation, one of which was in Exmouth

## 1948 – 1950: "Ryll Court" by Jeanne Boone

After WWII, the Government took over "*Fairfield*" (formerly a School) at the junction of Salterton Road, Carlton Hill and Rolle Road as an Emergency Training College. The purpose was to train, in just one year, mature students (mostly women from the Armed Forces) to become the teachers who were so much needed in the post-war schools. By 1948, the College had been renamed Exmouth Training College and it offered a 2-year course. The first of the 2-year students trained alongside the last year of the Emergency Students for the Teacher's Certificate of the University College of the South West (now Exeter University) [as the latter did not receive its charter until 1955]. I was part of that first intake of around 150 students doing the 2-year course at Exmouth Training College when I joined straight from school in Bexleyheath, Kent at the age of 18 in 1948. The principal, Miss Croft, had come from Avery Hill College in Hertfordshire, where I had also been offered a place. The *1948 – 49 Street Directory and Gazetteer for Exmouth* detailed:

EXMOUTH TRAINING COLLEGE

Two Year Training College for Women
Maintained by Devon County Education Authority
*Chief Education Officer*: W. E. Philip, M.A. Education Offices, Castle St, Exeter
*Principal*: Miss G. M. Croft O.B.E., B.A.

At present the College is housed on the main site in houses Fairfield (seen here), Brockhurst and Eldin, and outside the main site in St. Hilarian, Portland Avenue; Ferniehurst, Douglas Ave; Coonoor Lodge, Budleigh Salterton Rd and Ryll Court, Albion Hill. So far as the main site is concerned, that will be retained complete, but what houses in addition will be retained is another matter; most probably for the time being it will include all those buildings at present in use.

There was a core curriculum, which included psychology, health education, music and art, on top of which my two main subjects were English and maths. I recall that Mr Arnold taught art, Mr Illing music and Mr Floyd maths. I remember the latter once got a phone call during a lecture to say that his son had been born. [Philip M Floyd was born towards the end of 1949, his sister Judith I Floyd having been born in the summer of 1947. Both had been born in Devon Central, according to the *FreeBMD* website, whereas their parents,

Philip J Floyd and Enid P Bendall had married in Cheltenham in 1946.]

I was in the College choir, which was run by Mr Illing. He had a friend who lived at the big house, now a hotel (I can't remember the name) near Honiton, where he had a recording studio. We went there to record Benjamin Brittain's "Ceremony of Carols" but I don't know what happened to the recording.

The College scarf was pale blue and grey but that was thought to be too pale so it was later changed to blue, grey and red [see page 140]. At that time students were, of course, living and working in post-war austerity, with Utility furniture and food and clothes rationing under what would, today, be considered strict rules. I can recall the bomb-damaged sites where the Magnolia Centre now is in Exmouth. Cars used to park there, although there weren't so many about as there are now.

We had Friday afternoons off, and went to the Millican café, on the corner opposite Thomas Tucker department store. I liked to have a meringue, a great treat. My mother used to send me half-a-crown a week to help out as we didn't have much money.

I boarded at *Ryll Court* so played for them when we had a hockey tournament between the various halls on Maer Sports Ground in 1948-49. We won that Tournament so here is the winning team. I presume College had a team but have no recollection of it.

*Ryll Court*, a most attractive old house with one of the most beautiful gardens in Exmouth, covered the area where Ryll Court Drive and the new bungalows are now. Miss Cooper, a lecturer, was the Warden in charge and she was helped by Miss Samson who was not a lecturer but a friend of hers. All the Wardens were lecturers. I recall a garden party at Ryll on 3rd June 1950 – photographed here.

My room was on the ground floor and originally had six beds in it. Later, it was split four and two, and I was lucky enough to be one of the two. I am still great friends with the girl I shared with. There was one other bedroom on the ground floor with four beds in it and there were more upstairs, but I do not know how many. At one time we put magazine pictures all round our walls to brighten them up a bit, but we got told off and had to take them down again. It was rather like what I imagine a glorified boarding school would have been. Our room had sash windows to the ground and, one night, 12 of us climbed through them and went for a midnight swim in the sea. Fortunately, we were not caught, as we would probably have got into terrible trouble, bearing in mind that one student was sent down because her boyfriend climbed a ladder into her room. Miss Croft (and possibly students as well) lived in *Hasledene*.

Life was enjoyable, but disciplined. Miss Croft stood no nonsense – I think she had been in the ATS or something similar during the war and she knew how to keep order. If you went out in the evening you had to sign in and out, and special permission was needed if you were going to be out after 10 p.m.

*Ryll Court* had previously been owned by Robert Tucker Pain JP who died there 11th February 1942 at the age of 101. [Born in Kensington 9th August 1840, he married Emma Bayley in St George Hanover Square in 1870 and set up the Tucker Pain Nursing Fund in her memory in 1898 for "nursing attendance for the sick among the working class in the parish of Withycombe Raleigh". He married Harriett Emma Shirley Kennedy the following year and it was their second son, Arthur **Charles** Davy **Pain**, born 23rd June 1901, who made his fortune in Burma and India before returning to his home town of

Exmouth in the 1960s who founded the Pain Trust (before his death in 1971)], of which my son Howard is a Trustee. It provides bursaries for boys and young men, aged 11 to 21 years, who live in the East Devon area or 8 miles from Exmouth Town Hall to the east of the River Exe, to travel the world.

We used to sit on the stone wall which is still there at the top of Albion Street [Albion Hill] – the land was much higher on the *Ryll* side! The two white gate pillars outside one of the bungalows in Claremont Grove is all that remains of *Ryll Court*. I enjoyed the novelty of being away from home. As far as I can remember, I didn't manage to get back during term time and probably not even at half term. We did have an Open Day, when local people and parents were invited into the College to see our work. I remember that we dressed up in European peasant costumes and did some dances.

*Fairfield* was the main Administrative building of the College, but also provided some teaching and living accommodation. As well as the Lecture Rooms in *Fairfield*, there were more in other large old houses, such as *Brockhurst*, which was next door and *Eldin*, which is still standing today. We had more lectures in *Brockhurst* and *Eldin* than in *Fairfield* itself. In the latter's grounds were wooden buildings which acted as the Main Hall/Gym, a Dining Room and Common Room. We had all our meals in the wooden canteen building on campus, including at weekends. The only exception was a late supper, when we used to cook beans on toast in the basement of *Ryll Court*. We used to cycle between *Ryll* and Rolle.

While I was at the College I met my husband, Ray Mallett. He was not a student – we met at a dance at the Pavilion. There were quite a lot of those, often attended by male trainee teachers from St Luke's in Exeter and by the Royal Marines from Lympstone. Having gained my teaching certificate from the University College of the South West [which had been established in 1922 from Exeter Technical and University Extension College], I went back to Kent for a couple of years but then managed to find a teaching job in Okehampton. Ray and I were then able to get married in 1953.

**1948 – 1953 & 1976 – 1989: "The 'ten shilling' girls" by Hugh Jones**

My wife, Ingrid Lehmann, was born in 1930 in a hospital in Neukölln-Britz, a district of West Berlin. Her mother's family, the Szeklinskis, lived in the Neukölln Hermann Strasse at No. 58. It is divided into flats and it seems that several of them had been occupied at times by various members of her family. I visited her Uncle Heinz there. He could speak some English having spent most of World War II as a P.O.W. on a ship in the Mediterranean. Her father, Richard Lehmann, was a German intelligence operative who monitored the activities of American journalists prior to that country's entry into the war. He left his wife and two daughters at that time, disappearing without trace and Ingrid said that she never met, or heard anything about, any of his relatives.

She gave me to understand that she came to Exmouth when she was 18. She left Templehof in a Dakota military transport which had just flown in a load of coal to Germany during the Berlin Airlift [27th June 1948 to 12th May 1949, according to *Wikipedia*. However, boards at Imperial War Museum have 24th June 1948 to 11th May 1949 and Gatow is the airport mentioned]. The toilet was a bucket in a corner! On arriving in Hanover, she then travelled to a transit camp in England by rail and sea. From there, she was sent to Exmouth to work as a domestic in the Halls of Residence of the Emergency Training College and the local townspeople called her and her companions "Ten shilling girls" as they were to be treated on equal terms with English workers.

It was the British Military Administration of Berlin that had sent her to England and her papers, including the North Sea Scheme contract document, are now in the Devon Records Office in Exeter. *Wikipedia* suggests that our 1945–51 Government had decided to bring as many unemployed young Germans to England as possible and give them jobs here after the economy of West Berlin collapsed in 1945 so as to try and avoid conditions like those that existed after World War I, which then led to the formation of the Nazi Party. The men went down the mines and the women worked as domestics in hospitals and other institutions. Their contracts promised that they would be treated on equal terms with English workers and gave them the right to repatriation after 2 years' service. However many, like Ingrid, never returned.

[Diana Kay and Robert Mills in their 1992 book, *Refugees or Migrant Workers? European Volunteer Workers in Britain 1946 – 1951*, commented that, after the initial "special schemes", three somewhat larger ones followed during the Labour Government's period of office. The "Blue Danube" scheme recruited 2,341 Austrian women for textile work and nursing then, between 1948 and 1950, the "North Sea" scheme recruited 9,713 German women for various forms of domestic work. A further scheme, which began in late 1949 and was eventually discontinued in 1951, recruited 1,655 Italian women for various unskilled factory and domestic jobs.]

Ingrid and her companions were among those 9,713 German women recruited as part of the "North Sea" scheme and were billeted in *Ryll Court* at the top of Albion Hill when they arrived in Exmouth. None of them knew a word of English when they arrived and it appears that the College made no real attempt to teach them. However, they soon found a way to remedy that deficiency. It seems that they learned the language by going to the cinema every evening! [No television in those days!] but, apart from mentioning that fact, Ingrid did not really talk much about her life in the College.

[Auctioneer's description of Ryll-court, when it was to be sold by Messrs. Hussey and Son on Friday, 14th August, 1885 at the Rougemont Hotel, Exeter at 4 o'clock precisely, gives us some idea of the property where Ingrid found herself:

> all that charming FREEHOLD RESIDENCE known as **Ryll-court**, delightfully situated on a commanding position, overlooking the estuary of the Exe, and a long reach of the Devonshire coast as far as Berry Head, together with good walled garden, four fields of excellent pasture land, comprising some capital building sites, in the parish of Withycombe Raleigh, Devon, the whole containing 10a. or 31p. Near there is a small but suitable farmery, consisting of four-stall stable, coachhouse, with granary over; cow-house, piggery, and poultry-houses. The whole is within 10 minutes' walk of the Exmouth Station of the London and South-Western Railway, whence the city of Exeter is reached in 30 minutes and London in hours. From its high, yet sheltered position at the back of the improving town of Exmouth, it insures perfect privacy with the advantage of living near a centre of

population, and commands many views of land and water, hill and valley of surpassing beauty, and is in every way suited for the residence of a family of means. For orders to view, plans, particulars, and conditions of sale, apply to Messrs. Stamp and Son, Solicitors, Honiton; the Auctioneers: 14, Queen-street, Exeter; or to Messrs, J. and H. Drew, Land Agents and Surveyors, 15, Queen-street, Exeter. — July 7th, 1885.

The *London Gazette* of 23rd October 1942 provides further information as it carried a notice asking for those with a claim against the estate of Robert Tucker Pain, late of *Ryll Court*, Exmouth, Devon who died in February that year to submit their claims to the Exeter solicitors of his executor, Arthur Richard Pain of Frimley, Surrey by 25th December, after which time he would proceed to distribute the estate.

By 1947, *Ryll Court* was recorded as being an Exmouth Training College Hostel next to Marpool Hill and its phone number was 3281. A garden party for the Staff was held there each year as the gardens were so delightful. In 1949 the Misses Cooper and Samson were hostesses. Their cats Simon & Calligula are shown here with Pat in June 1950]:

Above Right: 2nd year students in *Ryll Court* grounds in March 1949

Ingrid was employed by what became Rolle College all her working life, apart from a short period when she was looking after her very young daughter. She had married a local man, John Middleton, who left her when their daughter went to Canterbury University. She was working part-time for the Cafe Wien at that time and commented that the "Austrians" who owned it were Germans!

Students in *Ryll Court* Gardens – 1949

Ingrid was still working at the College when I married her in 1987. I think she was in *Hasledene* then, 'though she seemed to know all of the Halls. When I met her, she had a companion, Brigitte White, still working with her (they are both pictured here). Brigitte had married a butcher who became the Manager of Dewhursts in Budleigh.

I cannot help too much with dates but I retired in 1996. Ingrid had retired shortly before then, possibly 1993/4 on health grounds as a result of osteo-arthritis, no doubt caused by too much shifting of furniture without assistance. She died in 2007 and, although I have none of her papers, I do have papers relating to my German widower's pension (Small!). They contain details of her contribution and pension records including dates. I cannot understand what the text is saying but I have extracted the following from a list of dates taken from just one page [translation follows each phrase]:

| | | |
|---|---|---|
| Versicherungsverlauf | : | Insurance Record |
| VAB Betrag aus, 06.06.47 – 31.12.47 | : | Amount from VAB |
| Glbh. Betrag aus, 01.01.48 – 30.04.48 | : | Amount from Glbh |
| Vereinigtes Konigreich (Grossbritannien) | : | United Kingdom (Great Britain) |

AUSL 06.04.48 – 30.04.48. (AUSL = "Ausland" – foreign)

## Chapter 4: ROLLE-TOP DESKS

### 1949 – 1951: "Coonoor Lodge" by Romola Pascoe

When I was accepted by Exmouth Training College to train for teaching in 1949, it was only four years after the war had finished, so things were still in short supply and rationed. In those days, I lived in Truro, Cornwall, which was very much a backwater. Consequently, I had not been further into England than Plymouth so the trip to Exmouth seemed to me a great excursion. I only knew I had been accepted by the College a week before term began. But that is another long story . . .

Being seventeen and attending the County Grammar School in Truro, I had thought of becoming a nurse. We had a pre-nursing $6^{th}$ form class and I was a keen first-aider in the School Red Cross with many medals. I can remember we wore them pinned to our tunics with badges for house, posture etc. Being very fond of Biology, I thought that would be the next best step for me but, when I discovered what was expected of the students – the physically hard work, long hours and pay – I changed my mind. That meant that I was late applying to the Colleges and, when the results were announced in March, I had not been given a place. My parents were not happy for me to stay at school for another year especially as my father had been very ill for two years and was only just returning to work. I therefore got a job in the Finance department of Cornwall County Council, working in the teachers' and school caretakers' pay department. I enjoyed the job but the comparison of my salary with those of the teachers made me long for something different. Basically, I still wanted to go to College but my parents wouldn't hear of it. However, I didn't take my name off the Clearing House list and, some months later, I received a letter from Exmouth Training College, asking me to attend for interview the following week. That was the difficult part as I was, by then, fully accepted by the County Council and settled in my work. I asked my current boyfriend what I should do and he encouraged me to persuade my parents to let me at least try or I would always be wondering if I was in the right job. There wasn't much time to lose and, eventually, I persuaded them to let me go to the interview, saying that, if I was accepted, it was to be and, if I was turned down, I would give up the idea permanently.

A trip to Exmouth was arranged for the following weekend and I set off to see Miss Croft (and her little Terrier, Judy). I was offered a place and asked to turn up the following Saturday for the beginning of term. That was the next trauma – trying to get everything ready in seven days and tying up all the loose ends. I was Church Organist, Sunday School teacher, Youth Club leader and County Council employee so all those groups had to be informed. With great excitement, and fear, I obtained a large trunk from my cousin who had just left St Gabriel's College in London to teach in Chacewater, Cornwall.

After what seemed like a long trip, I arrived at St David's station and asked the porter to take me to the branch line for Exmouth. What a beautiful trip it was! It reminded me of the Falmouth Branch line from Truro. There were others on the train – some chatty and others subdued. What was in store for us? Some of us were immature students, arriving from sheltered backwaters, not having travelled or moved around the country. That was particularly so for a Cornish student, as Cornwall was very remote those days.

We had all been through a six year war during the most influential years of our lives and had felt reasonably safe that far from London. Plymouth and Falmouth had been the nearest targets, though we did have one raid when a bomb landed on the hospital and bounced on to St Paul's Church roof. Today's children have no idea of the restrictions we had – the only activities available to us during those dark times were Church, Youth Club and Guides. Going to Exmouth was a huge step from home.

With other students we were taken to our Halls of Residence. I was to live at *Coonoor Lodge* on the Salterton Road, about 10 – 15 minutes' walk from *Fairfield.* It was a large stone-built house with gabled bay windows and an impressive front door with a conservatory to the right of that door. Set on the corner of Claremont Road and Salterton Road, *Coonoor Lodge* was not quite the farthest accommodation from the main College as the very impressive *Ryll Court* was much further along Claremont Road.

[Although we do not know the full history of how *Coonoor Lodge* came to be a Hall of Residence for Exmouth Training College, we do know from page 1141 of 20$^{th}$ December 1935 edition of *The Colliery Guardian and Journal of*

*the Coal and Iron Trades*, that "Mr Charles Wright, Coonoor Lodge, Exmouth, mining engineer, left £31,939, with net personalty £31,836." By 1947, *Coonoor Lodge*, Salterton Road is described as a Training College Hostel. Its phone number was 2483. It is photographed here in 2013.]

The upstairs of *Coonoor Lodge* was allotted to the 2$^{nd}$ years and downstairs to the 1$^{st}$ years. I was given a very basic room at the back which I shared with Dorothy Luxden. It had French windows out onto the back lawn and that fact was to prove very useful later on when students stayed out after curfew! We had iron beds, like boys' dormitory beds at boarding school. They were very uncomfortable, having mattresses with springs you could count each night! Dark charcoal coloured blankets and a cotton bedspread completed the look and there was a dark bedside table with drawers for clothes next to each bed, plus a very small wardrobe. All the furniture was dark brown – almost black – in colour. In the centre of the room was a table which Dorothy and I shared.

We went to *Fairfield* for all meals, sitting on benches like those in the Harry Potter Great Hall. All students were counted and ate at the same time, each table being for a selected house. Breakfast was the only meal you were able to omit without permission. Next to the Dining Hall was a Common Room where students would collect if they lived in houses not on Campus. Post was collected there and we made great use of its piano, showing off our prowess at duet playing and jazz, our favourite pieces being Mozart Duets and "Chopsticks".

We were divided into three groups: Infant, Junior and Seniors. I think the Infant group worked the hardest but were better trained for their future teaching. Miss Koegler (not sure how to spell her name) was an excellent teacher. During the week, 9 o'clock was the time to be back at your house as the doors were then locked. A book was kept for us to sign in and out. Looking back on it now, it was a bit like Prison!!

In our first week, we were given a maths examination set by Mr Floyd, a large man with untidy curly hair. He fancied himself as quite a ladies' man! I think he wore the same suit all the time. Fortunately, I did so well in the test that I was excused any maths lectures. So much for learning how to teach maths!

We had to choose our main study courses and I chose Music as that was my great passion at the time. I had been organist and choir mistress at Highertown Church for a good many years and I enjoyed choral music. My subsidiary subject was to be Art but, after a few weeks, I decided that I couldn't cope with the Music as I had not studied any theory and we had had no music lessons, apart from year group singing, at Grammar School. Writing an essay on style was too much for me. I had been given Music lessons by a Mrs Burnet but had somehow not studied the theory of Music. I realised that we had missed out because it was so difficult to get teachers during the war and, even some of those we did have, were shell-shocked from their experiences in the Forces.

Mr Illing was unsympathetic to my dilemma so I had to face my first meeting with Miss Croft and explain to her that I needed to change to another subject. Little did I realise in moving to Rural Science that I'd be taking on a most demanding subject as Mrs Leadley-Brown worked all her students to their limits in contrast to the adorable Mr Arnold, who took us for Art. I think those were the two extreme subjects as far as output was concerned.

The incredible Mrs Leadley-Brown expected us at lectures by 9.30, worked us all day and into the evening on special subject days. It was very annoying to be out tending the veggie plots and see your friends relaxing on the benches! We did a number of interesting things like rearing chicks, studying egg embryos, collecting honey, chasing swarms of bees, producing flower gardens, a woodland survey at Woodbury and trying out all the tasks we would be asking our pupils to do in the future. Mrs L-B did have a vintage Bentley car, in which she took us out to Woodbury Common and other places.

I think, as we were the first group of 2-year students to go to Rolle (Exmouth College as it was then), the staff were experimenting with us. Up till then, they had been training emergency students – mature students who were recently home from the Forces, having seen the world and been to places.

Because we had to travel to *Fairfield* every day, many of us brought our bicycles with us. That certainly made for a quicker journey in the mornings but it was hard work cycling home in the evening loaded with books and files! Our laundry was collected each week in a large wicker basket. We were allowed to change one sheet free each week but had to pay for anything else we sent. Each student had a Laundry book. There were no washing machines or fridges then. We hung the butter and milk out of the window in a muslin cloth on the cold side of the house. Sometimes the butter tasted quite rancid and the cheese grew interesting fungi, but we survived! [so did Laundry Books until the end of 1963 as this memento from one of my contemporaries shows]

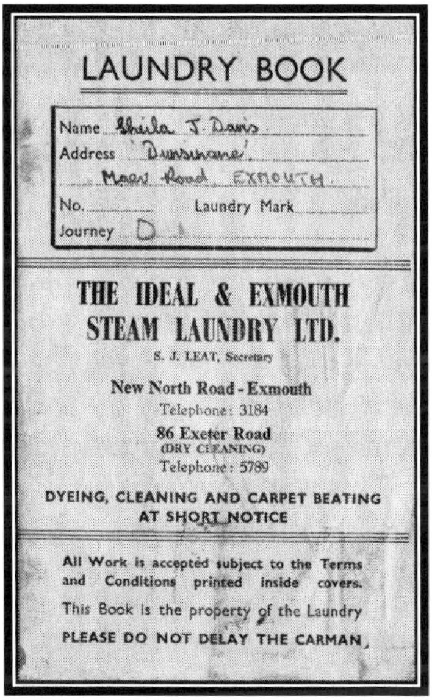
LAUNDRY BOOK

Name Sheila J. Davis

Address Dunsinane

Moor Road, EXMOUTH

No. Laundry Mark

Journey D

THE IDEAL & EXMOUTH
STEAM LAUNDRY LTD.

S. J. LEAT, Secretary

New North Road - Exmouth
Telephone: 3184

86 Exeter Road
(DRY CLEANING)
Telephone: 5789

DYEING, CLEANING AND CARPET BEATING
AT SHORT NOTICE

All Work is accepted subject to the Terms and Conditions printed inside covers.

This Book is the property of the Laundry

PLEASE DO NOT DELAY THE CARMAN

Commodities were only just beginning to come back into the shops and we had to economise. There was no paper to draw or paint on and we had to use kitchen rolls and newspapers for art lessons. We were also rationed to two packs of file paper a term at the local Stationer and pencils and pens were like gold dust. I grew so much in confidence during that first year and, as the photographs will show, I had a great time.

also brought over boxes of cigarettes to share – it really was the done thing to smoke then, especially with holders. I do not have any actual photos of *Coonoor Lodge* from that time, but, I have been looking at the satellite map of the area and retracing my steps from *Fairfield* up the Salterton Road to its junction with Claremont Grove and I am sure that the building on the corner, which is now split into two dwellings, is the old *Coonoor Lodge.* When I lived there, it had a conservatory on the left front where there is now a door to the split-off dwelling. My bedroom during my second year was top left.

The daily ritual was breakfast in *Fairfield* followed by lectures until 1 p.m. Most students then had the afternoon for "personal study", when:

Artists should be sketching
English students reading
Music students practising
Infant method students should be making apparatus

And Rural Science students working hard with Mrs L-B until supper at 7 p.m. However, most students were out shopping or on the beach as they interpreted "personal study" as meaning "time off"!

Other odd memories include:

Greek dancing on the lawn in 1950 – the final pose of which can be seen here with:

Top: Barbara, Isabel and Nancy Grey;
Bottom: Pam Naftel, Romola Pascoe and Heather Gosling.
Standing: Bernice Mahy

Our Peeping Tom in the bathroom window and trying to get a hot bath;
Growing lettuce and tomatoes for the house in the greenhouse;
and pruning the vine and getting grapes.
Someone hung a bra and French knickers on the lamppost outside *Dunsinane.* I didn't find out who!

I remember there was an Operatic Society that practiced near *Coonoor.* When I hear "Yeoman of the Guard", I always think of Exmouth as the same extract was sung over and over until we all felt we knew it better than they did!

The incredible Mrs Leadley-Brown expected us at lectures by 9.30, worked us all day and into the evening on special subject days. It was very annoying to be out tending the veggie plots and see your friends relaxing on the benches! We did a number of interesting things like rearing chicks, studying egg embryos, collecting honey, chasing swarms of bees, producing flower gardens, a woodland survey at Woodbury and trying out all the tasks we would be asking our pupils to do in the future. Mrs L-B did have a vintage Bentley car, in which she took us out to Woodbury Common and other places.

I think, as we were the first group of 2-year students to go to Rolle (Exmouth College as it was then), the staff were experimenting with us. Up till then, they had been training emergency students – mature students who were recently home from the Forces, having seen the world and been to places.

Because we had to travel to *Fairfield* every day, many of us brought our bicycles with us. That certainly made for a quicker journey in the mornings but it was hard work cycling home in the evening loaded with books and files! Our laundry was collected each week in a large wicker basket. We were allowed to change one sheet free each week but had to pay for anything else we sent. Each student had a Laundry book. There were no washing machines or fridges then. We hung the butter and milk out of the window in a muslin cloth on the cold side of the house. Sometimes the butter tasted quite rancid and the cheese grew interesting fungi, but we survived! [so did Laundry Books until the end of 1963 as this memento from one of my contemporaries shows]

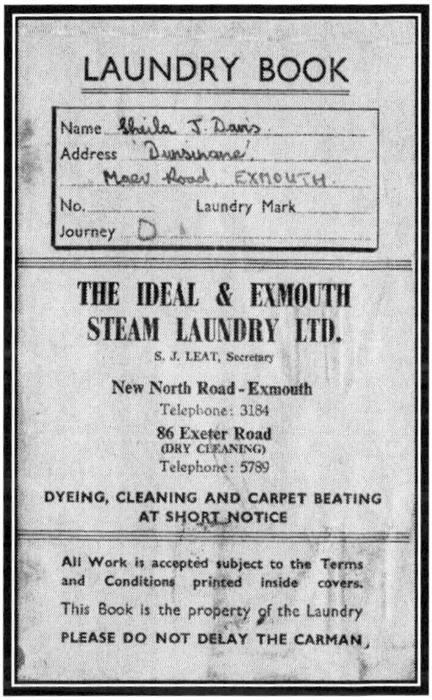
LAUNDRY BOOK

Name Sheila J. Davis

Address 'Dunsinane'.

Maer Road EXMOUTH.

No. Laundry Mark

Journey D

THE IDEAL & EXMOUTH STEAM LAUNDRY LTD.

S. J. LEAT, Secretary

New North Road - Exmouth

Telephone: 3184

86 Exeter Road

(DRY CLEANING)

Telephone: 5789

DYEING, CLEANING AND CARPET BEATING AT SHORT NOTICE

All Work is accepted subject to the Terms and Conditions printed inside covers.

This Book is the property of the Laundry

PLEASE DO NOT DELAY THE CARMAN.

Commodities were only just beginning to come back into the shops and we had to economise. There was no paper to draw or paint on and we had to use kitchen rolls and newspapers for art lessons. We were also rationed to two packs of file paper a term at the local Stationer and pencils and pens were like gold dust. I grew so much in confidence during that first year and, as the photographs will show, I had a great time.

[Taken by *Western Times Co. Ltd.*, the above photograph shows visitors outside *Brockhurst* enjoying the College Open Day on 27th June 1950. Jeanne Boone's parents (3rd row from front) are among them].

At the beginning of our second year, a new blazer was introduced – blue, edged with silver. There was also a college scarf, which was all the rage then. When we returned after the summer holiday, we were surprised to find new furniture in our rooms. Divan beds with drawers under, all made of beech wood. We had a new roll-top desk each to work at, with drawers underneath and a spacious wardrobe each to hang clothes in. This was a pleasant surprise and much more comfortable for us.

Being 2nd years, we had our rooms upstairs and Nancy Grey and I had the front room on the left of the house with good views up and down the road. It was at the end of the corridor so no one need disturb us at night.

One of the most interesting activities that year was our strike over weekend curfews. Some of us liked to go to the Pavilion dances on a Saturday night but, having to be back by 11, certainly curtailed the evening. We all worked to rule but attended no lectures and, after three days (I think), we got a concession.

During that year, materials became slightly easier to obtain and we began making our own dresses at College, developing new styles, using new lengths of dresses and skirts. Here is a photo of Isabel, one of our mannequins, on the lawn behind *Coonoor*, wearing one of the garments we made.

School Practices were in Cornwall, which suited me fine. My first was at St. Dennis near St. Austell and my second year one was in Camborne. We were there for four weeks and I was able to go home at weekends. Since the teacher I was observing sadly lost his wife while I was there, I took over the class and he had compassionate leave. That stood me in good stead as I could not write lesson notes for every lesson every day and I was excused that chore. The examiners came in but were very understanding. I think that "Baptism by Fire" was the best thing that happened to me as I learned so much so quickly, and gained confidence.

I have already referred to Miss Croft (with her little wire-haired terrier) as Principal. Vice-Principal was Miss Cooper, rather a large lady, who lectured in History and was in charge of *Ryll Court* – which was situated further along Claremont Road from *Coonoor Lodge*. She was very fond of a little tipple.

The Senior Lecturer in English was Mr Milne. Miss Menhenniot (who wore knitted dresses) lectured in English and was in charge of *Coonoor Lodge* and Miss Bell (Divinity) was in charge of *Dunsinane*. Mr Floyd, a large, scruffy man with untidy curly hair lectured in Maths. He liked the ladies yet always wore the same stained suit! I've mentioned Mrs Leadley-Brown for Rural Science and Mr Arnold for Art – he was a very quiet, kind man. Mr Illing (Music) expected students to sew on buttons and press shirts for him! Miss Smith taught P.E. Miss Koegler was an excellent Lecturer in Infant Method.

I lived in *Coonoor Lodge* throughout my course. Two of the girls there were from Guernsey and they had many tales to tell about The Occupation. They also brought over boxes of cigarettes to share – it really was the done thing to smoke then, especially with holders. I do not have any actual photos of *Coonoor Lodge* from that time, but, I have been looking at the satellite map of the area and retracing my steps from *Fairfield* up the Salterton Road to its junction with Claremont Grove and I am sure that the building on the corner, which is now split into two dwellings, is the old *Coonoor Lodge*. When I lived there, it had a conservatory on the left front where there is now a door to the split-off dwelling. My bedroom during my second year was top left.

The daily ritual was breakfast in *Fairfield* followed by lectures until 1 p.m. Most students then had the afternoon for "personal study", when:

Artists should be sketching
English students reading
Music students practising
Infant method students should be making apparatus

And Rural Science students working hard with Mrs L-B until supper at 7 p.m. However, most students were out shopping or on the beach as they interpreted "personal study" as meaning "time off"!

Other odd memories include:

Greek dancing on the lawn in 1950 – the final pose of which can be seen here with:

Top: Barbara, Isabel and Nancy Grey;
Bottom: Pam Naftel, Romola Pascoe and Heather Gosling.
Standing: Bernice Mahy

Our Peeping Tom in the bathroom window and trying to get a hot bath;
Growing lettuce and tomatoes for the house in the greenhouse;
and pruning the vine and getting grapes.
Someone hung a bra and French knickers on the lamppost outside *Dunsinane*. I didn't find out who!

I remember there was an Operatic Society that practiced near *Coonoor*. When I hear "Yeoman of the Guard", I always think of Exmouth as the same extract was sung over and over until we all felt we knew it better than they did!

We played hockey, netball and rounders – our 1950 rounders team included:

Dulce in the back row; Pam Naftel, Bernice Mahy in the middle and Nancy Grey and myself in the front.

I used the golf course near the sea-front. Issey, one of the girls in *Coonoor*, had a car, which she sometimes brought back and took us around Devon. There was very little to occupy us, except the coffee shop and the Pavilion at weekends or, as the next photo shows, acrobatics in the garden – that's me, bottom right with Nancy Grey leaping over me!

In our last term, we all made an evening dress for the end-of-term Ball. Tulle and silk were popular materials and the styles incorporated tiny waist lines and were "off the shoulder". My dress was blue with tulle collar/sleeve net over silk. I met an airman that night and he took me out on his motorbike the next day. We rode to Budleigh Salterton and did 'a ton' [100 miles per hour] on the way back. When we reached Woodbury Common, the road was wet and there were many leaves on it. The bike went out from under us and I slid along the wet road in my new mackintosh and tore the sleeve. We were lucky we had slowed down as we had no helmets or safety clothes!! I missed the Going Down service in the Church as a result.

[Early in the 1950s a Development Plan for the Rolle College Main Site was drawn up based on a Devon County Council Plan of 16th January 1952.

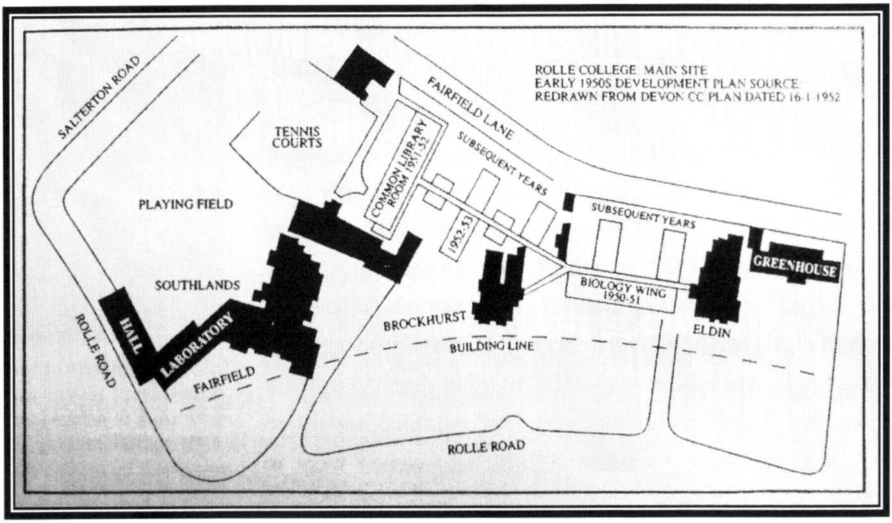


Layout of Buildings on Rolle College site in 1952 with proposed additions

The scheme involved building a Biology wing on land between *Eldin* and *Brockhurst* in 1950 – 51, followed by a Common Room and Library.]

I went on to teach in Somerset and Cornwall before becoming a Vicar's wife. Altogether, I taught for 25 years on and off when we had the family – at Chacewater School for seven years (it wasn't a County Primary then as we had pupils up to 15 years); Midsomer Norton for 18 months when my husband was at Wells Theological College; Twerton Primary at Bath when John was a curate there; Supply work at Cheddar, Mark, Badworth and Blackford – schools in Somerset where we had two parishes, Allerton & Blackford; and, finally, 15 years at St Ives County Primary Junior. Now retired, I live in Hampshire, having lost my husband in 2010.

## 1950 – 1952: "Change of name to Rolle" by Margery Wonnacott

My interview for a place at Exmouth Training College was at the Devon County Education Office, Larkbeare, Topsham Road, Exeter on Wednesday 30th November 1949 at 3.10 pm – I still have the letter which was written on the 15th! In the prospectus I was given, the College was described as having been opened in 1948 as a permanent Residential College for women who wished to become qualified teachers.

Being allocated a place in *Coonoor* Hostel, I can remember cycling downhill to College in time for breakfast on a daily basis but, of course, returning after lectures was a lot harder! While on the subject of food, I can recall eating herrings for dinner by candlelight during the one power cut we had. However, one much more elaborate event was an Elizabethan Tudor Christmas meal when we ate rabbit with our fingers (before the days of Myxomatosis!). Miss Cooper even introduced us to Mead.

Each year, we all travelled from Exeter on the Cornish Riviera Express for one month's School Practice in Cornwall. While there, I visited the Iron Age settlement, Chysauster Ancient Village. As well as visiting Cornwall, we did have a trip to London to see the film "All about Eve".

During our 2nd year, new rules had been introduced:

- No going into town in the morning (but, actually, we tended to spend more time there in the afternoons because we didn't have any double free periods in the morning).
- Being in our rooms Monday – Friday from 7 – 9 pm
- Always having to answer the register at the beginning of a lecture

We were not happy with those, so we decided to go on strike by going back to our hostels to study on Monday morning.

I can remember studying on the beach and on the College lawn then there was learning to play the recorder in Eldin on Saturday mornings – what a din! We had many funny moments. I managed to get myself stuck in a folding wooden chair in the gym when we had to practise swimming strokes. I laughed so much that I needed help to extricate myself! Even Miss Parry collapsed laughing. Another time in the library, Marie went to stand up to fetch a book but her foot had "gone to sleep" and she fell to the floor amidst loud laughter from everyone who saw what happened, including Miss Minhinnick, who eventually managed "Sh! Sh!" as no talking was allowed!!

It was while I was studying at the College that we were asked to suggest a different name for it. My group of friends came up with the name Princess Anne Training College as she had been born on 15$^{th}$ August 1950. However, the name chosen was Rolle College – a much better choice, I think.

We had promised ourselves a Knickerbocker Glory at Fortes before we left College but found it too big to eat all of it! We went to Exeter and hitch-hiked back – almost too late for the Going Down service.

[By the time the 1952 magazine was published in June, therefore, its cover bore the name **ROLLE COLLEGE, EXMOUTH 1952 Magazine** although the words "Exmouth Training College JUNE 1952" still appeared inside. Similarly, the *Tenth Edition Exmouth Street Directory 1952*, shows the Chief Education Officer and the Principal of the College on page 144 as being the same as for 1950 – 1951, but the College's new name was being used:

**ROLLE COLLEGE, EXMOUTH**
**TWO-YEAR TEACHERS TRAINING COLLEGE FOR WOMEN.**
**MAINTAINED BY DEVON COUNTY EDUCATION AUTHORITY**

| | |
|---|---|
| *Chief Education Officer:* | W E PHILIP, Esq, M A, |
| | Education Offices, Larkbeare, Topsham Road, Exeter |
| *Principal:* | Miss G.M. Croft O B E, B A [13] |

At present the College is housed on the main site in houses Fairfield, Brockhurst and Eldin, and outside the main site in St. Hilarian, Portland Avenue; Ferniehurst, Douglas Avenue; Coonoor Lodge, Salterton Road; Ryll Court, Claremont Grove; Dunsinane, Maer Road and Hasledene, Cyprus Road.

That same Directory showed an interesting fact on page 31 under 11 Carlton Hill on LHS leading from Sea Front to junction of Rolle and Salterton Roads.

Here is LOUISA PLACE. After numbers: 1, 3, 5, 7 & 9, we see:

**11 Old Southlands** Flat 1 – Miss V Wreford 3023
Flat 2 – Mrs W B Cormac, Miss H Cormac]

[13] born in Winchester in 1896, Geraldine Mary Croft died aged 66 early in 1962 in Plymouth

**1951 and 1952 – 1954: "Miss Croft and Sick Bay" by Betty Thomas**

I started the two-year course at Rolle College in 1951 and was allocated to *Eldin* Hall of Residence, which had, at one time, been a vicarage. In those days, we were immediately hurled into action as, after just a fortnight, we found ourselves on Teaching Practice for two weeks. I had been a Pupil Teacher before being accepted at Rolle so the quick initiation didn't bother me too much and I enjoyed my T.P. at the Episcopal Secondary Modern School, Exeter [closed 1972]. Unfortunately, I soon developed a facial paralysis which was followed by mobility problems. The College Principal at that time was Miss Geraldine M. Croft, who, having been an officer in the A.T.S. during WWII, presented a somewhat militaristic approach to life to most students. She lived in *Fairfield* and was extremely kind whilst I was in Sick Bay (also in *Fairfield*) and the medical people were deciding what to do with me, in that she gave me the use of her guest room during the daytime so that I had very comfortable surroundings and overlooked the beautiful gardens of that house – before the high boundary wall on the corner of Rolle Road and Douglas Avenue was altered. Soon it was decided that I should abandon the course at half-term and, hopefully, return in the next academic year.

When I returned to College in 1952, I was allocated to *Hasledene* in Cyprus Road where I shared a room with a girl from Exmouth and with whom I kept in touch until her death over fifty years later. Even though she lived in Exmouth, she had to live in College and the only people who were excused from this ruling were four older mature students whose homes were in the Exeter area. Because the re-decorations in *Hasledene* had not been completed by the beginning of term, four of us were billeted at 'Fernside' in Rolle Street. This property was dark, musty and eerie. Over the landing, there was a red glass sky-light which cast a strange glow over the already weird surroundings. Imagine our delight when, after two weeks, we moved to our beautifully decorated and newly furnished rooms in *Hasledene*. On three recent visits to Exmouth, I have stayed at 'Fernside', which has undergone complete renovation (a few owners later) and is now a pleasant small hotel. The proprietor was very interested to hear of my earlier stay and the red skylight is still there!

During my time at Rolle there were four delightful Polish students training with us (they were linguistically challenged) and I think there were also some Polish ladies on the cleaning staff.

Rules in those days were quite rigid (contrast with to-day's casual approach!) We were allowed out until 11 p.m. on Saturdays and until 10 p.m. at other times. On weekday evenings, we had to be in our study-bedrooms or the library from 7 – 9 p.m. From 9 – 10 p.m., there was much activity in the service room where we prepared night-time refreshment (usually in the form of beans on toast) and visited friends in nearby rooms. At 10 o'clock, we were back in our rooms again and 'lights out' was at 11 p.m.

We were not allowed to miss a meal and, if anyone arrived late, it was a case of having to walk through the dining-room to the staff table to apologise. The lecturing staff themselves were quite regimented as they paraded in behind Miss Croft and the Vice-Principal (Miss Cooper and later Miss Richardson) in some order of seniority. Then came the office staff and Nurse Doris Watson, affectionately known as 'Wattie' who, I got to know very well because of my earlier acquaintance with sick-bay. She frequently made beautiful arrangements of flowers grown in the college grounds and these were a very welcoming sight on entering the halls of residence. I kept in touch with her for many years. The office staff were Miss Phillips, bursar; Mrs Ryall, caterer (I am reminded at this point that we had to take our Ration Books to College); and I believe Miss Croft's secretary to have been a Miss Martin. There were of course very rigid rules in those days but I suspect that the parents of some students were glad to know that their daughters were under such supervision.

I attended Tower Street Methodist Church for both morning and evening services on Sundays. The minister there was Revd. Victor Surman whose daughter, Sheila, still lives in the town. After evening service about twenty students used to go to the Manse in Albion Hill for a 'squash' and that's the operative word! Mrs Surman would bake an enormous sponge for us and then cut it into as many pieces as there were students. Along with the plentiful supply of tea and coffee, the main attraction was that the Surmans had a television set (before Queen Elizabeth II's coronation!). We hardly ever saw the end of the Sunday night play as, just before 9.55 p.m., we had to make a mad dash to get back to our Halls of Residence and sign in by ten o'clock.

For my final year, I was elected President of the Students' Council and, during that time, I got to know Miss Croft even better. Her father had been a master at Winchester College where the motto was 'Manners Makyth Man' – I seem to remember her frequent references to that idea. Being brought up in Winchester probably accounted for her eye for beauty and her love of line in buildings. I can recall a local newspaper headline: 'Miss Croft Wins Fight Over Garden Wall' following her opposition to taking down part of the aforementioned *Fairfield* garden wall to improve visibility at the corner.

On Friday evenings, there was a compulsory lecture, usually by someone of note. Often the Vice-President or I would be invited to have dinner with the speaker and the Principal in her private dining room. The one thing I dreaded most about those evenings was having to drink coffee after the meal – as I wasn't a coffee drinker. My social skills have improved in that respect now!

The most daunting task I had was to address the students, about 200 in number, when there was a proposed strike over some issues relating to College life. This situation was completely out of my experience, however the strike was avoided after some negotiation. I did not approve of strike action then or throughout my teaching career, which ended in 1983.

I had wanted to stay at *Hasledene* for my final year but the Senior Student had to live at *Fairfield.* A facility for the use of all students was one pay-phone located in that house. My position caused a problem for the Valedictory service. Hitherto, it was always held in the Anglican Holy Trinity Church and the Senior Student read the lesson. The divinity lecturer and warden of *St. Hilarian*, Miss Atthill, known to us as 'Aunty At' sent for me and said that, as I was a Methodist, I could not read the lesson in the Anglican Church. The situation was resolved after contact with the Bishop who gave his permission! How things have changed.

One morning, a friend was summoned to the Principal's office at quite short notice. Wondering why, and looking down at her open sandals, we decided that the conspicuous bright nail varnish couldn't be worn for such an interview and might even be the reason for the summons, so we both set to and scraped the varnish off using a nail-file. It turned out that my friend was called in to be told that she had been offered a place at Cambridge! Through Mrs Alison Leadley-Brown, my special subject lecturer, I was offered a place at Exeter University to further my studies in Biology. I did not take this up for family reasons. In those days, the Biology Lab. was a greenhouse at *Eldin.* Mrs L-B was a real slave-driver and was known as 'Deadly Leadley' but a wonderful lady, who drove a Jaguar, always arrived carrying a large brief-case, was smartly dressed, had a very cultured voice and endeared herself to all those students who were prepared to work hard. I kept in touch with her for many years but her interest seemed to wane after I told her that I was changing direction and was going to do R.E!

On the evening before leaving College, it was time for the annual Students' Rag. Some horses which we had hired from local stables were duly delivered to the College and a group of us went as 'Rudolph Valentino and the Harem' (Jill Hearle is pictured here as Valentino on horseback) riding through the town and along the sea-front with a mounted police escort. On arrival back in my room, I discovered that a note from Miss Croft had been pushed under the door. It read, "Miss Thomas, before you leave to-morrow morning, will you please make sure that Fairfield Drive is cleared of horse manure!" Being a Biology and Rural Science student, that was no problem for me. I had been brought up on a farm and so quite happily shovelled the stuff on to a deserving rose-bed. Jill appears in a pram in another Rag photo – she is being pushed by Pat Goldstraw (left) and Jean Alder.

An Old Students' Association ran for several years after I left Rolle but gradually numbers dropped and it ceased to function. Several of us returned for reunions for the first few years. In 2004, a reunion was held in the College hall to celebrate fifty years since we left Rolle. One of our members brought a beautifully iced cake featuring the College badge. About 40 old students turned up and what chatter and reminiscing there was! Since then, six or seven of us have met up for lunch and afternoon chat at the Devoncourt Hotel on a few occasions – the latest being a sixty years' celebration in September 2014.

**1960s: "Rolle's PE & Art" by Jean Halton & Mary Beresford-Williams**

[Two Lecturers, whose time at Rolle College just overlapped, described their experiences there from the late 1950s. Jean Halton, a Physical Education tutor, wrote to Jenny Budden in May 2010]:

My first involvement with Rolle occurred in 1958/60 when I was appointed as a teacher to Withycombe Primary School. Rolle students were assigned to each class and the teacher of that class helped in their training, liaising with the tutor responsible for the student. In addition, some of the professional staff would 'borrow' my class to demonstrate particular skills.

Shortly after our fourth child was born in 1963, I was asked to join the Physical Education department at Rolle as P.E. was my specialist subject. I was then responsible for teaching P.E. to both young and mature students at the College.

During the 1960s and early 1970s, much interaction took place between the Town and Rolle. Students would visit families where there were children under school age and take back their observations to their tutors. The late Violet Madge and her staff were extremely influential at this time and they set up Saturday morning activities at the College, where there were wonderful resources available for young children. The Science Department was also 'hands on' with Primary School children and organised Science Weekends under the leadership of the Head of Department, Ray Jones.

Exmouth children were very fortunate to have all these facilities as were families from further afield. The County's Music staff used the resources at the College to bring together pupils who were studying a musical instrument. Rolle was used by many Exmouth groups such as the Music Society, Spanish and French Circles, the Dancing Schools' Concerts, Chess Groups and so on.

While I was working at the College, it expanded from around 250 to 1,000 students and became a Centre with established links to several countries overseas, especially Kenya – where there were lots of exchange visits by students in both directions.

Principals came and went – I remember Miss Croft in 1957 followed by Miss Spicer, but the most respected was Francis Cammaerts, a Belgian, who worked for the French Resistance during the Second World War. He was in danger of execution when captured and only survived because the war ended. He further opened up the doors of Rolle to the community, continuing contacts with Dartington College of Arts. Those who wanted to be specialist Secondary teachers did two years at Dartington and one year at Rolle while those wishing to be Primary specialist teachers did one year at Dartington and two years at Rolle. [Read more about Francis Cammaerts on pages 165-170]

I hope this potted version of my memories of Rolle College demonstrates the value enjoyed by the people of Exmouth when Rolle was an independent Training College.

ROLLE COLLEGE, EXMOUTH
October 1963

[In April 2012, Mary Beresford-Williams wrote]:

In about 1960, I taught Art at Rolle College. When I started, I taught in the old building which was later demolished [*Fairfield*, in 1963 – the above photo was the last to be taken outside it]. I thought that the students produced better work there than later in the more clinical space in the new building.

My boss was Frank Haddon who suggested I learn a bit of pottery with the students. I had never done any before, my training having been in Fine Art. I enjoyed it and am sorry I didn't go any further with it.

I left in 1964 as my husband, David, who had taught Geography at Exmouth Community College, was pursuing a headship, so I was not there for very long. [Like myself, Mary and David were graduates of Reading University].

## Chapter 5: ROCK 'n' ROLLE

### 1959 – 1972: "Thoughts on Rolle" by Principal Doris E L Spicer

> "I realise with humility that I have come into a goodly inheritance in this training college by the sea and on the fringe of beautiful country. Its amenities are a constant source of delight to me – attractive halls of residence with flourishing well-kept gardens, good teaching accommodation some of it temporary it is true, but all of it well equipped to foster an atmosphere conducive to learning, a new building pleasant and gracious in appearance, and an educational policy sound in its conception. It seems to me however, that the most precious part of this heritage is enshrined in the ever-growing community of people who teach, learn and work here. It is my good fortune to have come to a college characterised by the friendliness, good humour and devotion of all who work here."

So commented Miss Spicer in 1960 soon after her appointment as Principal of Rolle College and, on 18th July 2008, those words were displayed at the event to mark the move from the Rolle campus in Exmouth to the Rolle Building at Plymouth. After teaching in a Convent School and a Technical College, she lectured at Southlands Training College, Wimbledon before becoming Deputy Principal at Lady Mabel Training College in Yorkshire prior to her appointment at Rolle. On Friday 6th October 1961 at the time of the laying of the foundation stone of the new buildings, she commented:

> "The College, apart from the new block erected in 1958, consists mainly of adapted houses which have serious shortcomings for a modern College. At present, there are approximately 270 students. The Ministry of Education has agreed to development to provide for at least 400. It is also hoped that most of the new teaching accommodation will be ready for use in September 1963."

That 'new block erected in 1958' was officially opened on Thursday 9th July 1959 by the Dean of Winchester as the following article from the *Exmouth Chronicle Emergency Edition* of Saturday 11th July 1959 describes:

**Daw Building opened**

> The first instalment of the modernisation and enlargement of the college was officially opened on Thursday last by the Very Rev. Norman Sykes, Dean of

Winchester. He had been invited to open the door of the premises by Alderman B. G. Lampard-Vachell (chairman of the Governors and of Devon Education Committee) with a key handed to him by Mr Richard Fraser, a representative of the architects (Messrs. Louis de Soissons, Peacock, Hodges, Robertson and Fraser).

The building, which was to provide mainly teaching accommodation, was named to commemorate the interest of Sir John Daw, the former chairman of Devon County Council, in the development of the College since its inception.

When the building was opened, the gathering proceeded to the assembly hall where, following a lesson read by the Rev. G. E. Lawrence (Exmouth's Superintendent Methodist Minister), the dedicatory prayers and blessing were given by the Rt. Rev. Norman Clarke, the Lord Bishop of Plymouth.

The Dean was also the preacher at the Going Down service held later in the day at Holy Trinity Church, and which was conducted by the Vicar of Littleham-cum-Exmouth, the Rev. R. J. D. Newhouse.

Daw Building entrance taken on 2nd July 1965, just six years after its opening

Chairman B. G. Lampard-Vachell Esq., CBE, JP, CA, MA, LLD was again in attendance on Friday 6th October 1961 when it fell to Dame Mary Smieton DBE (Permanent Secretary in the Ministry of Education) to lay the foundation stone of further new buildings at 3 p.m. As with the Daw Building, Richard Fraser of Louis de Soissons and Partners was to be the architect and the contractors were to be Messrs. E.B.C. & Sleeman Ltd.

The *1961 Kelly's Directory* details the extent of the Rolle College site as being 1 – 9 Douglas Avenue with its telephone number as 2303. Each of the hostels had its own telephone number. There were three in Douglas Avenue – no. 4 (3838) [*Kingsthorpe*], 8 (2483) [*Seacroft*] and 19 (2670) [*Ferniehurst*]; 19/21 Cyprus Road (2817) [*Hasledene Hall and Cottage*]; one at 21 Portland Avenue (2528) [*St. Hilarian*]; one at 47 Salterton Road (2483) [*Coonoor Lodge*] and one in Maer Road (2030) [*Dunsinane*].

By 1963, Miss Spicer was able to write for the Rolle College magazine:

**"Principal's Foreword" by Miss D.E.L. Spicer**

It is impossible in this brief foreword to comment on all the developments and changes of the past year. It will be memorable because, for the first time, we have had three years of students in College. We shall all remember the first Assembly when over 400 students and about 40 members of staff managed to squeeze into the Hall. It was not an experience to be repeated!

The progress of building operations has been slower than we expected and accommodation difficulties have made great demands on the adaptability and ingenuity of staff and students alike. Fairfield ceased to be a Hall of Residence in September and study bedrooms are now temporary tutorial and lecture rooms. During the year, 110 study bedrooms have been completed and are now occupied by Third Year students who have gradually evolved a way of life for themselves in their houses. We have settled into the new Science and Geography Departments and have nearly forgotten the stresses and strains of the 'general post' experienced in the spring Term. At the beginning of this term the new kitchen and self-service dining-room were ready for use and memories of walks along wind-swept or icy roads to Fortes Restaurant on the sea front have faded. The upper dining-room and staff dining-room are finished and also the conversion of the old Science Laboratories into History and Mathematics Rooms. Disappointment caused by delays is compensated for to a great extent by the pleasure we feel in the attractive and gracious appearance of the new accommodation.

With so many physical upheavals in one year it might be thought that there could have been no stability and that the work and community life of the College must have suffered. I do not think that this has happened. Thanks to Miss Calveley and her staff the moves have taken place speedily and with the minimum amount of disruption. Our thanks are also due to Miss Parker and her staff for the fine job they have done in catering, not only for normal meals for so many people, but for the many and varied College functions held during the year. I must express my appreciation, too, to members of the academic staff for their cheerful and tolerant acceptance of difficult teaching conditions and to students who have energetically organised their social activities in cramped premises and have regarded these restrictions as a challenge. I am particularly sorry that the temporary Junior Common Room is so small and inadequate but I hope that early next session the new one will be available.

Students returning in September will be anxious to know what additional changes they will find. Probably we shall have moved into the new Administrative Wing and Senior Common Room and the Gymnasium should be finished. I am afraid that we shall not have a Hall for part of the session. New uses will have been found for some of the accommodation in Fairfield. For the greater part of the year we shall have to adjust to changes once again, but the completion of the buildings does seem now in sight. Some of the gardens which were delightful features of the Halls are in a sad state at the present but I hope that we shall soon be able to re-plan and re-stock them.

Inevitably there have been changes of staff. A year ago a number of members of staff left: Miss Martin, Miss Watson who is now at Dartford College of Physical Education, Miss Wilson who is enjoying a very active retirement, Miss Reed who is on the staff of the Unesco Training College in Lagos, Nigeria and Mr Goodall who has joined the staff of St. Luke's College. We wish them all success and happiness in their new spheres of work.

In September we were very glad to welcome to the staff Miss Sharpe as Deputy-Principal, Dr. Plack as Lecturer in Biology, Miss Anning as Lecturer in Physical Education, Mr Andrews as Lecturer in Drama, Mr Waddhams [Waddams] as Lecturer in English and Mr Cox as Lecturer in Music. Mr Malthouse joined us in January as Lecturer in Geography. Miss Hopkins has been Assistant Caterer since last August and on the secretarial side Miss Ward became College Secretary in November and Miss Greenfield has replaced Miss Rice as Junior Clerk.

And now as the College session draws to a close our first group of three-year students are about to leave and enter the teaching profession. They will take with them our sincere good wishes for their future. I must record here my thanks to Cora Williams who as President of the Students' Union has most competently and diplomatically led the students for two years, and to all students who have held office in College.

In a year which has presented so many problems it has been most helpful to have once again the advice and support of our Governors and the officials of the Devon County Education Committee.

D.E.L.S. (June, 1963)

That article tells us that the friends, Miss Martin and Miss Watson previously mentioned on pages 42 and 112, left Rolle in 1962. Wattie went on to Dartford College of Physical Education but we do not know what happened to Miss Martin.

Miss Spicer's first name was a well-guarded secret among students in my day so it is perhaps not surprising that the following song was sung to the tune of "Glory, Glory, Hallelujah":

We'll make old Dulcie Spicer smoke a Woodbine every day
We'll make old Dulcie Spicer smoke a Woodbine every day
We'll make old Dulcie Spicer smoke a Woodbine every day
When the Rolle revolution comes.

I could find no Dulcie Spicers and only one Doris E L Spicer when checking *FreeBMD* website, so realised that Rolle's Miss Spicer was born in Wilton, Wiltshire in the second quarter of 1913. Since her mother's maiden name was Saunders, there was again only one marriage possibility in the first quarter of 1911 between Beatrice S Saunders and Frank S Spicer in Wilton.

Checking out births to Spicer and Saunders between 1910 and 1930, I found that four daughters had been born to Frank and Beatrice in Wilton:

1. Gladys G M towards the end of 1911
2. Doris E L born mid 1913
3. Madge C H mid 1915
4. Beatrice J mid 1918

However, the *1970 Kelly's Directory of Devonshire Commercial Directory*, not only gives her Christian name as Doris on page 65 but also details that she was living at 8 Fairfield Road. By that time the following four hostels had been added: 6 Douglas Avenue (*Bonville*), 14 Cyprus Road (*St. Olans*), 17 Portland Avenue (*Kempston*) and 1 Salterton Road (*Carlton*) while 47 Salterton Road (*Coonoor Lodge*) had ceased to be maintained as one.

From the student union handbooks of 1967 – 1968 and 1969 – 1970, we learn that a new Sick Bay was being constructed next to *Seacroft* Hall of Residence during 1967. However, the original in *Langstone* had to continue in use all that year as the new-build had not been completed by September as planned. Entrance to Sick Bay was through the back door of *Langstone*, approached through *Eldin*'s garden. By 1969 – 1970, Sick Bay was located at *Bonville*.

## 1962 – 1965: "Brave New World of the 1960s" by Judith Atkinson

1962, the year I started at Rolle College, might still have been in the 1950s as far as attitudes and lifestyle were concerned although things had begun to change slowly. For a start the age of majority was 21 and the College was therefore "In Loco Parentis" which meant quite a lot of rules which students today would find ludicrous. Rolle was also in a state of change, moving from a 2-year to a 3-year course. This was the first year to have three sets of students but the extra accommodation and facilities were not yet ready and it was very much a building site with an odd mixture of new and old buildings.

At that stage the large house "*Fairfield*" was still in use. Next to it were other old buildings including the original dining room, which probably hadn't changed since the time there had been a school on the site. There were long tables with benches and dishes were brought down to the tables by the kitchen staff. There was never enough food and the quality left much to be desired. It felt very much like still being at school. It was during this period, while the third years were away on teaching practice, years one and two decided to stage a protest over food. We waited for the dishes to be brought down to the tables and then everyone got up and left. As far as I remember it was unanimous. Such behaviour was unheard of at Rolle in those days and was met with shock and fury by the Principal, Miss Spicer, and her deputy, Miss Sharpe. The 60s had begun to kick in! The rest of the year went on without further militancy as far as I can remember.

When I returned to College the following September to start my second year the new building was finished and, as far as I can recall, *Fairfield* and its adjacent buildings had been demolished [actually demolished early in 1964]. It was wonderful. Among other things we had a large comfortable **common room** and a light and airy self-service dining room with the luxury of new crockery and even Mappin & Webb cutlery. The food had much improved and we were no longer hungry. With the opening of the new building the whole atmosphere of Rolle changed. I had been seriously considering leaving during my first year, but what had been to me a depressing and old fashioned place had changed into a lively modern college well suited to the "Brave New World" of the 1960s.

## 1963 – 1966: "Education through Experience" by Daphne Barnes

According to Miss Spicer, I was one of the last batch of students to be interviewed by her in London. I discovered that fact when speaking to her a year after leaving Rolle at the first, and only, official Old Students' Reunion I was privileged to attend. My interview was on 30th October 1962 when my father and I caught the 9 a.m. train to Paddington and crossed by Underground to Westminster, which was crowded with people for the State Opening of Parliament. The interview was scheduled for 11.30 a.m. at County Hall but, according to my diary, "I did not go in until 11.55 a.m. – one lady examiner"!

I can remember my mother and I travelling into Reading the previous Saturday to choose a hat and suit (skirt and jacket) specially for the occasion, then, during the interview, spending time discussing with Miss Spicer, how much I could see without my glasses as I had foolishly mentioned that I used to go swimming regularly until my eyesight deteriorated!

We were not kept long in suspense after the interview as, by 19th November, I had received a letter offering me a place at Rolle College for the following September. At that stage, I had no idea what I was letting myself in for as I had never visited Rolle, nor even Exmouth. I knew that I wanted to teach and I had applied for Colleges that did not incorporate the words "Training College" in their title. Rolle was my first choice as it was on the coast and I had spent some lovely family holidays in Devon, which proved quite a contrast to Reading, Berkshire, where I was born and bred.

Unlike some students who had been interviewed in London, I had the opportunity to see Rolle before commencing my three-year Teacher Training Course as my parents chose to spend a family holiday in Exmouth during the August preceding the start of my course. By that time I knew that I had been assigned to *Dunsinane* Hall of Residence in Maer Road so, during the holiday, we decided to call round there on the off-chance of seeing more than just the outside. As a result, the second person I met with Rolle connections was Peggy, *Dunsinane*'s cleaner. She showed us all round the Hall and my parents were convinced that it was the interest we showed in the three-bed ground floor room with the magnificent sea view that clinched it for my eventually being in there with Ann Ashworth and Tricia Gibbs. Be that as it may, I was to spend a very happy first year in *Dunsinane* and I am still in contact with some of those who shared that first year with me in such a marvellous Hall. Here I am pictured in its attractive grounds:

Miss Bell (Divinity – pictured right) was our Warden and had the room next to Ann, Tricia and myself. I fondly recall the look of amazement on the face of the newspaper boy when he arrived during an early morning fire practice and there we all were in our night attire! Even for us students, it was the first time we had seen Miss Bell with her hair plaited for bed.

The first week at Rolle was an Induction Week to give us chance to find out about the many Clubs and other activities that were on offer, in addition to the work that would be required of us. During the initial briefing we were warned to respect the fact that "Exmouth goes to sleep at 9 p.m." Rules were quite rigid in those days. We were only allowed one weekend away from College each half-term and there was a signing-out book if we wanted to be out of our Hall later than 10 p.m. No male visitors were allowed in rooms after 7 p.m. and we delighted in seeing how many fathers and brothers could break that rule! That "freedom within a framework" (one of the Education essay titles that I remember to this day!) caused most of us more merriment than annoyance.

Although I had only met two people with Rolle connections – Miss Spicer and Peggy – before I went there, I had been contacted by my College "Mum" – Val Madle. I had not heard of such a system prior to being contacted by Val but found it a good one in that it put us Freshers' minds at rest on such points as not needing to buy all the books on the Book List – I ended up buying just those I could obtain second-hand!

I had managed to contact the only other student who was going from Reading to Rolle in 1963 – Jill Maggs – as a friend who attended Jill's school [Westwood] had put us in touch with each other. That meant that, on the first day of term, we were able to travel together by train from Reading. We soon realised that the girl sitting opposite us in the compartment was also travelling to Rolle. She turned out to be Margaret Payne from Wokingham so the three of us travelled on and had lunch together before heading up towards the main College buildings for the scheduled 2 p.m. arrival. Margaret was also in *Dunsinane* but Jill was in *Kingsthorpe* in Douglas Avenue.

I later discovered that those living closer to Exmouth had been sent a letter on 15th October 1962, which detailed that the cost for their bed and breakfast for the night prior to their interview would be 12/6 [12 shillings and 6 pence or £0.62½ in subsequent decimal currency], an evening meal in College 1/- [one shilling or 5p] and lunch on the day of the interview 2/3 [11p]. Their interviews were held a few days before our's – on 26th October – as Sheila Davis has the original paperwork in a scrapbook compiled at the time.

As someone once commented, "Everyone seems to recall exactly what they were doing when they first heard of President John F. Kennedy's assassination on 22nd November 1963 and, writing this fifty years later, I am, of course, no exception. I had been out that evening and arrived in *Dunsinane*'s kitchen to make my usual hot chocolate supper drink when the *10 o'clock News* chimes pealed forth from the radio. I realised afterwards that those who were already there had been waiting to see my reaction to the announcement, since they already knew its content.

Like many others at Rolle, I joined in as many social activities as possible. Fencing was a completely new activity for me. I had often acted so it seemed quite natural to be involved in "Alice in Wonderland" on 9th December. We finished making our costumes out of white crepe paper, decorated with red hearts, and red pill-box hats – over dinnertime ready to give a performance to schoolchildren at 2.30 p.m. and to adults at 7.30 p.m. – both in Exmouth Pavilion on the Esplanade.

The following day, the College Carol Service was held at Tower Street Methodist Church at 3 p.m. then, on the 11th, between tea and supper, I went to auditions for "Under Milk Wood" – a narrative reading which was to be held in January 1964. I was to read the part of First Woman but did not realise then that, among the 62 characters in Dylan Thomas' play, two – Waldo's wife and Third Boy – were to be read by fellow student, Pam Clements, who later went on to star in the television soap "Eastenders" under the name of Pam St. Clements – but more of that later.

I was not so interested in the many dances held, especially those of the more formal variety, so was intrigued to find that Exmouth Library currently has tickets for three Balls held in 1964. The Fancy Dress Rag Ball was held on Saturday, 23rd May from 8.30 p.m. until 11.45 p.m., when music was provided by *The Rejects* and tickets, priced at 5/-, included the cost of refreshments with proceeds going to charity. The Going Down Ball, less than a month later, was held in the College Hall on Friday June 19th, when Dinner Jackets were to be worn. Reception then was from 9 p.m. – 9.45 p.m. and dancing was until 2 a.m. Finally the Christmas Ball was held from 9 p.m. until 1 a.m. on Thursday December 10th. Again tickets were 5/- and dancing was to *The Rejects*, although Lounge Suits were the order of the day and a Licensed Bar was mentioned!

We were very fortunate as regards accommodation in the 1960s as we were in Hall during our first year; in digs for the second year and in Study Bedroom Blocks in our third year. Being in digs in the second year meant that we were able to choose those with whom we wanted to share and Sheila Davis, Janice Proctor, Hilary Warne and myself were even closer to College than we had been in *Dunsinane* as we were allocated to the Steiner family at 22 Portland Avenue so could leave from their side entrance in Fairfield Road, cross the road and enter College grounds near the greenhouses. Little did I realise at the time, that 45 years later, when my husband, Jim, finally retired, we would look across to that same house as we now live opposite.

Mr Steiner was a dentist and that proved fortunate for me when a filling came out of one of my teeth just as I was about to go on Teaching Practice. Later in the year, their elder son needed a room of his own for "A" level studies so Sheila and I had to move further afield for our final term in the second year. For hard-up students (full grants were £47 per term in those days with board and lodging paid for us), the moving of belongings meant, especially for Sheila and myself, the borrowing of a substantial wooden-based trolley from Rolle's porter, Mr Rix, so that we could trundle our worldly possessions between residences. The move, 'though, proved a good one for us as, in Raleigh Road, we had the luxury of our own lounge as well as a bedroom for the two of us and we are still in touch with the Dixon family to this day.

I actually spent part of that term on Teaching Practice in Falmouth while Sheila travelled daily and June Dixon (until her death on 12th February 2015), recalled that the iron was used for ironing maps for Teaching Practice more than for any other purpose by either of us! She also recalled that her carpet was cleaned quite regularly by us as a result of hot chocolate being spilt on it as we progressed from the kitchen to our lounge for supper!

We had all other meals in the Main Building at Rolle and I believe I gained quite a reputation for being the last to finish, possibly connected with the fact that I was often one of the last to arrive, especially for breakfast! Sheila's nickname of "Kipper" also stems from those days as she was the only one of us who seemed to appreciate kippers for breakfast and, as Joan Staples was from Grimsby, we were often reminded of that fact.

As we were training to be teachers, the highlights of our course were obviously the Teaching Practices. I had opted to teach the Junior/Secondary age group (9 – 13 year olds) so that meant that I spent a week observing in each type of school; a Teaching Practice in each; then, for final Teaching Practice, we were able to choose which we'd prefer.

I had two week's "Observation" in Exeter. One was at Bradley Rowe Junior Girls', the first time I had encountered a single-sex State Primary School [it was rebuilt in 2005 and given the new name of Wynstream Primary School]. The second was at Priory Girls' Secondary [renamed ISCA College in 2006]. At Bradley Rowe, I ended up teaching totally for a couple of days when a teacher was absent and I was given a box of chocolates as a "Thank You". My first actual Teaching Practice was spent in Totnes where I stayed with Mrs Ramsden, who had been the first lady Mayor of Totnes. I discovered that fact when she loaned me a ceremonial trowel to show my class of 10 – 11 year olds during the Building project I planned to do with them.

Since there are obviously less Secondary Schools in a County than Primary, I had to travel to Cornwall for my second Practice. This meant that my 21st birthday was spent partly at Trescobeas County Secondary School, Falmouth. As my main subject was Mathematics, Philip Floyd was my tutor and he had got to hear of this momentous occasion. Deciding to "mix business with pleasure", he observed lessons of Ann and myself on 17th May 1965, then invited us to a meal. Unfortunately, he had not reckoned on the fact that Mrs Toy, our landlady in Falmouth, would have prepared a special Tea with a birthday cake so, instead of going out to dinner that evening, the three of us went for a walk along the Sea Front and had ices. On his next visit, he brought me a box of chocolates to mark my birthday celebration instead of the meal he'd originally suggested.

My final Teaching Practice ended with a flourish as the ornithologist, Peter Scott, came to officially open Sidmouth County Secondary School on the last day of that Practice – 25th March 1966. That meant that there was no school that morning. During his tour of the school in the afternoon, I remember showing him how a piece of mathematical equipment worked.

In my third year at Rolle, I shared Tracy Study Bedroom Block near *Hasledene* Hall in Cyprus Road with nine others. Some of them can be seen here on the stairs in Tracy Block:

From top: Sarah Trickett, Chris Sisley, Heather Saunders, Pam Pope, Rosemary Ward, John (Chris' fiancé), Daphne Barnes, Sheila Davis & Jenny Willy – Judy Clark was in bed and Pat Munday took the photo

We again took part in a Rag Day float as I had while in *Dunsinane*. Rag Days were a very popular feature of life at Rolle in the 1960s. In *Dunsinane*, our theme was "Sunny Exmouth" whereas Tracy Block's was "Education through Experience in the Never-Never Land". One of those on the latter float has since become a household name, especially among those households that like "Soaps". Pam Clements, as she was then known, was in the same Junior/Secondary Education division as myself throughout our three years at Rolle but, whereas my main subject was Mathematics, her's was Drama and, after Rolle, she continued her drama studies at Rose Bruford College of Speech and Drama. She is now better known as Pam St. Clements, who starred as Pat Evans (née Harris, previously Beale, Wicks and Butcher!) in "Eastenders" from 12th June 1986 (just over a year after the show first aired) until her "death" on 1st January 2012. In 2008, the University of Plymouth had presented her with an honorary degree at its last Graduation ceremony held in Exeter Cathedral. From March to December 2012, she was a guest TV presenter on "This Morning" and, in February 2015, she published her first book – her autobiography, "The End of an Earring".

Rag Day 1966: Tracy Block's float. Pam Clements (as was) is the pirate standing second from the right while I too was a pirate – sitting in front of her

Although there was only one official meeting of the Old Students' Association after I left Rolle – Sheila and I had our Life membership subscriptions returned to us as the Association ceased to meet after that – I have still continued to meet up with others of my year, either at each other's homes; in Exmouth; or, early on, more often than not in London as that proved most central for Sheila from Bristol; Hilary from Tunbridge Wells; Janice from Chichester; Pat from Bahrain then Australia; Joan from Grimsby; Jenny Devon; Sandy Gloucester; and myself, Reading. Those were the most regular members of "Kidhaters" as we nicknamed ourselves but there have also been meetings with others, including a much larger get-together at Jean Capstick's (née Sherrin) in Bristol to celebrate our 25th Anniversary of going to Rolle.

This was held on 29th October 1988 and, in true teacher fashion, Jean had hung a Rolle scarf with balloons outside her house and put up a quiz about 1963 as she had been covering that period with her pupils. With husbands and children, 36 of us met then. 11 of the 16 former Rollers I had not seen in the intervening period but it was amazing how quickly we were chatting away as if it had been only yesterday that we had shared such happy times together.

Since my three years at Rolle in the '60s, I have obtained an Open University B.A. Honours Degree in 1979 and an M.A. in Education at the University of Reading in 1982, both studied for part-time while I continued to teach full-time in Berkshire Secondary Schools (In 1991, I received an award from the County for 25 years' continuous service). However, I have maintained more contact with my contemporaries at Rolle than with those I met through the Open University or the University of Reading, although I was elected onto the Committee of the University of Reading Society, having been a Year Secretary for the 1982 Graduates for many years and still attend the Annual Meeting of its Court to this day.

I am sure that we all appreciated the beautiful setting for a College and the trusting atmosphere that prevailed at Rolle. That aspect was particularly brought home to Sheila and myself when we visited a Welsh College during our vacation and a girl called out "Who are you?" That would never have happened at Rolle because, whenever we returned, no-one ever challenged our right to be looking round the campus. Staff, both academic and otherwise, proved similar to students in that regard and Sheila and I maintained contact with the lady who had cleaned Tracy Block – Mrs Pat James (pictured outside the block in 1966) – until she died in February 1990.

Although Sheila and I stayed at Rolle 'til the very last opportunity so that we could thank not only the staff with whom we had been most involved but also others connected with our life at Rolle – the Dixons and even a pupil and her family from Totnes – during our last week of College life, it is only since then that we have really appreciated what our time at Rolle meant to us. I should like to pay tribute to all those who contributed in any way to making it such an enjoyable experience and a memorable period of my life.

Top left – Leaving Rolle, Vicki Clements and I waiting for a taxi outside Hasledene.

Above – Trudie Potter and her family outside Hasledene Cottage – she had kept in touch since I taught her during my Teaching Practice at Totnes.

Left – June Dixon with son Geoffrey outside Tracy Study Bedroom Block at Hasledene.

In 2006, I approached the University of Plymouth to see if my year could hold a "40 Years on" Reunion to celebrate the 40 years since we had left Rolle. Its administrative assistant, Rebecca Liddington, arranged for those who wanted to stay in *Dunsinane* Hall of Residence over the weekend of July 1st – 2nd to do so. She also arranged a talk on the history of Rolle College, a lunch, a photographer and a guided tour and for many personalities from the University of Plymouth to join with us and we found the same welcoming atmosphere that we had experienced all those years before when we arrived in Exmouth at the start of our Teacher Training Course.

In the above photograph, Sheila Davis is showing Rebecca Liddington, Alston Kennerley, David Fallows and myself the contents of the scrapbook that she compiled when at Rolle while below is the group who attended the reunion

Jim and I were also able to join the large gathering on 18th July 2008 to mark the transference of Rolle Campus from Exmouth to the Rolle Building at the University of Plymouth.

There was a hog roast and a cake had been made to celebrate the occasion. *The Shanty Men* played and sang in the grounds near the new Owen Building, inside of which there was a display of Rolle memorabilia and photographs. A

Time Capsule was buried near *Eldin*, which had been used as the Student Union building since 1968.

Since then, we have visited the Rolle building at the University of Plymouth, as shown in this photograph:

When we chose to move to Exmouth in September 2009, we were amazed to realise that the bus tickets then being issued still gave "Rolle College" as the destination for the first stop in Salterton Road even though the site had been renamed Rolle Campus of the University of Plymouth for many years. We took that as a sign that the College was still held in high regard by the people of Exmouth, particularly the Bus Company

– can't have been anything that those from my era were responsible for as I can't remember travelling by bus much in Exmouth in the early to mid '60s as we walked everywhere, or used the train to travel further afield to Exeter.

Although we used to sing, with gusto, College songs to well-known hymn tunes, such as the following to "*What a friend we have in Jesus*":

> When we leave this Training College
> Oh! how happy we will be –
> No more getting up for breakfast,
> No more wishy, washy tea.
> No more getting up for lectures,
> No more waiting for the bell.
> When we leave this Training College,
> It will be like leaving BLANK! BLANK! BLANK!

we knew that the life that awaited us post-Rolle could in no way replicate the charmed existence we had experienced while there.

Thc following chant should remind those of my era of various lecturers and other staff as well as the Revues that were performed at the end of most terms:

John Williams

**Summer Revue 1965**

10 Rolle lecturers sitting down to dine.
One ate Miss Parker, then there were 9.
9 Rolle lecturers got there rather late.
One found some students, then there were 8.
8 Rolle lecturers talking about heaven.
One got caught by Williams, then there were 7.
7 Rolle lecturers wanting Mr Rix.
Fred couldn't find him, then there were 6.
6 Rolle lecturers going for a dive.
Miss Cray forgot her costume, then there were 5.
5 Rolle lecturers wanting something more.
Floyd already had it, so there were 4.
4 Rolle lecturers longing to be free.
One met Mr Lee, then there were 3.
3 Rolle lecturers feeling very blue.
Miss Jackson suggested dyeing, then there were 2.
2 Rolle lecturers looking at the sun.
Ray looked too closely, then there was 1.
One Rolle lecturer feeling all alone.
Went back to teaching, then there was none.

Philip Floyd

## 1962 – 1988: "Expansion of Rolle" by Keith Waddams

I didn't keep a diary of my experiences during the many years I spent at Rolle so this will not be an autobiographical contribution. However, the story of the emergence of a small Emergency Training College founded shortly after the Second World War into an integral part of one of the largest of the 'new' universities some forty years later is a fascinating one.

I was recruited to the staff in 1962 at a time when Rolle was expanding from a small training college for 270 women to cater for some 400. Thereafter, there were many other significant shifts in its status and function. Rolle became a College of Education then a College of Higher Education, offering (under the auspices of Exeter University) B.Ed. degrees when the 'training' period shifted from two to three years (and, later, four). Soon after, B.A. degrees in a limited number of subjects were introduced. At some time [September 1966], the college became mixed when male students were admitted to study for those degrees. Building programmes were developed to cope with the considerable increase in numbers brought about by such developments.

Then, of course, Rolle College ceased to exist as a separate institution when it became part of Polytechnic South West – a single county-wide institution that also incorporated Plymouth Polytechnic, Exeter College of Art and Seale Hayne Agricultural College. Later, Polytechnic South West was 'promoted' to university status as the University of Plymouth, with the Exmouth campus serving as the site of the Education and Humanities faculties. The decision to move those faculties to the Plymouth campus means that we may soon have a Rolle Centre on the former College site. [Written in May 2012, Keith died 17th June 2014]

A significant part of the history of Rolle occurred during the 1980s when the College was threatened with closure and was reprieved by the then Secretary of State for Education, Shirley Williams, after a vigorous campaign mounted by many groups – the students, staff, the community of Exmouth and Devon County Council. Being Branch secretary of the staff union/association NATFE at the time and therefore considerably involved in the campaign, I accumulated a file of documents (mainly correspondence) that gave some insight into the ways in which the campaign was developed. However, I handed on the whole archive of NATFE documents to my successor so I'm afraid I don't know where it is now – but it must be lurking somewhere!

## Chapter 6: ROLLE OUT THE BARREL

### 1950s & 1960s: "Carlton ablaze" by Chris Humphries

My memories fall into two categories. Firstly, I grew up in Exmouth during the '50s and '60s and, as a child, was aware of the old house that was formerly Southlands School standing on the site on the corner of Rolle Road and Douglas Avenue. As I lived in Freelands Close, off Drakes Avenue, I frequently took a no. 40 bus, which travelled up the Salterton Road and, from the top deck, I could see the campus. In the early '60s, I can remember the demolition and rebuilding that took place, in particular the large crane used in the construction of the lecture hall. It was fascinating to see the progress as the new, attractive buildings took shape.

One incident that lodges in my mind from my childhood must have happened one Tuesday evening around 1960. I had been to choir practice at St. Andrew's Church and was cycling home. Going up Rolle Street, I had just reached the Post Office on the corner of Bicton Street, when I was aware of thick, acrid black smoke billowing down Rolle Road and getting denser the further I went. When I arrived at Rolle Road's junction with Salterton Road, I saw the cause. On the corner of Rolle Road and Carlton Hill, the old house was well ablaze and fire engines were in attendance. We were told it was *Carlton Hall* of Residence [see page 60 – *Carlton Hall* is in the top left corner of that aerial view] and it was suspected that a discarded cigarette had caused the blaze. A few weeks later, some of us ventured inside and witnessed a scene of utter devastation. In particular, I remember the panelled interior doors half-burnt through. It wasn't long before the old house was demolished and the present block of brick-built flats was erected on the site.

My family left Exmouth in 1964 on account of my father's job, and moved to Barnstaple. The following year, I decided to become a teacher and started looking for a Training College. At first I discounted Rolle as I knew it was a Ladies' College but, when I heard that it was to become co-ed from September 1966, it became my first choice. I think Miss Spicer found the arrival of hordes of young men a culture shock. She was nearing retirement anyway and tended to keep in the background, leaving her Deputy to deal with us. My three years at Rolle College from September 1966 to July 1969 were very happy and, of course, I was able to meet up with old friends from the town. Rolle had a beautiful campus and was small enough to be friendly rather than impersonal, as larger establishments tend to be. The males lived out in digs which were vetted very carefully and they were very good. I spent two years in Morton Road and the final year in Ashleigh Road at the home of a lovely lady who was a mature student at Rolle. During my second year in Morton Road, I was often given a lift by a student who owned a Jaguar XK140. It was interesting to hear some of the comments made by the old Colonels about students and student grants. Needless to say, the car owner wasn't on a grant.

I was lucky with lecturers at Rolle College, especially my Education tutor. Mr Pete Burnham was a lovely man and a good teacher with a marvellous sense of humour. Other lecturers I remember were: Keith Waddams, Peter King, A.J. Jones and Terry Jones. I was also a student librarian and the tutor librarian was another Jones, James Owen Jones, known as "Jones the Book"! At first, there was no Bar but, following much demand, one was established in *Eldin* in 1968. [An application for a temporary Bar in two rooms in *Eldin* was submitted to the Magistrates early that year when Keith Waddams and Phil Livesey were the Staff Representatives on the Bar Committee – *Insight No. 19* of 22nd January 1968. Photo shows Bar in *Eldin* during 2006 reunion]. I was surprised when my son followed in my footsteps and went to Rolle College in 2002 to find how little the buildings I knew had changed, although I didn't know the Spicer Building – that was being built during my last year in 1969.

We were all highly amused by an incident which happened in 1967. At our digs we had a student called John Smith. He was extremely quiet and studious and as honest as the day is long. One morning, just before 8, he was walking from his digs along the seafront to go to breakfast at College. As he passed the "Deer Leap", he was stopped by the police as there had been a break-in and, for some reason, they thought he looked suspicious! They asked for his name and, of course, he answered, "John Smith". He didn't have his driving licence or his student union card on him and they refused to believe him. They ended up bundling him into a panda car and taking him up to College and asking a student, "Do you know this man?" Fortunately, the first student they met did. The joys of being a small and friendly campus!

**1967 – 1970: "A view from Down Under" by Linden Kilbane**

I was part of a small group of male students at Rolle College from 1967 – 1970. Every so often, we had meals with the staff and we got really good food!! Mind you the meals were fantastic anyway and plenty of them. We used to get dripping and/or banana sandwiches for morning tea – they were popular then but I wouldn't touch a dripping sandwich now!! The meals at the College were brilliant and plenty of food was available. On Sundays, we always had a roast. However, what was happening sometimes, especially at weekends, was that friends of the students and others joined the queue and got free meals!! That led to us eventually having a metal disc system to stop the food disappearing to non-students.

My years at Rolle were very happy and I remember that, from our lecture room, we could see the estuary, which was nice. We had three lecturers in the R.E. department and they all began with the letter B – Barraclough, Baker and Bell. My Education Lecturer was Peter Horner who lived on Woodbury Common – I often wonder if he is still around. I remember Miss Spicer as the Principal even 'though she was almost never seen by the students!! The Principal after her was a man, whose name I have forgotten – he had a bushy beard and we used to call him "Moses"!! [John Williams]. At the start of each year they went through all the different Student Organisations and the relevant person had to say a few things about their group. Every so often, we had to line up near the Hall to get our grant cheques from our Local Authority.

I lived in *St. Hilarian* Hall – which is now gone, I believe [approval was granted in March 2000 for its demolition and the erection of 16 high-class apartments on the corner of Portland Avenue with Douglas Avenue. However, the name was retained. *St. Hilarian* had been the home of the Hon. Georgina Cicely Pellew ($18^{th}$ December 1885 – $17^{th}$ May 1930), eldest child of $4^{th}$ Viscount Exmouth. Her only brother, Edward Addington Hargreaves Pellew, five years her junior, became $5^{th}$ Viscount Exmouth until his untimely death, aged 32, on $16^{th}$ August 1922, when a cousin succeeded to the title. Their mother was Edith Hargreaves of Arborfield Hall, Berkshire. Nowadays, the replacement for Arborfield Hall is "Aberleigh", the home of the Vice-Chancellor of the University of Reading, which you will recall was where W F Morris was lecturing prior to becoming the first principal of Exmouth Training College in 1946. "Green Hollows", where Jim and I have lived since September 2009 was built in the gardens of the original *St Hilarian* in 1931].

Several newspapers were delivered each morning and there was often a scramble to get a copy. I looked forward to reading the different papers, especially the Sunday ones with their coloured magazines.

One day, all students were summoned to the Hall – we had no idea why – and were given a telling off for letting lights stay on in the evening by the Principal whose name I have forgotten. At the back of the College were propagating buildings [pictured here on 26th March 2014]. As I used these, I developed an interest in plants, which has stayed with me till today.

There was a real character when I was at Rolle, one Norman Baker. He was the oldest student at Rolle – aged around 50 when he started – whereas the vast bulk of the 1,000 odd students were around 18 – 20 years old. He is still alive, aged 84 and lives at Weston-Super-Mare.

I live in Western Australia now and teach Special Needs children in Perth but I still have my old College scarf in the wardrobe!!! I trained in Primary Education at Rolle, before going "down under", where I branched out into Special Education. We don't have any dyslexic children in my School – all of them have intellectual and physical disabilities. Some of the students are in wheelchairs and we have a lot of autistic children who also have intellectual disabilities. I have only ever met one student from Rolle in all my time in Australia, which is over 30 years now.

This scarf was brought to the 2006 reunion by former student Lyn Pattinson (Plyn)

## Chapter 7: ROLLE PLAY

### 1967 – 1970: "Classed as a Mature Student" by Mike Cole

I entered Rolle College at the age of 23 after seven years at work so was classed as a mature student (!) I had been an apprentice in Plymouth dockyard then worked in an assortment of jobs, including the Civil Service, which I found really boring. Entering Rolle was perhaps the best decision I ever made and, as I had worked previously, I had a decent grant so felt reasonably well off. I had had to go to Evening Classes to secure an "A" level before I could be accepted by the College. Having taken two but only passing Geography, I had a bit of an inferiority complex when I arrived and approached the three-year course with some trepidation. However, it turned out to be possibly the best years of my life.

I was billeted in Victoria Road with five other Rolle students and we all remained there throughout our three years. My personal tutor was Ray Jones – his wife, Megan, still lives in Exmouth. I had originally been accepted to study Geography as a main subject but I could see the Drama students having so much more fun so asked if I might swap. Rolle was one of the few colleges to offer Drama as a main subject and, although we produced some obscure plays, Mr Bosence made the course really interesting. We did have some very arty types as some had started their training at Dartington College and were very talented.

The Aesthetic Studies week at the beginning of each term in the 1st Year was fascinating for me as all first year students had to study Dance, Drama and Art then, whatever their actual main subject(s). The idea was for everyone to get to know everyone else but I was interested in watching how a 6′ 4″ guy studying Maths would cope with performing Dance!

Obviously Teaching Practices entailed stays away from College and I was amazed to be sent to an all-boys Primary School in Falmouth where a master actually washed a boy's mouth out with soap after some profanity was uttered! Despite plenty of rehearsals and line learning in between course work and visiting schools with Children's Theatre, I soon settled into College life. Situated just a few hundred yards from the beach and outnumbered ten to one by females (we were only the second intake of men!), free from signing in or clocking on, it was the nearest thing to heaven you could imagine – pure luxury for me!

Because the numbers at Rolle were comparatively small (about 600), it felt like being a member of a very special community. The opportunities for self-development were countless. Unlike those who had come straight from School, I didn't miss any lectures as I felt privileged to be here. I played football, ran the team in my last year; represented Rolle occasionally at basketball and hockey and, of course, performed regularly in plays.

The highlight for me was the involvement in a venture partway through the course when a small group of us got together and wrote a Late Night Revue Show "And So To Bed", which was performed in the Common Room every couple of months. It was a series of sketches and one-liners on a particular theme with a bit of music thrown in. It turned out to be quite popular and both the BBC and ITV came to view it. Fellow actors were John McGrouther, Phil Walker and Chris Lillicrap, with lecturer Colin Davis and his wife. When our course finished, we moved to London with it, instead of going straight into teaching. After three or four months of limited success, we disbanded; returned to Exmouth; did the sensible thing – became teachers and got married – although Chris Lillicrap is still in Show Business.

It was John McGrouther who took many of the photos I have of that period in my life. His comments included:

"Having a camera at College was not very common in those days (1967 – 1970); nor were cars, or any personal means of playing music, 'though, being the '60s, there were a lot of guitars! (but all acoustic).

John's Morris Oxford in the snow outside *Kingsthorpe*.

"As can be seen from the photographs on the next page of *Kingsthorpe* in Douglas Avenue (left) – just opposite the College Admin Building – and St Aubyn's in Hartley Road (right), there was quite a covering of snow at that time and some students certainly took advantage of it for a snowball fight.

[A large snowfall that stayed around is something quite unusual for Exmouth as, during the three years that I was at Rolle from 1963 – 1966, I can only remember around 20 minutes of snow falling, and that did not settle.]

"I was one of the few with a car as I had worked for three years before going to Rolle but it didn't last long on a grant! However, cars did continue to feature throughout my time at Rolle as can be seen here:"

1969-70 Rag day "float" – Vestal Virgins – on Cortina along Exmouth seafront.

John's photos really remind me of how glorious my three years at Rolle had been. After seven years of clocking on or signing in for fairly uninteresting work, here was an environment which offered so much scope for learning and being creative. During those three years, I hardly missed a lecture – so eager was I not to miss a moment! I hardly missed a meal either as it was such an opportunity to socialise. In my time, all meals were provided at College. Digs (mine were in Victoria Road) just provided accommodation.

As well as Drama, I became heavily involved in the sporting scene, especially football, during the three years and I still have copies of "Insight" from

2nd October 1967 and "Rolle Sportlight" from 1st October 1969 along with a scrapbook of other memorabilia collected during my time at Rolle. "Rolle Sportlight" reminded me that additional buildings east of the main College were then ready for occupation. The four-storey building near *Fairfield* Road housed the Students Union. As well as a Cafeteria and study accommodation, it also offered hairdressing, washing and leisure facilities for the use of day and lodging students, many of whom lacked them. A permanent cricket square had been laid out at the College Fields in between the football and rugby pitches by then but, as the men's changing rooms had not been finished, those of the women to the side of the gym had to be used for visiting men's teams for part of Saturday afternoons. Later a table tennis table was installed in the Recreation Room next to the Hairdressing Salon in the Student Centre.

I particularly enjoyed: playing "away" football matches, when we visited lovely local villages by way of coach; putting on the Arnold Palmer course; walking down to the beach inbetween lectures; and Rag Days – always greatly supported by the people of Exmouth. [1968 saw Rolle's first attempt at a Rag Mag – RAGAMUFFIN] I have so many happy memories of Rolle!

I had to leave teaching when I was 52, having taught in Surrey then Sussex. A heart attack at school meant that I needed a by-pass operation then, early in 2012, I had another so needed stents fitted. I am still in touch with twelve or so of my year and, since I was able to move back to Exmouth six years ago and now live in Douglas Avenue – opposite the football field – I was able to organise a reunion in *Dunsinane* for them.

Being at Rolle was a richly fulfilling experience. The College had a unique atmosphere. Its smallness gave it an intimate, special feel, which lecturers and students seemed to enjoy being part of – small was beautiful and the ambiance of the place made it special. Its demise is very sad – thank goodness we were able to enjoy it in its prime.

## 1968 – 1971: "Floods and power-cuts" by Maggie Morbey

One of my first impressions when I arrived at Rolle College to do a Cert. Ed. course in 1968 was of the age of Exmouth's population. It was nearly a whole term before I saw someone pushing a pram (outside Hudson's bookshop in Rolle Street). Everyone was OLD. The presence of College students must have been quite a strain for the locals, especially in the alternative times of the 1960s and early 70s. It seems very different today when we visit friends there.

In the summer of 1969, reflecting on the dress code of hipster jeans and cut-off tops adopted by the female students of that time, the Deputy Principal had taken time from an Education lecture to remind us that we must cover our midriffs and wear footwear to all lectures. Scholl sandals and flip-flops were permitted but bikini tops were not. I was in *Seacroft* Hall during that first year.

At the end of it, my room-mate left all her lecture notes and essays – beautifully written in fountain pen – locked in a trunk full of clothes in the cellar. There was a lot of rain during that summer break and the cellar flooded. The trunk was pulled out of the water but could not be unlocked until her return in September. Consequently, her clothes had gone mouldy and her notes ruined and unreadable – fountain pen is not waterproof and there were no back-up copies in those days! As you can imagine, she was devastated.

Some of the highlights of Rolle's social calendar were the drama department's Reviews. Students would queue along the two corridors leading to the main hall, or in the Junior Common Room. I can recall the romance of sitting in the dark in the JCR with candles during the power-cuts caused by the miners' strikes. Today Health and Safety would have put a stop to that! On one occasion, the show could not start until power was restored.

Other highlights of our time at Rolle were the Teaching Practices when we were taken to the far reaches of Devon and Cornwall by coach and deposited there for four to six weeks in 'digs', clutching suitcases, rolls of card and hamster cages. There was no M5 and the main roads went through all the villages then – it seemed to take forever. My friends returned with tales of doing preparation on scrubbed kitchen tables in farm houses though I was more fortunate. I had four weeks in Salcombe in Spring 1969, in the village school where the class teacher's tweed suit had a scorch pattern from leaning against the guard around the coal-burning stove in the classroom. One little boy, a farmer's son, was not very bright academically but he could identify every plant in the hedgerow and knew all about the farm animals. In my second year, I was in Camborne and used to borrow the landlord's bike to ride through the lanes and explore. I only learned from the next-year's student that it is considered very unlucky to bring bluebells indoors in Cornwall – they were too nice to tell me! A group of us took the landlord's daughter to the Helston festival. My last practice was in Plymouth where I took my class to the Zoo – I don't think it exists now [19th April 1962 – 8th January 1978]. Our maths topic was decimalisation which was occurring about then.

Ken and I met when he came to college in 1970, having got bored with working in Insurance in London. I was then in my third and last year. We met through Christian Union connections – but he went out with another girl for eight months. When that ended, he asked me out – though by then I had got my first teaching job in Kent starting in the September. Needless to say, British Rail and BT did quite well out of us for the next two years! As this was before mobile phones, we would arrange a time by POST then I would go out to a nearby phone box to ring Ken who would arrange to be by the phone in the Students' Union Building at Rolle! I can also recall long train journeys when I would write LETTERS or sew a maxi-dress for a college dance.

We were married in 1973 and lived in Topsham for a year while Ken finished his degree and earned holiday money helping build the M5, and I taught at Bradley Rowe School in Exeter – an experience I would not like to repeat. Then we moved to Birmingham – a new adventure. On one occasion at Rolle, I had overheard one lecturer say to another, "I wonder how long these girls will stay in the profession – until they get married and have children I suppose". Forty years of teaching and our own children and grandchildren later, I often reflect on how much the world has changed since then!

## 1970 – 1974: "President of the Students' Union" by Ken Hazel

My first observation when I arrived at Rolle College in 1970 was how many girls there were – girls of all shapes and sizes. For a bloke, a ratio of 6:1 was a very attractive set-up! I was in *Hilarian Hall* for my first year and the place was always full of young women, even though it was a male hall!!

Rag Week happened each year. At the end of my first, June 1971, the boys of *Hilarian Hall* decided they would spice things up a bit. Overnight we painted the word 'RAG' in white paint on the road along the sea-front. A friend and I then broke into college and took all the seats off the girls' toilets, locked all the doors from the inside, then put the toilet seats in various places in the college – including on the Principal's chair in her office! In the morning we all went in to breakfast (normally unheard of!) to observe the fun as people ran about putting them back! *Hilarian* also had the best Rag 'Float' that year, a pirate ship. We captured several girls and put them on the float!

I was in the Religious Studies department at Rolle and, once a year, we spent the day with the Drama department. We were given exercises then the whole department was given a scenario which we worked out as if in real life. I found I loved such activities and role-play in general. I never really used it in schools but often included it in a Youth Club setting. I directed ten pantomimes using the technique and also used it in a variety of Christian settings as it was an excellent way of developing people and their talents.

I played for the college football team throughout my four years at Rolle. Every Saturday for two terms of the year, we toured Devon and played in a succession of villages I had never heard of. The men we played spoke a language I didn't understand (such as "where you be to?") and played a brand of football I came to understand only too well. As a Centre Forward ('Striker' in today's language), I played with my back to the goal. The ball would be passed to my feet and I would either turn and run with it or pass it elsewhere.

1971 – 72 Rolle Football Team: Dan; Mike Biscombe; – ; Ken Hazel; Andy; Andy
(Front row): – ; Roger; – ; Keith Urrow; Paul Bucci.

The opposing Centre Half wore large boots with toe-caps and, whenever the ball was passed to me, he would lunge for it and, if my leg or ankle happened to be in the way, then tough luck on me. (The tackle 'from behind' has now been banned). My memory of Saturday evenings is of bringing the bruises out with cold then hot water – Nurse Bendle from Sick Bay recommended that. On Sunday, I would shuffle about in great pain and, on Monday and Tuesday, hobble in late to lectures. Through the rest of the week things would gradually improve then, on Saturday, the cycle would restart! Devon Centre Halves didn't like students much! However I loved every minute of every game – the camaraderie, physicality and scoring goals gives a wonderful feeling! I scored over 100 in four years so like to think I got the better of those defenders.

Our's was the era when students were in conflict with Government ("Maggie, Maggie, Maggie, out, out, out"!). Even in sleepy Devon, we voted for a 3-day strike over Government plans for student unions. One day was meant to be for explaining ourselves to the local community so we advertised, hired a big hall in town and laid on refreshments. Three turned up and we ended up sitting in a circle, explaining our position to the three of them! Most students spent the day on the beach! However, the government backed down (probably the only time Mrs T did so) – our efforts must have terrified them.

When I was President of Rolle's Student Union in 1973, we negotiated a new lodgings policy for Year 2 students. There was a clear list of expectations for people who let a room to students, which included a key for the student to get in and the freedom to come and go as they pleased. The Lodgings Officer had been at the job for years when the college had been all girls (who seemed to do as they were told and be in their rooms by 10.00 pm). We had one girl who was not given a key and, if she returned after 10.00 pm, was locked out! When we complained to the Lodgings Officer on her behalf, she agreed that the landlord had contravened the agreement, but refused to do anything about it. She said, "You keep saying it is unacceptable but I am not sure what you can do about it". (I was so livid I can remember her exact words 40+ years later). So we found the student a spare bed in a Hall and moved her in with all her belongings. Once she was settled, I rang the Principal and informed him of our action. He was supportive and promised to deal with his employee.

I think that episode shows the contrast between the 1960s and the way things were changing by the early '70s. Students were no longer boys and girls prepared to just do as they were told. The *Exmouth Journal* was notoriously anti-student at that time and sniped continuously at the long-haired 'louts' in their midst. At one Union meeting, we voted NOT to support a 'Union for School Students', although some of its ideas (such as no physical violence to students) would seem normal today. Some students from Rolle anonymously sent details of the proposed Union to the *Journal*. A vitriolic editorial, which only had half the facts, caused me, as President of the Students Union, to write a reasoned but firm letter putting the facts straight. The editor published my letter unabridged. Several (well 5 or 6!) lecturers saw it and congratulated me on taking on the editor, with comments such as "It's time someone took him on", which made me believe it was one up to us students.

I made two speeches at the National NUS Conference. In one, I took on the executive and we won the vote! (What on earth it was about I have no idea). The experience of student politics with Caucasus and positions made me decide not to get involved in Party Politics when I left college. The way that conferences worked meant that taking part was essentially a game, rather than being about ideas and issues. The best game-players won! People also seemed to dislike each other. I went from there to a National Christian Conference where people loved each other – the difference was stark! I went on to teach RE, be a Year Head and finally Assistant Head – all in large inner-city comprehensive schools.

## 1970 – 1974: "French Studies" by Rosemary Earl

It was a beautiful, warm, spring-like day in January 1970 when I stood on Exmouth sea front with my parents, wondering whether my dream of living by the sea would come true. My pessimistic mood was contrasted by the delights of the weather. Rolle College – modern, forward-looking and well-sited [see here for plan of Campus from 1969–1970 Student Union Hand-

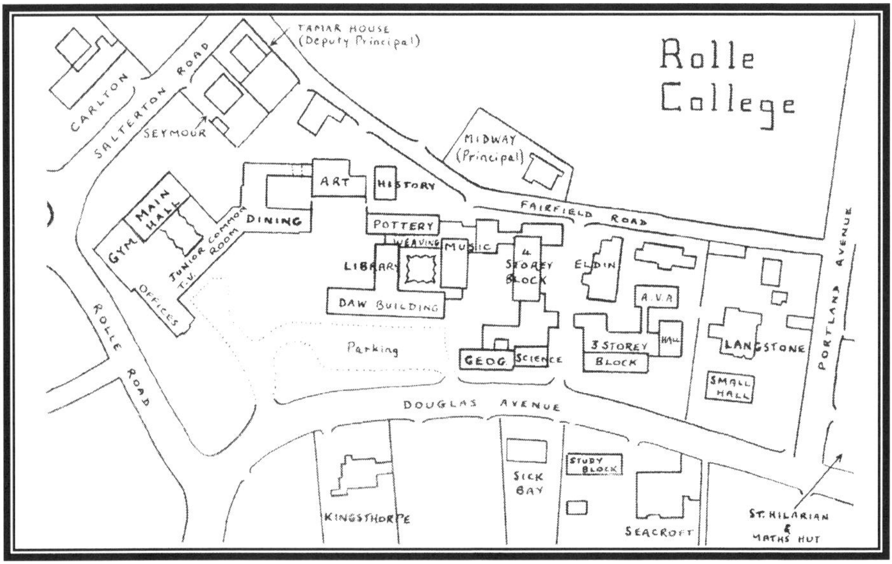


book and below for an aerial view of it and adjacent area from 1973–74 Prospectus] – seemed the ideal educational establishment for my Teacher Training but I felt my interview had gone badly so my hopes were in tatters.

Earlier that morning, I had waited patiently outside a small tutorial room in the French Department, located in the Main Reception Block, which housed the Senior Common Room and Administrative Area. As a young girl of seventeen years, I was highly nervous for my expectations of myself were high and my limited experience of life made me shy. I was only aware of shiny floors and empty corridors when Mr Wilfred Perry, dressed very smartly in suit and tie, invited me into his den. This small, sharp-featured, dapper man in his 40s attempted to put me at ease by pointing to a chair. His diction was very clear; his English sounded upper class but that window of comfort did not last long. Within moments, he was explaining in French that the interview would be 'tout en français', sending cold shudders through my spine and a desire for the nearest escape route! His expressive face, his lively eyes (which rapidly assimilated every snippet of information) and his boundless energy, seemed overpowering. Yet there was a friendliness and warmth about him that, all in all, made him a most interesting and colourful character.

He asked me basic questions that would be expected in an interview but I struggled to respond quickly and confidently and, the harder I tried, the more flummoxed I became. I knew he was thinking that my oral French (my weakest aspect) was not at the desired standard hence his final question, posed in very optimistic tone, " . . . and have you been to France?" (*tout en français*, of course!) to which I replied in downbeat mode and then excitedly, knowing only too well that a negative response would not be received gladly, "No . . . but I have been to Algiers!" Mr Perry received this news with sheer joy and enthusiasm before asking, " . . . and how long were you there for?" My heart sank into my stomach. My face must have said it all as I meekly answered, "Twelve hours!!" Clearly, this was grossly insufficient time to acquaint me with the culture or to improve my language skills. Mr Perry's subsequent

loud chuckle has stayed with me to this very day. Somehow, I managed to pull myself together so that he could show me his treasured Language Laboratory, quite newly-installed, I believe, where almost all French sessions would be conducted and which would be open most of the term time to enable students to use it freely and independently.

A few days later, the dreaded envelope came through the post and I feared the worst! Maybe that final question posed by Mr Perry had turned matters around though because I was accepted to study for a "5 – 9 years teaching certificate" with French as my Main subject, albeit with a strong recommendation that I should visit France and improve my oral French skills. At that time, many Secondary Schools were installing Language Laboratories but my Grammar School was not one of them, so I felt disadvantaged. Nevertheless, all that was to change as I embarked on the challenge of using Rolle College's language laboratory – the technology was a challenge in itself, let alone the difficulties of working in a foreign language!

The French Department consisted of Mr Wilfred Perry (Head of Department); Mrs Marie-Thérèse Crowle (a French native speaker and part-time lecturer in her 40s); Mr Charles Marie (a bachelor from Lille, probably in his 30s) and Miss Sheila Smith (in her late 20s to early 30s and who, I believe, had come from Exeter University). All spoke fluent French and all teaching was conducted solely in French! You can imagine how hard this was for us students, particularly in the first year and, especially, when some sessions were double ones lasting at least two hours. The concentration needed was very demanding for, not only were we listening in French, but we had to take notes in French and at lightning speed as time waits for no man!

Sessions were divided into at least four areas: *langue*, *littérature*, *civilisation* (geography, history & customs) and *pédagogie* (teaching methods). Looking back, the provision was broad and included a wide, varied knowledge of France. The methods were quite innovative. Sometimes we would transcribe the words of a traditional or modern French song by listening to it over and over again on the tape recorder and, in that way too, we acquired a repertoire of French songs we could later teach in school. I remember many of them to this day. Such was our repertoire that we gave a French concert at Dartington Hall, Totnes to teachers of French on a residential weekend course. Rolle Arts/Crafts Department made all the participating female students a variety of *coiffes* (traditional French headdresses) to wear on the day as, not only did we sing, but we performed French traditional dances as well. Somehow, word spread of our excellence, resulting in us travelling to Plymouth to the Westward Television Studios where our performance was recorded then broadcast that evening on the local News.

Mrs Crowle, whom we called *la poupée en porcelaine* as she was very *petite*, seemed to be at the heart of these many, enjoyable musical activities. Mr Perry regularly organised French bistro-style *soirées* with wine, cheese and music, the smell of 'Camel' cigarettes pervading the atmosphere. A play was

performed annually by the Department staff and a few students. Molière's "Le Bourgeois Gentilhomme" was one of them. It was performed in 1973 and the cast consisted of: Peter Henson Trudgill; Sheila Smith; Marie-Thérèse Crowle; Gerard Poulet and Ottman Hamayed, the last three of whom can be seen in the above photograph performing in front of an audience.

Each year we would also have the advantage of a French native speaker, an *assistant* attached to the French Department to support its work. All students studying French were obliged to spend at least part of their summer holidays in France, either independently or on a suitable course at a French university. Students were also encouraged to spend three terms at a French university prior to embarking on their final B.Ed. year. Clearly, the French Department worked hard to ensure high standards and we responded by working hard too. However, it wasn't without some dissatisfaction on the part of the students from time to time. French, as a Main Subject, was known amongst all Rolle students to be the hardest subject to pursue, the discipline with the most follow-up work. As if the course work and homework weren't hard enough, we also had to fit in the reading of one French novel per fortnight in order to give a *résumé* and to answer questions in a 20 minute or so tutorial. My tutor for that was Charles Marie (a Boris Johnson look-alike) and I recall the perpetual worry of waiting outside his room when, although conscientious by nature, I just hadn't been able to complete the task. He was a very 'deep' thinking man and there was no way you could pull the wool over his eyes!

Every summer, towards the end of term, the French Department would organise a residential week at The Prince's Hall on Dartmoor. This was during Mains Week, when all Departments set up activities away from College for their students as a form of enrichment. We always envied the English Department as they would go to London or some big city and spend time viewing theatrical productions. For us, there were no visits to France at that time – only the experience of being isolated in the middle of the Moors in order to benefit from *un bain linguistique* (total immersion) in French. That was the best the Department could provide in those days. Once again, we had to speak solely in French, and the whole days of activities were organised around reporting on the latest French news by listening to the radio, watching French films, playing games, singing songs etc. We would be driven to a location on the Moors where we would set off in groups to find out about the area by asking local people or by researching in churches or wherever we could. The small group would then write up a report or re-enact the scene in French to the whole group in the evening. We even went on a night 'treasure hunt' type trek over the Moors.

There was always plenty of cross-curricular work, and opportunities to perform to an audience abounded. This undoubtedly assisted me in my quest to acquire greater self-confidence but it also caused me much worry as nobody likes to make a fool of themselves! On occasions, fellow students would revolt against some of the demands. Being cooped up together and confined like prisoners for a week in the middle of the Moors did not always go down very well with young students, who naturally sought freedom and wished to veer towards bright, city night-life. Only about a year after we all left, Mains Week was rescheduled to a residential week in Brittany!

I was always very stiff at the end of the first week of each term during my first year as we had to be very physically active during the Aesthetic Studies Week (Dance, Drama, Art)! Initially, I resided at *Kempston* Hall in Portland Avenue in my first year. [Margaret Buchanan was the sub-warden at *Kempston* and she can be seen in this 1972 photograph in her graduation gown outside the Hall].

After that I was in lodgings in Raleigh Road, then Avondale Road, near Littleham, in my second year; and in Study Bedroom Blocks [below] on the *Hasledene* Campus during my final two years – in Peverell then Carey. Meals were taken in College throughout – what mammoth meals they were!

I used Stone's Bookshop in Rolle Street; belonged to the College Choir for a while; appeared in the first year revue in the main College Hall and attended some of the balls and discos. Two friends and I hired the main Common Room to celebrate our joint 21st birthday party.

My Education tutors over the years were: Mr Horner, Mr Bob Louis and Mrs Katie O'Connor. Teaching Practices were spent in Barnstaple, Teignmouth and Plymouth. We were shipped out in coaches, or a College Bedford like this one, and returned to College at weekends, as it was apparently cheaper to do things that way. Other tutors I recall: Mr Draper and Mrs Yvonne Wardrop (Maths); Mr Wood (Humanities); Mr Tony Jones (English); Mr Tushingham (P.E.); Mr Gordon Crone (Drama); Miss Early (Art/Needlework) and Miss Violet Madge (Divinity).

I loved Exmouth, frequently walking on its beach; had cream teas at Newton Poppleford; saved money in order to have a cheap Chinese meal in the Strand with College friends at the end of some of the terms; often caught the train to Exeter on Saturday for shopping; frequently went to Clapp's – a coffee house in the Strand – where we would have lovely, milky coffee and cream cakes! I don't have much in the way of photos as I didn't have a camera at the time.

I recall going to Bystock Court for a weekend to help paint the house with one of the Rolle student groups. This project had been organised by students so we cooked our own meals; sang songs with guitar accompaniment in the evening and had a bonfire evening/barbecue with a twilight walk. Quite a lot of us slept on the floor in sleeping bags for a couple of nights!!

During our second year, a group of us would go to Marpool Primary School, Exmouth, where we took it in turns to teach part of a French lesson to pupils at the upper end of the school. Members of our group would observe us and, on return to College, each student teacher would be appraised by lecturers and fellow students alike. We had become familiar with the two main schemes of work for teaching Primary School pupils in our *pédagogie* sessions, namely *Bonjourline* and *En Avant*. In our final year, we taught the younger pupils in Exmouth Community College. That proved to be harder as pupils were more self-conscious at a slightly older age. Two of us would prepare a lesson in French and deliver it while the rest of our year group and at least one tutor watched and evaluated it for subsequent discussion back at College.

I assume that it was through the developing relationship between Rolle French Department and Marpool Primary School that three students, accompanied by Miss Sheila Smith, were able to spend a week at the *Maison Familiale* in Tailleville, a small village near Bernières-sur-Mer, not far from Caen in Normandy, with about 34 pupils from Marpool and a group of about six pupils and their headteacher from a village primary school near Crediton, Devon. I was very fortunate to be one of those three students! Much time was spent with the children at mealtimes, informally teaching them small differences between the customs of England and France. For example, they were taught about using bread to mop up the sauce on their plate; to keep their knife and fork for their next course and how to leave them at the end of the meal. At that time, many Marpool pupils were going abroad for the first time and were not widely travelled as today's youngsters are. Children were not as exposed to European or global influence then so the differences between the two countries were more apparent. Much of what we did therefore focused on observing and identifying those differences.

While in Normandy, we would visit Caen, a local market, the war graves at Omaha Beach and a diverse range of places to interest and extend the knowledge of all. The children would have opportunities to use French money (*francs* and *centimes*!) and to use simple French language for shopping. This helped to develop their confidence and independence. We also made a visit to the local village school where the Marpool and local French children quickly overcame the language barrier using a combination of sign language and simple words and phrases to teach each other common playground games, resulting in new friendships.

Groups of elderly French people often stayed at these *Maisons Familiales*. They adored having the children around them at mealtimes and, since the children then had a real purpose to speak French in response to the elderly people's questions or comments, they constantly sought French words or phrases to maintain a conversation. The resultant bonding led to the children putting on a concert and the elderly French people responded by singing traditional songs wholeheartedly as a thank you gesture!

I acquired so much from the visit that, a few years later, I felt sufficiently confident as a fully-fledged teacher to organise my own trips to the *Maison Familiale* in Bernières-sur-Mer. By then, I knew the places to take the children on excursions, had a wealth of acquired French songs to amuse them and, of course, had some experience of the organisation and pastoral care required for dealing with large groups of youngsters. In the years that followed, I went on to organise at least 20 residential weeks with primary school children in Normandy, Belgium and the Netherlands. I have also been involved with the Plymouth/Brest Twinning Panel since soon after leaving Rolle, so its influence continued to play a part in my life.

There were 12 – 15 of our year group in the French Department and the other year groups were similarly sized, except for the fourth year students staying on to work for a B.Ed. degree. A fellow student who wanted to take the degree course persuaded me to stay on for a fourth year so there were just the two of us. I enjoyed French and wanted to achieve a B.Ed. in Psychology of Education and French but it was very hard work. I did not mind that but I thought failure was a potential reality and could not have borne that! [No doubt, Rosemary had seen 25th October 1968 "Insight" No. 33 where the comment was made that, of the 23 4th year B.Ed. students, only 13 passed, 6 failed and 4 were referred. As a result, the second intake of B.Ed.s had reduced from 50 just a year before to 16]. However, we supported one another through the torturous journey to success. I could do very well in examinations but, if I did not feel confident on the initial reading of the questions, I was inclined to panic and then perform below par. I was therefore pleased that Rolle College had used continuous assessment over the three year course. Sometimes, at the end of a term or block of work, we were given a written test as part of the assessment but these were usually manageable and did not affect my nerves too much! In the fourth year, though, it was different! Then, we had to prepare for lengthy three hour examinations.

As there were only two of us, some of our lectures took place at St. Luke's College in Exeter, which meant travelling there a couple of times per week. At least once per week, St. Luke's French students came to Rolle. Our B.Ed. examinations took place in Exeter. The first one was the oral examination held at Exeter University – alien surroundings for us! The examiner was a total stranger. Once again my confidence failed me, for this was my weakest aspect, even though I had by then been to France a few times. What I do remember is that in the French Literature examination paper, it stated quite clearly that St. Luke's students should answer in English and Rolle College students should answer in FRENCH! It seemed hugely unfair and I recall trying to be as accurate as possible, endeavouring to find alternative phrases and means of expression that were not prone to errors.

During the year we had to research and write a thesis, which would form the other part of the assessment for our degree. I decided to study and write about the social conditions of pre-French Revolution agricultural workers. I thoroughly enjoyed this but was sad to learn that, once the thesis went for assessment, it could not be returned to me for a few years. Apparently it then sat on the shelves somewhere at Exeter University. When it was finally returned to me, I found it riddled with deep pencil underlinings as if someone had used it for their own study and this was quite upsetting. It was the same for my thesis in Education.

My years at Rolle College contributed enormously to my development as an adult and as a teacher. Those years were some of the happiest in my life! On leaving Rolle, I acquired a teaching post in a Plymouth primary school, which, at the time, was one of the few primary schools in the area to teach French. I taught my specialised subject to junior school children, establishing an annual residential visit to Normandy. However, when funding for maintaining French teaching was cut, inevitably the teaching of it across the city stopped. For many years thereafter, I tried to keep a voluntary French club running outside school hours.

Around 1991, I attended a reunion at Rolle for former students of my era. In 2003, I volunteered to be part of the Steering Group in Plymouth to set up the teaching of Modern Foreign Languages in city primary schools. My enthusiastic work led to my becoming the Chairman of an Academic Council to implement the policy that the Steering Group had written. This resulted in me supporting half a dozen primary schools in the throes of establishing a new subject to teach to their pupils. By the time I retired as an assistant headteacher in 2010, after 36 years in the same primary school, Plymouth was well advanced in its implementation of the legal requirement. I feel that my Local Education Authority has benefited from my years at Rolle College and, therefore, thanks are particularly due to the members of Rolle's French Department for their enthusiasm and inspiration – a special thank you to Mrs Crowle with whom I have kept in contact since our first meeting in 1970.

As well as the photograph taken of the players in "Le Bourgeois Gentilhomme" on page 153, here are four further scenes from French plays produced by the French Department at Rolle during my time there:

## 1971 – 1973: "An A-V Technician's Memories" by Felicity Kirton

Known as "Diddy", I worked at Rolle College as an Audio-Visual Technician from 1971 to 1973. Those were the days of slide and film projectors (and even the epidiascope), Gestetner and Banda copiers, and tentative moves towards educational television. I have watched the development of Audio Visual Aids and the gradual disappearance of my relevant skills with interest in the intervening years and thank God for the interactive white board!

My memories are of lugging Bell and Howell projectors (see centre of photograph on page 161) from the technician's cupboard to the hall, to waiting students, praying that the film wouldn't break or the bulb go whilst projecting. I spent a great deal of my time in the dark, printing or developing staff photographs in a peaceful Victorian house surrounded by roses.

I remember my good friend, Karen Ayres, who worked as a science technician in the wonderful greenhouses and how I had to look after the ghastly Axolotls [large aquatic salamanders found naturally only in parts of Mexico] and other beasts when she was away. As long as Don Leech, my boss, wasn't around, I used to borrow a rat to sit on my desk and keep me company!

I had done a course in Educational Television at Plymouth Art College and was really pleased to get a relevant job in such a lovely place and near enough to Exeter so that my husband could finish his Teaching degree. Rolle College was in such a wonderful location and the layout then was very quirky, and therefore interesting, with several old Victorian houses (*Langstone* and *Eldin*) as classrooms. I only remember beautiful weather there and the wonderful views over the sea, but then I have moved to Suffolk now!

My colleague, Alan Gentle, was a tremendous help and encouragement and Tony Rogers and Bob White became good friends. I also made friends with one ex-student who was temporarily working as a technician, Bill Bailey, who remains a good friend today. It was a good first job, fun and interesting but I spent most of my time trying to be innovative and creative in a position that didn't really allow such leeway. I later moved on to work at Exmouth Teacher's Centre (now razed) with Philip Brookman, a tremendously supportive and inspiring man, who later took the Centre up to Rolle and worked there, I believe, while I became a Careers Guidance Adviser.

## Chapter 8: ROLLE OVER?

### 1966 – 1986: "Closed–circuit television at Rolle" by Don Leech

My own experience of Rolle College of Education in Exmouth started in 1966 following 20 years working in Secondary Schools, mostly in Essex. The Department of Education and Science had decided about 1964 that there might be a practical use for closed-circuit television in the Training Colleges. Initially, 11 Colleges or Departments of Education in Universities were given money to experiment with the idea. Lecturers and technicians were appointed and asked to offer their expertise in developing courses and training for staff and students. A report was subsequently published by those employed to participate in the experiment and, not surprisingly, it was decided that this was a promising and successful idea. Money then became available for several similar establishments to appoint a lecturer and equip his department to develop television teaching. I was that person at Rolle. The architects of the modern part of the College came to discuss with me the design of a TV studio. A building already planned was to be modified so that it could be adapted to those new needs. The architects were very proud of all their work and had talked very professionally of the need to retain a similar style throughout the College. They were very proud of the appearance of the site and resisted firmly any attempt to "spoil the line" by random building.

Immediately after those new appointments around the country, someone had cold feet and required that all new appointees had better spend a term gaining real experience in one or more of the 11 "original" establishments. I therefore had to go to Coventry where I found the course interesting but not very enlightening as everyone was still struggling to gain recognition for his work in an educational context. Many colleagues were openly cynical. My own experience had been in film-making and using the educational TV studio in Essex. It was interesting that not all people on the course were actually intending to operate TV equipment when they returned to their own College. It was never required that the trainee should be the person in charge of TV!

The pattern of work for most Staff was that they taught in their "subject" according to the needs of that department. There were regular lectures, of course, to the various groups of students on each course. Tutors also held back-up sessions (or tutorials) for small groups of students. Some general subjects, mostly in the field of educational theory and practice, were taught to whole year-groups in the large lecture halls. My work was partly to create, operate and maintain closed-circuit television (CCTV) with its technicians, studio and mobile unit. However, half the time was to be spent in teaching practicalities concerned with audio-visual systems, equipment and resources.

A Resources Centre was developed which was allied to the library and provided students with much of the audio-visual material that they needed in schools. Whole year-groups went out into the schools of Devon and Cornwall

for a period of about six weeks once a year. There was a complicated system of organising the way tutors visited those schools to advise and assess the work of the students. We were often away for three days at a stretch to visit our more distant students and to spend sufficient time with them. There were three "practices" a year; most tutors being involved with two of them and they interfered a lot with the work we had to do at the same time in College.

There was a busy social life for everyone at Rolle. Apart from the sports activities, there were dances and special events, regular performances by the Drama Department, concerts by members of the Music Department and less formal events about once a month in which many students showed their entertainment talents in Revue-like Evenings. Those shows were very popular and many students demonstrated considerable skill.

In the earlier days, staff were still responsible for the care of the students "in loco parentis" up to the age of 21. However, when a change in the law [1st Jan 1970] brought the age of responsibility down to 18, many students chose to be independent and rent their own rooms in town rather than live in College accommodation. That meant that there was extra space to accommodate other students, many of them from abroad, who would attend courses designed especially for them. These included refresher courses for experienced teachers, training courses for school inspectors and various specialist courses in particular subjects, such as a one-year training course for Post-Graduates who wished to teach their particular subjects in School. We had many visitors from Botswana, I recall, but also from other parts of the world as well.

At that time, Rolle students studied for a degree of the University of Exeter. Later, the administration of the College was to be taken over by the University of Plymouth and a rumour soon developed that Rolle would be closed and the students (and staff, presumably) transferred to Plymouth. Many tales of mystery crept into the Senior Common Room and there was much talk about what might be happening. As things became more and more indefinite, many of us, who were able, took the opportunity to take retirement and so lost the thread of events that eventually led to the point when Rolle's closure was finally announced. Life there had set the pattern for 20 years of my own life and I found it sad to realise that its happy atmosphere would no longer be available to the people of Exmouth and its visitors from all over the World.

**1966 – 1985: "Families of staff" by Edna Ireland & Joan Barraclough**

Among the many people with Rolle College connections with whom I've kept in touch over the years is Don Leech, who started at Rolle at the same time as my husband, John Ireland, in 1966 though he was on the technical side. John had applied for the post of Lecturer in Education at Rolle on completion of his second degree – a research one – at Cambridge. At the time, the family knew nothing about Exmouth – did not even know that it existed – so we told our daughters that there were four miles of sand there and plenty of fish!

Miss Spicer, who interviewed John, was a lovely lady. He told her that he suspected the post was not particularly relevant to his experience but she told him that, although it was too low at that time, there was to be a big expansion so she wanted to appoint him in readiness for that. She had put everything into getting men as students as she wanted the College to survive and grow. John, a Historian, had spent two years in the Forces in Cannock Chase where he was a Squadron Leader in charge of the Education Corps and it was that experience that enabled him to realise how few of the personnel could read. On leaving the Forces, he found a job in Cirencester. Eventually, he became one of Miss Spicer's senior staff – Principal Lecturer in charge of post-graduate students. In fact, he was the third down in seniority and he used to comment on how, even the dregs among the students, seemed to blossom at Rolle. However, that is racing ahead and I've not even told you of how his proposed move affected the family.

We came down by train and stayed in a caravan for three days while looking for a suitable place to live. Fortunately, the 4-bed turn-of-the-century house we bought for £5,000 in 1966 is still ideal for me even though John died in 1985 and the girls have obviously flown the nest. It was built on the Rolle estate. I feel really blessed that all the houses nearby have remained as private family homes – not been sold and converted into apartments, or demolished then replaced by blocks of modern flats. Tony Jones, another of Rolle's Senior Lecturers, lived next door until he died in 2011 – I was godmother to his youngest child.

John had gone on ahead to Exmouth, leaving me to deal with the move from our previous house by myself. On the strength of that experience, I vowed I would never move house again by myself and, fortunately, I've not needed to.

As you can imagine the move to Exmouth was not the easiest to achieve with the education of two young daughters to be considered. Sue, our eldest, had completed her first year at Grammar School in Cambridge but she had done that a year ahead of her age group as she'd been recognised as gifted from the age of four. That meant that, although Exmouth Grammar School said they would be delighted to have her, they only had a place for her with their first year intake. We therefore had to look around for other alternatives in the area, including Exeter. Eventually, we settled on a Convent Boarding/Day School in Exmouth. It had a very good Head and she even accepted our younger daughter, Josephine, aged seven, at a reduced fee when she didn't settle well into the local Primary School and we couldn't afford fees for both of them.

As a result of the move and settling the girls into their school, I did not return to teaching during our first year in Exmouth, but I used to walk children from Exeter Road School to Rolle College swimming pool. We encouraged both girls to attend the Saturday morning sessions at Rolle so they would get to know more children from Exmouth. The sessions were organised by the students for local children but all Sue and Jessica seemed to remember, when I asked them about them recently, is that they were "made to go and listen to twee stories" but at least they liked the person telling them!

Another opportunity that presented itself was that Ray Pocock, Head of Music, allowed anyone from the town to join Rolle's orchestra. Sue joined as a violinist while still at school so that was another gain she experienced.

In Doris Spicer's time as Principal, the Balls were very formal. We had to wear Ball gowns and long white gloves and line up to be presented. Altogether, they were great 'do's! No. 8 Fairfield Road had been bought as the Principal's House during Doris' time so her successor, Francis Cammaerts (right) and his wife Nancy, moved there with their family after her retirement in 1972. Francis was a complete change from Doris. Having been dropped behind enemy lines during World War II, he was known throughout the country. He was great – the best thing that could have happened to Rolle at that time. The 11$^{th}$ December 1971 *Exmouth Journal* announced his appointment the previous Monday with the heading: "War hero to be Rolle College principal".

Aged 55, Professor Cammaerts had been educated at Mill Hill School and St. Catherine's College, Cambridge, where he read English and History. The end of September 1972, *Exmouth Journal* gave a further description of him:

**New principal settles in at Rolle College**

SETTLING DOWN now at Rolle College is the new principal, Professor Francis C.A. Cammaerts – a man who was dropped into France during the last war to join the French resistance fighters, and who was subsequently awarded the D.S.O., the Légion d'Honneur, the American Medal of Freedom and the Croix de Guerre [with which he was presented after the war, as seen in this photograph].

Professor Cammaerts has come to his present appointment from a position as Professor of Education at the University of Nairobi, Kenya, where, during the six years of his tenure, student numbers rose from 70 to nearly a thousand, and teaching strength from two to 50. He was the first professor of education at the university.

He has a wife, Nan and three grown-up children, Nicola, Joania and Paul. They are accompanied by their grandson, Kia, 8, but two of their children remain in Nairobi and one in Switzerland.

Before going to Nairobi, he was principal of the City of Leicester College of Education from 1961 to 1966; and before that he was headmaster of Alleyn's Grammar School, Stevenage New Town, from 1952 to 1961.

**OPPORTUNITIES**

In 1948, Professor Cammaerts became the body's first director when the Central Bureau for Educational Visits and Exchanges was set up – and remained in charge until 1952. "The major task," he said, "was to provide opportunities for students and teachers to go abroad on exchange visits. We helped schools and individuals to gain particular information as to how the needs could be met. Language training was of course a very important part of it, but the range was wide – if someone wanted to learn Japanese painting, for example we could ensure that he did it 'on location'."

Professor Cammaerts was selected for the Rolle College appointment from a total of 115 applicants.

"My father was Belgian and I had always been bilingual," he said, "so in February

1943, after volunteering for the task, I was dropped in. My main job was to arm and train guerrilla fighters and instruct them in communications sabotage."
In May 1944, he was arrested, along with three other officers suspected of resistance activities, and was sentenced to be shot. Their lives were saved, he relates, by a Polish woman agent, Christine Granville, who had been dropped into France to work with Mr Cammaerts.

[In Beaulieu's Secret Army Exhibition, Francis Cammaerts is described as "a talented organiser, being one of the SOE's leading agents in Provence who led around 10,000 resistance members in south-eastern France. After the invasion of France he was arrested at a routine road-block and his courier, Christine Granville, had to blackmail a German officer to secure his release." He had trained at Beaulieu in October 1942 in F section (France) at the School for the Special Operations Executive where he was given the code name Roger.]

**'.. OR ELSE'**

"She went straight to the Germans," he said, "and more or less told them 'You'd better free the prisoners, or there will be trouble for you'!" Fortunately for the three agents, the Germans were virtually defeated in France at the time, and they took the point and released the prisoners. If Mr Cammaerts and his fellow agents had been arrested earlier, there would have been no escape.
"Tragically," he said, "Christine Granville was murdered in London after the war." It was too early said Professor Cammaerts, for him to have "identified" very much with life at the college. The students were not back, but he had been able to meet some of his staff colleagues.
"The college is in a beautiful situation" he said, "I particularly like the fact that the students live in a variety of accommodations – as opposed to the monolithic halls of residence of the past, with which I disagree."
It was not the first time he had been to Exmouth, or to Rolle College, he pointed out. He had been on a teacher's course at the college in about 1964 when it was still a women's college. Also he had formed an acquaintanceship with Devon "as a youth-hostelling lad".
Asked his leisure activities, Professor Cammaerts said he was not "a performer in any particular activity". He liked sailing and had taught it at Leicester – but maybe I'm past it now!" Also he regarded golf as "an agreeable pastime" but his handicap was "a lot higher than it should be!"

**FULL–TIME**

"But primarily," he explained, "my leisure has always been very closely connected with my job. I enjoy the task of education and it's a full-time one."
"I've already become very fond of Exmouth," he said, "and I believe the town has a lot to gain from the college, and a lot to offer to it."

Professor Cammaerts replaces Miss Dorothy [Doris] Spicer as principal. Under Miss Spicer, who is retiring, the college has grown during the last 14 years from a small establishment for 250 women to a mixed college for about 1,000.
Miss Spicer, a lecturer in education, was formerly vice-principal of the Lady Mabel training college, Yorkshire, a physical education college for women which provides a three-year course.

Many quality concerts were held during Francis' principalship. The young Jacqueline du Pré gave a memorable concert – she really put everything into it. That must have been early in his principalship as she had to cease playing the cello after February 1973 when, during a concert in New York, her final piece had to be cancelled because her fingers could no longer perform. It was in October that year that she was diagnosed with Multiple Sclerosis.

Francis saved Rolle College in 1977 when the big chiefs were going to axe it. He wrote a letter, which was published in 24th July 1976 *Exmouth Journal*:

**ROLLE COLLEGE 'FAVOURED' NOT 'VICTIM'**

Sir, – Last week you printed a report of a personal statement by Mr Michael Miller, chairman of the Exmouth Chamber of Trade and Commerce, concerning the future of Rolle College. In this statement Mr Miller said that he was "led to believe" that Rolle College had already been threatened with closure, had been reprieved, and was once more threatened with closure.
We at the college are most grateful for Mr Miller's interest and concern and we also fully appreciate that any "threat to the college" involves not only those directly employed by the college but also the economic well being of the whole Exmouth community. The money spent by staff and students in Exmouth and the contribution to the social and cultural life of Exmouth of this college is, we hope and have reason to believe, very widely appreciated in the town.
However, Mr Miller's statement if read without comment may give rise to great anxiety among those who are wholly or partly dependant on the college particularly at the beginning of the holiday season, when for a number of weeks they will not be in daily touch with staff and students.

I would therefore be grateful if you would assist me in putting the record straight by publishing this letter.

Since the publication of the previous Government's White paper "Education a framework for expansion" in December 1972, it has been apparent that the continual fall in the birth-rate would produce fewer children in school and therefore a declining need for qualified teachers.

During the past 3½ years plans have been drawn up and discussed locally, regionally and nationally on the reorganisation of initial teacher training. This culminated in August, 1975, by all institutions receiving a target figure for 1981 of teachers in training.

**STUDENT REDUCTION**

Rolle College numbers were to be reduced from 850 to 600 students for teacher education of which 120 would be serving teachers on induction or in-service programmes. Many colleges of comparable size were reduced to 500 or less and a number of colleges were informed that they had to close.

Under the pressure of the present financial constraints the programme has been speeded up and further controls on input and output of students have accelerated the procedure to reduce the output of teachers.

The target figures for students to be admitted to colleges in 1977 were received last week and no doubt precipitated Mr Miller's statement.

**DIVERSIFIED**

In all this period of planning and reduction of student numbers, the continued existence of Rolle College has never been questioned officially. The South West is an area which is not overprovided with colleges, and Rolle College is the only Local Authority Maintained College between Weymouth and Land's End.

Plans are in hand to use the additional college space for diversified programmes of studies for students who will not be preparing to be teachers.

Throughout this period the college has been strongly supported in its plans for the future by Devon Education Authority and also by the neighbouring counties of Cornwall and Somerset who do not have a similar college.

There are at least 65 other institutions in England and Wales who in terms of size and planning are as susceptible or more susceptible to closure than Rolle College.

**ROLLE MAINTAINED**

I would simply like to stress that we plan to retain in Exmouth a college of a size comparable to Rolle College at present and that there is no reason to believe that the recent figures issued to colleges in any way single out Rolle College or a group of colleges including Rolle College for threat of closure.

Our continued existence in these hard times will be greatly assisted by the interest and enthusiastic support of our town of Exmouth, of the County of Devon and of the South West in general.

Whatever our personal opinions may be on the rights or wrongs of present Government planning for teacher education, and whatever we may feel about the closure of some excellent colleges, within the context of the national picture Rolle College has been treated with favour rather than being a "victim".

*F. C. A. Cammaerts* *(Principal)*

I can remember one Easter, when we had taken my old Mum (who lived 'til she was nearly a hundred) to a cottage in Cornwall. John always seemed to be on call and that time he received a call from Francis, "Please will you be in London Education Department tomorrow. It's vital – we're fighting for the College". John had to catch the milk train up, having had no more time than that to think what he'd say. He got back at 2 a.m. but at least the College had been saved! He was certain that Rolle would have got the push if Cammaerts hadn't been around at that time.

By the time Francis Cammaerts left Rolle College, it had expanded terrifically as reported in the $25^{th}$ September 1981 *Exmouth and East Devon Journal*:

**Rolle College Principal off to Africa**

Mr Francis Cammaerts has retired after nine years as principal of Rolle College at Exmouth. But he's off to Africa to help start a new teacher-training college in Botswana. A presentation was made on behalf of the college to Mr Cammaerts and his wife Nan by Mr Phil Livesey, dean of students at Rolle.

Mr Livesey described Mr Cammaerts as "an impressive man with human qualities of integrity, sincerity and concern for the well being of everyone in the college".

He stressed that Mr Cammaerts had been instrumental in saving Rolle College when it was threatened with closure in 1977 and had worked during his time at Rolle for the personal and professional advancement of those studying and teaching there.

**THE PROBLEMS**

Mr Cammaerts pointed out the failures and successes he had encountered during his time as principal; the problem of the exam assessment system, the teaching of languages and the handicap of compulsion for children to stay on at school.

He saw the advancement in primary education as a step in the right direction, with the teaching of science and mathematics.

He thanked Mrs Althea Ratcliffe, a long-standing governor of the college, for her service.

Mr Cammaerts is going to Africa where he plans to visit Botswana to discuss setting up a new teacher-training college over the next few years.

A floral presentation was made to Mrs Nan Cammaerts, Mrs Ratcliffe and Miss Terry Parker for her 25 years' service as catering officer at Rolle.

Francis finally retired in 1987 when he and Nan returned to live at Le Pouget in the south of France where he died 3rd July 2006, aged 90 years and 14 days, having been born 19th June 1916.

A year after John Ireland arrived at Rolle with his family, Tony Barraclough was appointed as Lecturer of Religious Studies, joining Deaconess Bell, a long-standing member of the staff who was mentioned by Linden Kilbane on page 139 as two-thirds of the R.E. Department's 3Bs – Barraclough, Baker and Bell. Tony's wife, Joan, recalled that Tony always invited all his main subject students to supper, which she prepared. Numbers of students varied between ten and 42 over the years due to changes in Government policy. Degree courses often changed with very little time for consultation.

Joan commented that families of staff were entitled to use the swimming pool on the sports field and their children were also able to go to a Saturday Club at the College. She taught her children to play tennis on the courts at *Hasledene* (below) and a former Dartington student, who came to Rolle to complete her teaching qualification, taught her daughter oboe and piano. Staff from Rolle's Modern Languages Department went with Marpool School pupils to France.

**1967 – 1981: "Erstwhile Housekeeper" by Ruth Rockett**

Ken and I came to Rolle in 1967. He was in the Music Department and also a Warden while I was asked to do a brief stint as housekeeper until a new one could be appointed. In actual fact, I stayed 14 years and a few anecdotes spring to mind from that experience.

In the '60s and early '70s, women students were somewhat restricted in their evening excursions away from their Hall of Residence. They had to sign 'The Book', stating their destination, and be back by 10.30 p.m. (I think) whereupon the Sub-Warden would lock and bolt the door to ensure all her charges were safe from any wandering male with evil intent! Legend has it that one Lothario thought he would visit his girl in spite of this and attempted to penetrate Castle Adamant by going the scenic route via a small skylight. Sadly, he got stuck – and had to be rescued by the Warden – with a ladder! So embarrassing!

*Ferniehurst* was one of the Halls of Residence in Douglas Avenue (1990 Photograph)

As well as cleaning Halls and Study Bedroom blocks, two of my domestic staff also serviced several teaching areas by renewing towels, soap etc. two or three times a week. One of them came to me in mild distress one morning:

"I'm sorry but I can't do it, Mrs Rockett."
"Can't do what?"
"Towels in the Animal House."
"Why can't you do the towels?"
"'Cos I can't get in."
"Oh, is it locked?"
"I don't know – only I've been three times this week and each time I knock, somebody says 'You can't come in'."
"Right, let's both go and find out what the problem is."

So off we went, knocked on the Animal House door and, sure enough, were told, "You can't come in".
Not quite sure what was going on in there, I knocked again, gently opened the door and stuck my head round. Not a soul in sight!
There were lots of cages of small mammals – gerbils, mice – and zebra finches – and then, behind the door, I caught the gaze of a rather malevolent-looking Mynah bird. Mystery solved! I'm afraid that I may have added a little to his vocabulary!

Albert Rix had been the head porter and caretaker throughout my time as housekeeper and, when he retired in March 1978, this article appeared in the 1st April 1978 edition of the *Exmouth Journal* under the heading:

**Leaving, but he's not forgetting Rolle College**

CHEERFUL smile from Mr Francis Cammaerts accompanied the farewell cheque presented recently to Rolle College's retiring head porter and caretaker, Mr Albert Rix.
Mr Rix, who retired after 15 years at the College, received an electric fan heater and a book on the history of Exmouth from the students, and a tankard from the clerical staff.
Before moving to Rolle College, Mr Rix served as a senior C.O. in the Royal Air Force during the war, after which he joined the Mersey Docks and Harbour Boards as a motor engineer for marine and dock maintenance.
During his retirement he hopes to remain in close touch with the activities of the college and the students' union. His interests include walking, cycling and motor cycling and these will enable him regularly to visit his family in Somerset and Lancashire. He will also have more time to enjoy his other hobbies – reading books on anthropology and Egyptology and "messing about with cars".

## 1971 – 1989: "Changes in Religious Studies" by Dr David Keep

I was appointed to the Religious Studies department at Rolle College in 1971, together with John Highfield, as Deaconess Bell was due to retire in 1972. The college was expanding and the intake reached about 240 (from which peak it was rapidly cut to 100) and we had to contrive a B.A. degree course. John and I were appointed for New Testament Greek as Exeter would not allow an Honours degree in the Theology Department without a study of two books in the original language. This was eventually reduced to a few chapters and my final student got a first. I used to tell my students that it was the only knowledge they could be sure of when they graduated! John taught Hinduism and I was responsible for Church History and Philosophy while the late Tony Barraclough took Old and New Testament. We were a happy team and remained friends even though John returned to teach in Africa and then Liverpool.

Under Principal Doris Spicer, our day started at 9.15 a.m. as she had abolished Prayers. We had four long sessions for main subject, later cut to four hours and finally to four 45-minute sessions. We continued with four elements to the main subject course and, when I began to teach history, I discovered why our students complained of their workload. At one stage we had free afternoons and twilight classes, after which, on Thursdays, I used to have dinner before singing with the choir. I had assumed there would be a lively Senior Common Room, but ate only with the assistant housekeeper and Annmaree Kain, a temporary lecturer in Geography, who moved to Exmouth School (and with whom I still sing). The hotplate contained all the alternative meals for each of us! The music at Rolle gave me a great deal of pleasure. In my early years, we collaborated in a formal carol service. This was taken over by the always flourishing Christian Union outside the College day. One lecturer would never allow her class to miss a lecture in the penultimate day of term. A far greater loss of time occurred when Wallace Arnold offered a cheap coach to London on Friday afternoons when I was teaching Professional Studies.

One third of the students' course covered a main Academic Discipline, another third was Educational Theory and the third, Professional Skills, which included three half terms in school. Those three elements to the course eventually became all graduate. We rapidly realised that, if we changed our usual C+ to B–, all our students could attempt a degree. The Education Department theorised about practical issues and, in 1971, I was regarded as conservative. However, by 1988, I was liberal, and my views had not changed at all!

Teaching Practice was usually very enjoyable, especially in Cornwall in May! I had had only Grammar School experience, yet was given mainly Infant supervision!! That didn't matter too much as I had had some training and a lot of experience of talking to small children in Churches. In general, the students knew what they were doing as they were often following their mothers! However, I do vividly recall one girl panicking and rushing out of the room. I looked at 30 five-year-olds and they looked at me. Fortunately their teacher sent the girl straight back and she played finger games for the last ten minutes and saved her career. Another student whispered at her class and I thought depended on the teacher in the next room who had, in fact, gone to the hospital with a sick child. That student went on to use the same technique at Exmouth School with equal success!

More energy seemed to be spent in trying to keep students in School rather than failing them, though there were a few who would not acknowledge that they could not cope. We were sometimes misled by mature students as experience with a family or in the Armed Forces did not always translate to competence in the classroom. I used to assure students that they could ring me at any time. Fortunately, very few did, 'though I still recall one midnight complaint from a former engineer, "All they want to do is play." Sometimes a change of School was all that was needed to solve the problem.

French play L'Avare – November 1982

I am not sure how far leadership can be taught but it can be learned by experience. Selection for entry to College, and so potentially to the profession, was by a joint interview and we generally agreed. The question to a brilliant candidate "Why do you want to come to Rolle?" was sometimes answered by "My boyfriend/fiancé is at St. Luke's." That relationship was strong in the '70s with joint Gilbert & Sullivan and the occasional French play. I took part in the last of the latter in 1982 as the subject was being dropped at Rolle and in Primary Schools.

When the course was continuous assessment, a few learned to play within the rules. Since they had to average a 'C' grade, it was possible to skip an essay if an 'A' had already been achieved. One mature student moved to Religious Studies from Dance and did not even know that there was more than one translation of the Bible. Her first love was Art, but she produced a few brilliant pieces of work in Church History. One student taught me a valuable lesson at the end of my first course of carefully prepared lectures, when she commented, "We have your lectures, but we haven't learned anything." That inspired me to move to getting the students to do the work and then teach one another. A couple of our students transferred to the University Department of Theology and did well.

One of St. Luke's Halls of Residence – Killerton – is now a National Trust property and in May 2008 a group of "Kidhaters" came across Terry Jones, who had been a Senior Lecturer in English at Rolle, volunteering there.
Daphne Barnes-Phillips (née Barnes); Terry Jones; Joan Mercer (née Staples); Janice Walter (née Proctor) and Jenny Newman (née Willy)

In our later years of working with St. Luke's, main subjects were merged for students preparing to teach Infants. Something called a 'domain' was contrived and three of us went very unwillingly to St. Luke's to produce a syllabus. History had years of experience with Geography within Environmental Studies and was not interested in English, let alone Theology. However, both those subjects had taught the U.S.A. and U.S.S.R. for years and the other two of us had learned military Russian so, tongue in cheek, we proposed "The U.S.A. or U.S.S.R. since 1945". This went through on the nod proving relevant and popular since it came on stream in 1984 with Glasnost.

I was persuaded it was my duty to support the Union. We three Theologians passed a vote with one other colleague against a pay rise during rapid inflation but, despite this, I became chairman and negotiated a deal with Mike Preston, largely preserving the status quo. I also became chair of the Academic Council, including a packed meeting voting to join Plymouth Polytechnic with only the Principal and I abstaining. Rolle might have succeeded alone ...

[Mike Preston had been Rolle's principal since 1981 when the *Exmouth Journal* of 14th November gave a summary of his previous achievements:

**Dr Michael Preston new principal of Rolle**

DR MICHAEL PRESTON is the new principal at Rolle College.
Educated at St Bartholomew's Grammar School, Newbury, Dr Preston trained for teaching at Borough Road College, gaining his M.Ed and Ph.D. at the University of Leicester. His teaching career covers posts in primary, secondary grammar and secondary modern schools, followed by posts in higher education at the College of All Saints' and Charlotte Mason College.
Dr Preston's professional interests include the curriculum of the primary school and curriculum structure, and mathematical education. His personal interests include rugby football and sport in general, the National Trust, the RSPB and art and craft appreciation.
He sees a major role for Rolle College in the Southwest, and is very optimistic about its future. The community role of the college is very important to him, and he has already liaised with Mr Philip Thorne, headmaster of Exmouth School and Exmouth Adult Education Organiser, Mr Colin Joliffe, with a view to expanding this side of the college's activities. Dr Preston's wife Betty has obtained a post as a senior mistress at Colyton Grammar School. Their two children John, aged 16, and Ruth, 14, both attend Exmouth School.]

With that experience, I was promoted Acting Director of Resources for six months and did the job for over two years until the merger with the University of Plymouth. From being on my own in Religious Studies, I had three academic colleagues and over twenty technicians. I was totally ignorant of computers and was mainly a consumer of the library but we had a unique catalogue of teaching resources in R.S., which I adapted. My main task was to set up a Resources Centre accessible to the public and negotiate longer staffing hours, both of which I managed with loyal support. We made some good appointments. I had great respect for the well-qualified cleaner to whom I offered a post in the library. She turned it down so she could be available to her children.

Being ignorant of computers, David no doubt appreciated the manual library system in evidence in this photo of 1983

I managed to write a paper most summers, often for the Ecclesiastical History Society. I found the typists did wonders with my handwriting and rough drafts. One unfortunate lady did retype the material on the reverse of the used sheets I was using! For a few years we had Youth Opportunities workers. Two made a useful index of *Studies in Church History* with guidance and I found one giving a Teaching Practice tutorial on *Judaism* but we were not too grateful to another, who begged some paint and left our storeroom white and sticky! It was a good scheme for building confidence and several moved to proper jobs but we could not continue as we had no formal training element.

Very few staff left Rolle – although one did return to teaching – and we were staid as a community. Ray Jones organised a reading of *Under Milk Wood* every year or so, but there was not much social life even at the end-of-year Ball. In the 70s, there were children's parties where the hat competition was more between the mothers than the children. One child complained that there was no sound to a black and white film. The party ended with Kate Hadley telling the story of *The old lady who lived in a vinegar bottle*!

We had a quiet farewell when many of us left on generous terms in 1988. I went back for a year to teach for a morning a week, so that was a very pleasant wind-down.

[David omitted to mention that his family took part in the BBC's "Ask the Family" quiz programme while he was a lecturer at Rolle but thanks to administrator, Linda Meikle's collection of newspaper articles, we know about the occasion from the 21st February 1981 *Exmouth Journal*:

**Keeping it in the family!**

> THE KEEP family of Woodbury with their pet cat Domino, pictured this week after their recent trip to London to take part in the BBC's "Ask the Family" quiz programme.
> Dr David Keep, a lecturer in Religious Studies at Rolle College, is seen here, with his wife Carolyn, a chemistry teacher at Exmouth School, son Nicholas, 14, and daughter Philippa, aged 12, who both attend Exmouth School.
> Last September they successfully passed the initial interview at the Royal Clarence, Exeter, which took them to London for the pre-recording last weekend.
> The family spent last Sunday afternoon at the BBC studios at Shepherds Bush for the programme which will be screened in the spring. Whether they won the first round remains a secret as the family have been asked not to say.

Another interesting article in the light of David's comments about leaving on generous terms in 1988 is the following from the 24th May 1986 *Exmouth Journal* as it seems in direct contrast to what actually came to pass:

**Boost for Rolle College**

> ROLLE College has received a major boost – Secretary of State for Education Sir Keith Joseph has announced.
> By 1989 the number of annual intakes of students for initial teacher training courses will leap from 160 to 220.
> "It really is a major boost for employment", said a delighted Mr Ray Owen, the college's head of faculty of teacher education.
> Mr Owen said he anticipated around 12 more academic tutors and lecturers' would have to be employed, plus a large number of ancillary, clerical and catering staff.]

## 1988: – "heralded change to Rolle Faculty of Education"

David Keep's mention of leaving Rolle "on generous terms" in 1988 then returning to teach one morning a week for a year probably needs a little explanation to those not familiar with various changes in Education as it relates to the financial provisions made at the time of the merger between Rolle College and Plymouth Polytechnic. I was able to take advantage of a similar scheme in 1996 when schools were being awarded grant-maintained status. Then, any members of the teaching staff who were over 50 years of age could apply for early retirement within two years of their school becoming grant-maintained. This was not an automatic right as it depended on how many applied and whether the school could accommodate such changes. In my case, Hugh Faringdon R.C. School in Reading had previously been voluntary-aided and four members of staff applied for early retirement. Two of the latter were close to age 60 so the school governors agreed that they should be granted retirement first – at the end of 1995. I was next in age (52) and was granted four years' enhancement when I left in July 1996. Having taught fulltime for 30 years, my pension was therefore calculated as if I had completed 34 years' teaching service. Since such arrangements were obviously expensive for the school, the governors felt that they could not agree to allowing the youngest, barely 50, the privilege of early retirement as well. However, they generously allowed him to lessen his work-load by choosing one of his two job titles – Head of Geography or Head of Careers – but retaining his original salary.

In the case of Rolle's merger with Plymouth Polytechnic, the arrangements were somewhat different because as 17th June 1988 *Exmouth Herald* reported:

> **College chiefs quit over merger plan**
>
> It is understood that up to one third of the college's staff will also be leaving because the merger plan gives them an opportunity to take early retirement on two-thirds of their salary.

Rolle College Principal since 1981, Dr Michael Preston, and his deputy, Frank Aldred, who had been there for 16 years, were among those who opted for early retirement. They knew that, under the merger plan, Rolle College was likely to become a Faculty of Education for the new polytechnic so it would be administered by an Assistant Director of the Polytechnic at Plymouth rather than by a Principal on the Exmouth site as this advertisement in the

*Times Higher Education Supplement* of Friday, 24th June shows:

**DEAN OF FACULTY OF EDUCATION**

**(Assistant Director Designate)**
**(located at Rolle College, Exmouth)**

**Salary: Within the range £25,710 to £28,164 until 31st March 1989; (£29,687 from 1st April 1989)**

Rolle College at Exmouth will shortly be merging with Plymouth Polytechnic along with Exeter College of Art and Design and Seale Hayne at Newton Abbot. Rolle will become a Faculty of Education, and the Polytechnic is seeking to appoint a Dean of Faculty (Assistant Director Designate). The appointee will be a person of good academic reputation, probably of a professorial calibre, who, at a time of substantial change, can provide the Faculty with strong academic leadership and management.

Application forms, to be returned by Friday 22 July 1988, and further details are available from the Personnel Department, Plymouth Polytechnic at the address below, or by telephoning (0752) 264639. Any further clarification can be obtained from the Deputy Director (Academic Planning and Control) by telephoning (0752) 264638.

Plymouth Polytechnic

**Drake Circus, Plymouth, Devon PL4 8AA**

AN EQUAL OPPORTUNITIES EMPLOYER

It was thought likely that 19 members of staff would leave through ill-health, retirements or technical redundancies, including several senior and principal lecturers, many of whom had given more than 20 years' service to Rolle College. While leaving staff were to be replaced, there were likely to be a few months when the college would have to rely on part-time staff and associate tutors until new appointments were made.

The above had been reported at the end of an article entitled: **Rolle moves into a new era** in Saturday, 25th June, 1988 edition of *Exmouth and East Devon Journal* which had started:

> Rolle College – Exmouth's largest employer – is to join with Plymouth Polytechnic and Exeter College of Art and Design in September.
> The College will become the Rolle Faculty of Education – and Mr Ray Owen of Douglas Avenue, has been appointed its acting dean.
> A former head teacher in Lancashire, Mr Owen has been at Rolle College for 22 years. His wife, Fernley, is a former teacher at the Exmouth Church Primary School, and their 21-year-old son Jonathan was educated at Exmouth Comprehensive.
> Plymouth Polytechnic, Exeter College of Art and Design, and Rolle will merge on September 1. Next year Seale Hayne College will also join the new institution. In a joint statement this week, Rolle College Principal Dr Michael Preston, and governors' chairman, Mr Peter Thorpe, said the college was in its strongest position

> ever to go forward into the new institution.
> Dr Preston and Mr Thorpe also denied that they were opposed to the merger.
> They said they hoped their acceptance of places on the institution's new board of governors and on its formation committee would demonstrate their "total commitment and interest" in the merged institution.

There had been much less time to arrange things for the Rolle lecturers than schools were allowed if the articles in the *Exmouth Herald* are anything to go by. As a result, it was really not surprising that this was dubbed the "retire one day, back to work the next" policy in the 24th June edition of that paper:

> **Lecturers to retire, then return to work**
>
> Some senior lecturers at Rolle College, Exmouth, will be retiring early on up to £12,000 a year on August 31st – and then going back to work at Rolle part-time the next day.

In fact, more than two years of planning had gone into the proposed merger, but the college authorities seemed suddenly to have been given the go-ahead by Education Secretary, Kenneth Baker, in June, and the move had to be completed by the start of the new academic year on 1st September.

The merger involved altering the job descriptions of most of the staff, and that allowed some of them to qualify for an early retirement scheme known as *Crombie*, under which they were paid up to two-thirds of their salary until they reached the age of 65, when they would revert to normal half-salary retirement. A county council spokesman said that the *Crombie* scheme allowed for any extra payments lecturers received, and would be based on any extra they might be paid for that sort of work. He added:

> Senior lecturers at Rolle could be on a salary scale of £14,800 to £18,500. This would mean pensions of up to £12,000.
> In the interests of the students, you have to keep the courses going. If that means using lecturers on a part-time basis to finish things off, that is a sensible arrangement.
> They will be used as sparingly as possible. It is possibly for two terms while some of the courses are finished.

The consequences were therefore seen as:

> Because of the speed with which the merger is moving, Rolle will be unable to find suitable replacements for everyone who is leaving, until next January at the earliest Devon County Council confirmed this week that Rolle had been instructed to "endeavour to use any arrangement which does not involve re-employing the

> existing staff."
> But it admitted that if there was no other way, existing staff would be taken back. And already about 10 of the 15 senior academic staff who have so far agreed to take early retirement, are expected to resume part-time lecturing in Rolle.

Just as schools in the 1990s were to find it baffling that experienced teachers could be replaced with cheaper-to-employ younger colleagues, Barry Willoughby, Exmouth Town Committee Chairman and member of Devon Education Committee described as "incredible" the 1988 Rolle situation:

> I am not very happy about this state of affairs at all. Every bit of the education budget is under extreme pressure. We are trying to save every penny we can.
> If they cannot find anybody to replace them, they should not have been made redundant.
> The sooner Rolle becomes a local financial management centre and manages its own affairs within its own budget, the better. If that were happening, they might be a little bit more careful.

Some of the governors of the college were opposed to the polytechnic merger, and it was agreed by only a small minority to back the scheme.

> The merger also incorporates Exeter College of Art and Design, and Seale-Hayne College of Agriculture, in Newton Abbot.
> It will create one of the largest polytechnics in Britain, with new management structures being introduced next spring.

John Bull, Plymouth Polytechnic's deputy academic director, said the merger would safeguard the future of Rolle College, Exmouth's largest employer, at a time when Government policy was making small institutions vulnerable. As well as lecturers, four senior administrative staff opted to retire.

Dr. Preston said that Monday's press conference would give "more detail about the merger so that people can be reassured. I am not very happy about the idea of Rolle College becoming a 'satellite.' We want to explain it carefully so that we reassure people and at the same time give a clear indication of what is happening." He commented that, as well as talking about the development of the merger and the way forward, the situation regarding other staff at the college would also be revealed. One member of staff at Rolle College told the *Herald*: "The staff here are very excited by the new courses we are starting and the new ideas which are being put into operation."

Linda Meikle's collection of newspaper articles, accumulated while she was administrator at Rolle from 1982 to 1997, has facilitated this history as this article from Monday 3rd April 1989 *Western Morning News* shows:

**'Sell Campus' plan to beat cash cuts** by Julian Joyce, Education Correspondent.

Governors of the Polytechnic South West – formerly Plymouth Polytechnic – have drawn up money-saving plans involving cuts in staff, and student numbers and even involving selling off entire campuses.

The plans, discussed at a recent Governors' Finance Committee, were confirmed by a polytechnic spokesman last night.

But he said: "These are only options to be considered if the polytechnic fails to reach its financial targets. At the moment we are confident that we can survive without putting them into effect."

**Discussion**

Like every other polytechnic in England and Wales, Polytechnic South West was given "corporate status" on April 1. Under the new Education Reform Act it is now required to run as a commercial concern, just like a profit-orientated company

But polytechnics are to receive less Government funding than previously to encourage them to raise more of their own revenue. Governors at Poly South West have been told to expect an under-funding of £1.9 million over the next two years.

The money-saving measures, contained in a report for discussion by Governors, include:

- Shedding students from "non-cost effective" courses.
- Students to pay extra "fee surcharges" for their course.
- A reduction in the number of academic staff.
- A greater use to be made of cheaper, less experienced staff.
- A "reduction" in the number of poly campuses – possibly selling off valuable sites to raise extra cash.

Meanwhile poly authorities are pressing ahead with a campaign designed to attract more students and their valuable Government grants.

There are also proposals to extend the academic year so greater use is made of capital resources and to persuade the Government's new Polytechnics and Colleges Funding Council to fund more students.

If these measures are effective governors hope to save £5.05 million over the next four years – and do away with the need to put the more Draconian measures into effect.

**Radical**

Academic staff at Poly South West have warned that courses and students will suffer if the Poly tries to employ less experienced "coolie-labourer" staff and have called for a radical rethink of the way the institution is run – including doing away with the Director's office and replacing it with a co-operative style structure.

Paul White, Polytechnic South West spokesman said: "It is only sensible planning to have these fall-back options in the eventuality of our revenue targets not being reached."

He said the poly was looking at the value of its four campus sites at Exeter, Newton Abbot, Exmouth and Plymouth but stressed: "Any organisation is going to look at the value of its property to see if they are worth something."

A couple of months later, we read in 28th June 1989 *Western Morning News*:

**Retiring chief accepts Chair**

Devon's chief education offic[e]r, Joslyn Owen, who is to retire at the end of September, has accepted an invitation from Polytechnic South West to be the first holder of the new Rolle Chair in Education.

The visiting chair represents a part-time commitment, and will involve Mr Owen in research, writing, inquiry and involvement in the work of the Faculty of Education and of the Polytechnic.

Unfortunately Joslyn Owen only lived for a further 2½ years following his appointment. His Obituary, written by David Sample, appeared in *The Independent* of 7th February 1992 as follows:

Following his retirement in 1989 he became Professor of Education in the Rolle Faculty of Polytechnic South West, an institution which he had been helping to create, with independent status, before the 1988 Education Act made such development the norm. It will be interesting to see whether his vision of the comprehensive public-sector university, which motivated his efforts to develop higher education, is fulfilled after the granting of university status to such institutions. His involvement in higher education and the arts had recently taken a new step forward with his acceptance of the chairmanship of the Governing Body of Dartington College of Arts, following many years association with the college.

*Summary: Joslyn Grey Owen, educationalist, born 23 August 1928, Assistant Education Officer Croydon 1959-62, Somerset 1962-66, Joint Secretary Schools Council 1966-68, Deputy Chief Education Officer Devon 1968-72, Chief Education Officer Devon 1972-89, Deputy Chief Executive Devon County Council 1975-89, married 1961 Mary Patricia Brooks (three sons), died Exeter 19 January 1992.*

**1972–75 & 1986–1990: "A Haven from the World" by Dave Gwilliam**

I retired in 2008 after a 30-year career in education. Attending Rolle from 1972 to 1975, my memories of the College are very vivid. It was a wonderful experience and life-shaping. We were taught all the idealistic theories of the Plowden Report and given the opportunity to develop and mature into world-challenging young teachers. I left Rolle with an optimistic and informed attitude which gave me the sense of mission to tackle some of the toughest schools and work with challenging children.

Rolle was almost like a haven from the world, nurturing creative and caring people! . . . The social life was fantastic. I can remember the Rag Processions and the top-rate bands we used to book in the main Hall. I learnt to socialise and entertain, skills that I've found useful all my life. We lived in a community and shared food, Halls of Residence and even clothes! In the bar and the tutor groups, I learnt to share ideas!!!!!

A typical Study Bedroom from the 1980s [could have been the 1960s!]

Returning to Exmouth in 1980 to teach in Exeter, I did a Certificate of Advanced Professional Studies course (known to us as C.A.P.S.!) at Rolle in 1986 and a Dip. Ed. in 1988 – 1990, so have had a lot of contact over the years. The College seemed to change a lot when it moved its links from Exeter to Plymouth and broke off those with Dartington.

Losing the Docks, the College, the shoe factory [1999] and the presence of the Marines, I fear for Exmouth's future. It could become unbalanced in its mix and fall victim to E.D.D.C. I stood as Labour candidate in the local elections last year, in Littleham, and trebled the vote but was soundly beaten by the 'sitting' candidate so I guess that most people are happy with the status quo.

[Around the time that David was studying for his Diploma in Education, one of Rolle's lecturers was part of a three-man team visiting China to explain British law to the Chinese. In the 9th July 1988 *Exmouth Journal*, the following was reported under the heading:

**Rolle lecturer Les Johnston to lay down the law to Chinese**

> Exmouth Rolle College lecturer Dr Les Johnston will be crossing the world this weekend to lay down the law to the Chinese.
> His trip to the Orient is as part of a three-man specialist team to explain British policing to the Chinese, and broaden their own knowledge of policing in China.
> Dr Johnston, who lectures in policing as part of the sociology course at Rolle College, and also at the Centre of Police Studies at Exeter University, was due to leave today (Saturday) for his two-week visit.
> Also in the team are former Chief Constable of the Devon and Cornwall Constabulary John Alderson, and Bill Tupman, director of the Centre of Police Studies.
> The team was invited over by the Chinese to talk about changes in British policing, with an emphasis on community policing, Dr Johnston told the Journal.
> He said they would be talking about crime in Britain, police/public relations and patterns of consultation.
> "We will also be describing forms of public accountability and to what extent the police are accountable," he said.
> This is Dr Johnston's first trip to China.

The following April, the *Western Morning News* reported under the title:

**Mild winter a real lift**

> A lift is to be provided this year at the former Rolle College, Exmouth to help disabled students – thanks to the so called "Greenhouse Effect."
> Devon County Council has decided that it can afford to fund £37,000 for the work because of major savings on its heating bills during the mildest winter this century.

## Delighted

The total saving on the education budget alone up to the end of March is expected to have been as much as £600,000. The lift will be provided at the Rolle Faculty of the Polytechnic South West.

It will particularly benefit the four disabled students who will join the college in the autumn.

They will stay at Kempston House, the East Devon Cheshire home at nearby Portland Avenue.

Peter Thorpe, spokesman for the home's appeal committee said he was delighted to hear the work will be carried out this year.

"We must obviously thank nature for its help," he said.

Mr Thorpe praised the county council for its assistance to the disabled, saying that £70,000 had already been spent at the college to help them.

The cash windfall will also be used to offset the loss of money from the Training Agency.

The agency has decided to reduce its contribution towards "work related" further education in Devon by 14 per cent. That is the equivalent of £320,000 with further losses in future years.

Outline permission had been granted September 1984 for a Leonard Cheshire Home to be erected on the *Kempston/St Olans* site. Following the submission of detailed plans in July 1986, permission was granted in October that year.]

# Chapter 9: ARCTIC ROLLE

## 1990: "Rolle becomes a 'Finnishing' School"

It was in the 1970s that Rolle staff began to extend the Courses offered to students. Among nine new Courses developed in 1973, were degrees in North American studies and Russian/European literature as well as expressive arts, urban studies, mathematics and society, community studies, environmental studies and a certificate in theological studies. The following statistics reproduced for the minutes of the Governors' meeting held on 6th March 1979, shows that the total student body had dropped by 200 in a year – from 735 to 535. There were nine students enrolled for the first year of the BA in Urban Studies. While there had been 38 students from Kenya studying at Rolle in 1978, that figure had dropped to 31 in 1979 and the African studies course submitted to the Council for National Academic Awards (CNAA) in 1979 was not successful.

| Student numbers as at 26 February 1979 | | | | |
|---|---|---|---|---|
| | Men | Women | Total | (1978) |
| Teacher Education Yr 1 | 11 | 59 | 70 | (123) |
| Teacher Education Yr 2 | 19 | 97 | 116 | (195) |
| Teacher Education Yr 2 (o/s) | 19 | 1 | 20 | (11) |
| Teacher Education Yr 3 | 27 | 152 | 179 | (228) |
| Teacher Education Yr 3 (o/s) | 11 | 0 | 11 | (27) |
| Teacher Education Yr 4 | 14 | 37 | 51 | (47) |
| One year Professional Teachers | 15 | 31 | 46 | (68) |
| Teacher Education Post Graduate | 11 | 21 | 32 | (36) |
| BA Urban Studies Yr 1 | 6 | 3 | 9 | |
| Special English | 1 | | 1 | |
| | | | | |
| Totals | 134 | 401 | 535 | (735) |

Key: o/s = overseas students (Kenyans)

No doubt, there had been some changes to the College Prospectus by then as the September 1966 one stated under **Qualifications for Admission**:

> Candidates should be of British Nationality.

Rolle had built up links between itself and Africa with groups from Kenya and Botswana studying there while the William and Mary College of America had brought exchange students to England for periods of study at Rolle. It was to be ten years or so before links made with other countries would be formalised. In the 6th April 1990 edition of the *Exmouth Herald* under the title: "**They're Lapping it up at Rolle**", we learn that:

> EXMOUTH has a link with Lapland – which should come in handy at Christmas.
> Polytechnic South West's Rolle Faculty of Education – the old Rolle College – has negotiated a five-year agreement for academic collaboration and student and staff exchanges with the University of Lapland.
> The University is at Rovaniemi on the Arctic Circle in northern Finland.
> The two institutions agree to cooperate to develop a programme of activities in teacher training and research and this could include conferences, field trips, research projects and comparative studies.
> Mr Ray Owen, consultant for overseas links at Rolle, said: "We have been working with the Finns for three years and receiving their students for two years.
> "We have another group of 18 Finnish students in May for a two-week course.
> "These are small beginnings. In the long term we would expect Finnish students to come to us for six to 12 months at a time in a Bachelor of Education programme and do their practice in schools here.
> "We also hope to send Rolle students there on exchange."

Another partnership scheme was set up later that year as reported by Gabrielle O'Neill, Education Correspondent of the *Western Morning News* on 2nd November under the heading:

**School's industry link**

> POLYTECHNIC South West's education faculty is setting up a partnership scheme aiming to link West country primary schools with local industry.
> The Exmouth-based Rolle faculty is inviting industry and business representatives to two breakfast events to launch its Industry and Education Action programme on November 14 and 15.
> Organisers stress the scheme will not promote "blatant advertising" of local firms in schools, but will work to the mutual benefit of those involved.
> Prof Michael Newby, dean of Rolle, said: "We do not support the kind of involvement with a company which results in blatant advertising by sending children home with such things as a Filofax, geometry set or exercise book bearing a company logo.
> "We are aiming to establish a real commitment from industry towards education for the future."

Education consultant Janet Roberts said the scheme might involve school trips to local firms, or companies providing school equipment. She added:

> "I have seen far too many schools going along to businesses and expecting donations as a kind of charity. I don't think we can do that."

**1988 – 91: "Lifelong friends made at Dunsinane" by Debbie Winship**

I was apprehensive about University. It seemed too big and impersonal so I applied to Rolle College of Higher Education. Three years later, I graduated from The University of Exeter, having been at Polytechnic South West in the Second Year and The University of Plymouth in year 3. It was all the same place but it changed its name and status every year at that time.

Being in *Dunsinane* Hall and having a sea view, I was able to witness gorgeous sunsets. The first night there, although very apprehensive about meeting people, I chatted to all in my Hall, gathering around people's portable TVs to watch "Neighbours" in the Kylie and Jason years. One girl I chatted to was Alison from the Midlands and, by the middle of the week, we had met two blokes – Mike and Jez. There were others in our gang and we all went around together talking about our homes and families. Although very shy, I built a base of good friends.

I loved the fact that when we had finished our work or lectures we could walk to the beach or to the docks and see the big boats come in. We got so slow with the pace of life in Exmouth, we sometimes almost stopped. Every day, the whole Hall would watch "Neighbours". We had parties in Hall and in the nightclubs – *Sams* being where the Marines hung out but I preferred *Oscars* on the side of *The Deer Leap*. The rest of the time, we lived in the Student bar – at 15p for a glass of milk or lime and soda, it was a good way to be sociable. My time in *Dunsinane* was very happy but, in the 2nd and 3rd year, we all lived up Exeter Road next to the CO-OP and felt more part of the town. Student antics were no longer fun but I knew Devon was the place to stay. One of Rolle's lecturers, David Keep, had persuaded me to become a Methodist Local Preacher and I became recognised as such in 1995.

Unfortunately, in 2014, *Dunsinane* is a pile of rubble but I loved the place, the town and its people. I'm married to Jez, Mike is married to Ali and I'm Godmother to their 16-year-old son. They live in Totnes and we live in Exeter.

**1990 – 96 & 1974: "Polytechnic to University" by Nicholas Goddard**

Whilst in the 6th form at Exmouth School, I joined a group of pupils interested in teaching. We met in one of the Rolle College out-buildings – a wooden hut just south of the Student Union Bar Building – to plan a bizarre Drama based upon Pirates and Aztecs to take into schools. We then took it into Littleham and Withycombe Raleigh Primary Schools. At the latter, a class of 6-year-olds participated in the Drama with us and, afterwards, they went back to their classroom and wrote about it. That was my first taste of teaching and of Rolle College and I thank Roy Pryke for that fortnight's wonderful experience as a 16-year-old in 1974. I went on to voluntarily help at Withycombe Raleigh Primary School for six years.

The book's author in front of the Art Block & Library

By 1990, Rolle College had become part of the Polytechnic South West. I was working and living in Rugby, Warwickshire then and I made a last-ditch application to do a teaching course. My first choice was Rolle Campus, Exmouth and I was accepted to start a B.Ed. in Theatre Arts (Drama) in 1991. Drama came under the Expressive Arts domain, which included Art, Music and Dance, so I used the Rolle Campus site extensively – the Drama Studios for performances such as "Early Morning", "Mid-summer Madness" and a solo performance featuring a Jew persecuted and imprisoned for healing and doing good, as well as the Art Studios, where I constructed a kite sculpture for an outdoor performance and a Forget-me-not rose.

The Polytechnic became part of the University of Plymouth in 1992 whilst I was in my second year. The teaching side continued to blossom and we took science experiments into Brixington and Marpool Schools. Children came to Rolle College Playing Fields to learn how to play tennis and to the gym to learn how to make routes on the apparatus. I can remember children finding out what made the best shopping bag.

This photo of a Rolle Art Studio was taken during the 2006 reunion when those attending were given a guided tour by current students

I had two wonderful Teaching Practices, being placed at St. Nicholas and St. Lawrence School at Weymouth and Montgomery School at Exeter. At the first of those, I recall a fantastic lesson on the environment and the eco system when the children in my class performed for the younger ones about the dangers of smoking. At the latter, I became Mr Waddington looking for new games and had the class perform a drama I'd written based on the life of an Indian village.

Because I had to redo part of my Drama module, in reality that meant that I gained an extra year at Rolle. However, in 1996, I graduated with an Honours Degree in Theatre Arts and Education from the University of Plymouth. The graduation on Rolle Playing Fields in Douglas Avenue was the pinnacle of my education. My wife, and parents, saw me receive my certificate with all the pomp and ceremony it deserved. I can remember particularly the staff, fully robed, processing to the reverberation of Walton's "Crown Imperial".

I thank Rolle for bringing me home, giving me a wonderful teaching experience and helping me reach that pinnacle but I am saddened by its demise. Surely it has still got something to offer to today's youth – the wonderful facilities and setting are a Godsend.

**1996 – 2001: "Light Operatic Society" by Joseph Lewis**

I initially came to Exmouth as part of a Combined Honours BA Degree. Having completed my first year at Somerset College of Arts & Technology in Taunton, years 2 and 3 were held at the University of Plymouth's Campuses at Queen Street, Exeter and Rolle College, Exmouth from 1996.

Graduating with a 2:1 in Media Arts in 1998, I returned to Exmouth in September of that year for a Postgraduate Diploma leading to a Master of Arts qualification, which I gained in July 2001.

During June 1999, I enjoyed the University of Plymouth Light Operatic Society's production of *Oklahoma!* which was held at the Pavilion Theatre on Exmouth Sea Front. That encouraged me to join the Light Operatic Society and take part in its next production – the Christmas 1999 Variety Concert, which was held in the Main Hall at Rolle College. There seemed to be a long-standing arrangement whereby the Christmas production was held at Rolle and the summer show at the Pavilion.

Our Variety Production was great fun, 'though demanding, as we had to learn the words to songs from the shows and corresponding dance moves, such as "The Deadwood Stage" from *Calamity Jane*. Most of our auditioning was done in Room D117, which I believe was in the Music Block. Quite a few of my fellow 'treaders of the boards' were on a 4-year Teaching Practice course. I had supplied hats and scarves for the sketch "Merry, Merry Christmas". That Christmas Variety Show was filmed to video tape.

*Me and My Girl* was chosen for the June 2000 summer production. I found that particularly interesting as I played the part of posh Sir Jasper Tring with 'sprayed' grey hair, an ear trumpet and the immortal line "Eh?" Taking to the comparatively large stage of the Pavilion Theatre was initially rather daunting but we did have a number of rehearsals and finally a dress rehearsal.

It was the year after I left that the *Exmouth Journal* reported on 12$^{th}$ November 2002 that the University shake-up could see colleges shut down. However, the University of Plymouth said, at that time, that its education centre would remain at Exmouth because of its geographical location of student placements.

# Chapter 10: ROLLE's ROYCE

## 1989 – 2004: "A Lecture Theatre for Exmouth" by Dean Mike Newby

**In the beginning …**

Not, of course, the *very* beginning. I'm talking about the beginning of the last phase of what was Rolle College, the moment when, in the autumn of 1988, it became one of four constituent centres of Higher Education – the others being Exeter College of Art & Design, Seale Hayne College of Agriculture [it was renamed *Hannahs* in 2010. See photo below] and Plymouth Polytechnic – in a new organisation named *Polytechnic South West.* In January the following year, I arrived to take up my post as Dean of the Rolle Faculty of Education so here are some thoughts and memories of what it was like to be the senior person at Rolle from then until I left in 2004.

The four merged centres, which straddled Devon from east to west, had been the responsibility of Devon Education Authority but government legislation had freed them of such links. It was the same all over the country. 'Public sector' providers of HE (subject to the same rules and regulations, and run from the same County Hall offices, as Primary Schools and youth clubs) became independent *HE Corporations*. In constitutional, legal, financial and academic terms, all had become free to make their own way in the world. The first Director of our new federation of educational centres, John Bull, ruefully reminded those on his senior management team: "We are now free to go bankrupt!" and this set the tone for much of my time in the organisation. Along with all such institutions, Polytechnic South West found itself on constant guard against the possibility that the difficulties and dangers inherent in those new financial circumstances might overwhelm us. Understanding the last years of the College becomes possible only when taking that into account.

**Faculty disputes**

So, we were 'newly incorporated', that is, a new *HEC.* Many on Rolle's staff assumed I was the new Principal, for this was the model they knew. I wasn't!

My title was *Dean* of the 'Rolle Faculty of Education' – not the *Principal*, nor the boss of all bosses (that was first the *Director*, later the *Vice-Chancellor*, at Plymouth) – but his most senior member of staff at Rolle. I soon discovered (a little to my surprise) that a third of the operations at Rolle fell outside my brief. At the point of merger into the new institution, faculties had been created, and the departmental structures at Rolle were translated into a large Education-based Faculty and part of another one entirely, based around Humanities and Performance. Its staff had little to do with Teacher Education except when they received Education students into their sessions alongside students reading for BA degrees, as part of the 'subject studies' component of their BEd course. The staff involved took direction from another *Dean*, based in Exeter and, until the merger, *Principal* of Exeter College of Art & Design.

It was an organisational nightmare – we had *two* English departments (one in his Faculty, one in mine), *two* History and *two* Drama Departments. Managing the scant resources of those duplicates was all but impossible. (Who was in charge of timetabling of rooms, for instance? What happened if there was a clash: which group should take precedence?) As the changed organisation at Rolle began to find its way in the new world, this was a constant difficulty, made worse by the fact that staff in the other Faculty were sometimes reluctant to work with Education students, whom they (rightly) considered to be only partly engaged in their subjects because the students' main concern was to enter Primary School teaching. Staff too: tutors from one side found it difficult to work with those from the other. I discovered that most had been uneasy colleagues for years in the old Rolle College days and the new circumstances (two Deans) didn't help in trying to forge more productive links. Indeed, when required to do so, the response was usually grudging and sometimes straightforwardly rude. The main locus for this other group was *Langstone* House (photo – left), at the eastern limits of the campus.

Rarely did staff based there come west, all the way over to the Staff Common Room! An Education colleague once announced, beaming, that he'd just had occasion to wander across to *Langstone*, where he had witnessed some tiff between staff in the English department. "They're so confused over there", he said, "that they're going round stabbing each other in the *front*!"

For this Dean, at least, it quickly became clear that we needed to establish a new culture at Rolle if it was to move ahead – one based on respect for each others' disciplines. Academic and professional groups (of which there were many in the Faculty) naturally enough stuck together and found having to work alongside others from different parts of the academy challenging, particularly when, as they often saw it at Rolle, those colleagues came from a Primary School background rather than an academic one. It was a barrier too high for many to cross and, by the time I left, I don't believe I had achieved any real success in helping staff make the leap because they didn't want to.

Nonetheless, we made progress in other ways. In 1992, it was decided that the faculty situation I have described was untenable and so the *Faculty of Arts & Education* was created to encompass all the work at Rolle and also in Exeter. I became Dean of that much larger, multi-campus Faculty and we all began working in the bigger, more complicated, organisation. Though problems abounded, opportunities for the sharing of resources and ideas became possible. Student numbers began to rise. We got used to the new ways of working, not always much liking them, but accepting them as a part of the way the world was then going. Though many staff remembered the old Rolle College days with nostalgia, there was a general sense of grim optimism as we learned to become part of a new regional organisation and to work on a different scale. Indeed, the name 'Rolle' was itself coming to be questioned as being a throw-back to a time almost vanished. In the new Faculty of Arts & Education, what had been the Rolle *Faculty* became the Rolle *School* of Education, and there were many in it who even suggested dropping that 'Rolle' altogether as being inappropriate to the new situation. ("What or who was 'Rolle', anyway?", asked some. "And how is it pronounced – to rhyme with 'pole' or 'doll' or even with 'Polly'?") So it was that Rolle College came to be known as 'the Exmouth campus' by most who worked there and, I think it is fair to say, by practically no-one else in Exmouth who didn't!

**The University in the far West**

In 1993, the Polytechnic became a University in name as well as in practice – the *University of Plymouth*. In the weeks when the whole institution was engaged in a *faux*-consultation to choose a new name for itself, and before a final decision was taken, we referred to ourselves as 'The University of X' and, for those of us working in Exmouth and Exeter, this offered us a *frisson* of unwarranted and short-lived satisfaction. For, of course, it wasn't to last. Soon, it was agreed that we should become 'The University of Plymouth' and so started a slow trickle of confusion which lasted throughout my time as the "Dean who worked sixty miles east of that grey city". Interviewing for new members of staff was a case in point. On more than one occasion, the short-list was smaller than expected because candidates had presented themselves at the Reception Desk in Plymouth instead of at Exmouth or Exeter! We got used to explaining that, though the 'University of Plymouth', we were actually either in or only a few miles from Exeter (that ancient cathedral city and county town of Devon). In mischievous mood, we would occasionally even remind our Plymouth brethren that the Faculty of Arts & Education had campuses over an hour closer to London by train than did our distant, less metropolitan, colleagues down on the border with Cornwall.

**The campus**

For those in Plymouth, we were a long way away. It was at least understandable that, when money was tight, preference was given to developing the Plymouth campus (by far the largest of the four) and investment in new building in Exmouth was, until the **Owen Building** was completed in 2002, insignificant. Devon County Council had not maintained the place well in the days before incorporation. (Knowing they would soon lose it, I suspect they did not think there was any point at all in throwing money at a vanishing asset.) The hot water supply leaked into the ground and rain came in through the roof. The science laboratory was an old, dark room – more like a storage cupboard than a modern teaching space – and the general ambience often reminded me of an antiquated leather armchair: bagged-out – comfortable enough, but with the horse-hair stuffing coming out in large handfuls!

My job was to run the academic work of the Faculty while the Estates Department ran the campus, caring for the place and all its fabric. The Exmouth estate was really quite extensive because, as well as the campus itself, the Halls of Residence and the games fields just down the road off Douglas Avenue, all needed attention. The clamour for money to do things was always intense, not only because we wanted the best environment for our students and staff but because campus improvements implied confidence from Head Office. I recall once asking the Vice-Chancellor to build us something on the Exmouth campus. "A new bike shed would do!", I pleaded. "*Anything* to prove you still think of us as being worthy of investment!" It took a very long time before he agreed. For the last decade of the twentieth century, Plymouth spent most of the money allocated to Exmouth on patching up the place – on repair and maintenance and health and safety as necessary. However, real commitment to new buildings and major refurbishment – not really, not often, and never enough! The Owen Building marked a change of heart and a victory. Finally, it seemed, we had made our case. The danger, though, was that we'd 'had our turn' and that that would be it for another ten years. Throughout my time at Rolle, I always harboured the suspicion that, if they could, the powers-that-be in Plymouth would quite like to close us down.

Former students and their spouses gather inside the Owen Building during their "40 years on from leaving Rolle" reunion in 2006

As Plymouth people became more accustomed to the fact that they now had responsibilities across the county, they grew harassed. All that money going to Exmouth, to Exeter, to Seale Hayne! Think of the books in *our* library we can't afford any more! I once had a conversation on just those lines with a *very* senior Plymouth-based colleague, having to remind him that Rolle, Exeter and Seale Hayne were all now part of his institution, all playing for the same team. He took several years to properly understand what I meant.

Once, in the middle of a harsh winter, staff members were complaining when the heating broke down in Exmouth. One phoned me mid-morning: "I'm taking a group of professional teachers on an in-service course," she said, "and we're all sitting in the room in our overcoats! Can nothing be done?" Having no powers myself to mend the heating system, what could I do but telephone Plymouth? I remember the exasperated impatience in the voice of another *very* senior colleague in charge of 'resources' (which included estates, part of which was our heating system in Exmouth) when I told him that I had a room full of professional teachers trying to learn in what were Arctic, and probably illegal, conditions. After a pause, during which I could almost hear the cogs of his mind running through the possible courses of action he might be forced to take, including spending more money, he spluttered, "Well . . . well, they're only Primary School teachers!" before, with much huffing and puffing, sending someone off to investigate the problem. This was an unusually graphic, though not unique, illustration of the difficulties Plymouth had with Exmouth and, in particular, with its Primary Teacher Education mission. Ten years later, I recall another *very* senior Plymouth-based colleague expressing surprise on learning that *Primary* Teachers needed to have a degree before being allowed to qualify for the profession.

By then overseeing multi-million pound budgets, Plymouth's Finance Office early on drew the line at the flowerbeds which were one of the features most enjoyed by people at Rolle. It wasn't so much the cost of the flowers but of

the gardeners that they baulked. "Gardeners will have to go!" and, alas, they did – and the flower beds [see photo on left from 1983/4 Prospectus] with them, as did that other throwback to the glory days of Rolle College before the Fall – extravagance in the kitchens. I still remember lunches of Michelin-star quality served in my first year at Rolle. But where was the money coming from to reach those standards? It couldn't last! After a year or so, as the new organisation began to find its way (and to look unblinkingly at the books), food at Rolle was taken over by the Catering Department (Plymouth-based, of course) and from then on it consisted of good, nourishing and carefully-costed portions served in straightforward works-canteen style and entirely without flourish. So much for calling our dining room 'The Refectory', in recognition of our academic status as part of a university. It was still a canteen when all was said and done!

Dreams of an existence redolent of an Oxford College were brought smartly to an end when my secretary asked shortly after I had arrived, "The kitchens want to know what sort of wine they should get in when you entertain visitors to lunch". "Hmmm! What a lovely question!", I mused out loud. "Well, I suppose we could buy in some crisp Sancerre for the warm summer months, and how about some thoughtful Burgundies for the cooler ones?" "No, no" was the response, "they want to know whether you want white or red!" It was a salutary moment. Rolle College had, since its inception, gained a reputation as a delightful, happy, creative place within sight of the sea, not too far from mystical Dartington, with elegantly relaxed staff and dreamy students, scented music drifting from the open windows, a very strong tradition of preparing Primary School teachers for the kind of creative, child-centred, post-Plowden classrooms of the middle years of the century – a kind of educational paradise down in the south-west. Not that it ever actually happened (not in my time, anyway, and I doubt in anyone else's) but the myth was that, at the end of each day, staff would gather, perhaps on the lawn outside the Principal's study, for tea and cucumber sandwiches, engaged in languid conversation until, at 5.30 pm, the bar opened and those who wanted to could continue their discussions over stronger stuff. Perhaps a little cut off from a larger world (virtually no ethnic minorities among staff or students), it was a happy place. To survive, however, it was forced to move into this new, incorporated, money-driven world and it was not always a comfortable transition.

Many smaller colleges, notably Teacher Training Colleges, had been closed down in the 1970s as being non-viable. In fact, Rolle itself had survived such a threat, but only just. Many found that the way to survive was to allow themselves to be subsumed into a larger organisation, satellites in the greater Russian embrace of university or polytechnic. That way, economies of scale would allow their operations to continue, albeit not in the old, comfortable ways. It was the same with many Art Colleges, not least Exeter College of Art & Design, by then a part of my faculty along with Rolle. Such institutions needed to achieve a state of *critical mass* before they could *wash their faces* and be *self-sustaining*. The price for survival was the loss of many of the old ways of working and a significant element of an erstwhile, often proud, identity. The task was to find ways of preserving something of the valuable spirit and tradition of Rolle College at its best with the newer virtues which marked English HE at the end of the twentieth century and beyond – the more sober ones of financial probity, student choice within modular degree schemes, an energetic pursuit of verifiable quality, and an opening up of HE to a much larger proportion of the population. It was a difficult balancing act.

**Money**

Money was, of course, the new master. HE was learning the harsh lessons of a new educational economics. The language of university management changed to reflect the new realities drawn from industrial and commercial situations, with talk of *student through-put* and *efficiency gains*; of courses no longer being *taught* but being *delivered*, with *Course Delivery Systems* where before there had been tutors; of *resource packs* where hitherto we had used books; of *mission statements* (and – oh dear! – sometimes of *mission drift*); of *niche and mass markets*; of *quality-this* and *quality-that*. "We've got to get more quality academics on the staff!", we were enjoined, though how they might differ from those we already had we were not too certain. The organisation developed a preference for the balance sheet over the book. I recall one staff meeting when the Vice-Chancellor and (ominously) the Dean of the Business School confronted polite but puzzled Arts lecturers with a presentation consisting almost entirely of numbers. "This", we were told with enthusiasm, "is the Future! The Plan! So – over to you!"

The University's money came from the two funding bodies with which we worked (the Higher Education Funding Council – HEFC – and, in the case of Rolle, the Teacher Training Agency – TTA). The University was paid an annual block grant by each of these two quangos, together with student fees, normally paid by the student's Local Education Authority. Everything went to the central University coffers and then, each year, meetings were held to decide 'top-slice', a term which became one of the most important items in my lexicon throughout my time as Dean. 'Top-slice' was a centrally-imposed 'tax' (we were urged to try to remember to call it a 'contribution'!) from the money-earning parts of the organisation (mainly the Faculties) to the centre. That contribution was used to pay for all the centralised services like Estates, Finance, Personnel (later 'Human Resources'), Marketing, Student Services, the Vice-Chancellor's salary and so on. The list was a long one and all the Faculties called upon their services to support their operations. Once the 'top-slice' rate had been established (notionally around 40% of student income but actually much more), the money was handed out to the Deans on the basis of the number and type of students they had recruited. That budgeting process took many, many weeks. Indeed, while it was going on, it filled the sky with portent and the stormy clouds of uncertainty, for the outcome was extremely important to the quality and extent of the work to be done during the following academic session. It was a time for intense scrutiny of spreadsheets as, working with our finance staff, I tried to find ways to make the money go round. Intricate formulae, incomprehensible to all but a few, allowed me to offer a small group of staff over there a tiny amount of budget more than a larger group here, because they had increased their percentage of weighted full-time student equivalents by more than the target since last year. Explanations of my calculations, however, usually caused eyes to glaze over.

**Efficiency**

Government took a hand, of course. Although it left the two funding bodies to do the donkey work, it was the Treasury which determined the amount of public money to be devoted to Higher Education and, each year, the pressures were ferocious to become ever more *efficient.* Institutions had to achieve annual 'efficiency gains'. This meant that they must do the same amount of work for less money and that, in turn, usually meant teaching more students than the previous year but for the same funding. Under such a regime, the pressures were considerable to recruit more students than we really had room for, to be taught by fewer staff than were really needed. The measure for such efficiencies was captured by the *Staff Student Ratio (*SSR). There were a great many ways to work out the SSR, but the basic idea was simple enough: for one tutor to teach 10 students was a lot less efficient (and so much more unaffordably expensive) than if he or she were to teach 20. Or 30 – for, as the years went by, so the target SSR rose to become more and more difficult to achieve. After all, there was only so much space on the campus, unless new building was to be erected (which, until the Owen Building was built, it wasn't). So, in common with the whole of the Higher Education sector, timetabling the teaching sessions became increasingly difficult unless one was prepared to push everyone into one big lecture theatre and teach them *en masse*. And until Owen was built, there was no lecture theatre in Exmouth.

We could, of course, have doubled the teaching space by teaching at night. After considering this idea, we rejected it because, for many of our students, night-time working would have been impossible as they had families to look after. Many studying to become Primary Teachers were married women whose children had gone off to school, leaving their mothers with the time – just about – to train for their chosen profession. Others also had family responsibilities and, for the majority with none, there was still often a need to earn money. At the end of the lecturing day, many students would go off to their part-time jobs as waiters or bar-staff as the only way to make ends meet. They, too, had to make their own efficiency gains.

**Effectiveness**

The move for ever greater efficiency created, in its turn, a real problem of professional values. Staff believed that the most effective way of teaching students was to meet them individually (the old 'tutorial' system) or in small groups (of no more than a dozen or so, perhaps). In such a situation, people could talk together, spend time teasing out ideas, asking questions, risking opinions with their tutor and their peers – in other words, engaging in the kinds of activity which characterised good learning in Higher Education (and, indeed, good education at most levels). During the 1990s and beyond, that way of teaching was superseded by what many referred to as 'massification of Higher Education' as government required universities to take ever more students. Its ambition was that 50% or so of British school leavers would have the opportunity to study at Higher Education level so as to be in line with our major international competitors. Rolle had been comparatively small with fewer than 1,000 students but, by the time I left it in 2004, full-time student numbers in Exmouth were approaching 1,600, with many more at Exeter, and around 2,000 part–time students, mainly teachers, on in–service courses spread right across the south-west. We were bursting at the seams!

As well as wanting to enjoy a close working relationship with their students, those working in Higher Education recognised the need to be 'research active' but you can't do everything. Staff at Exmouth felt the conflict because, if you're spending all your time with your students, you won't be able to work on your own research. Squeezing teaching into a smaller part of your working week by pressing students into ever larger groups, or teaching them less, seemed the only alternative with the pressure of increasing numbers. Once again, a balance was needed between help and support for students (particularly those learning how to become professionals) and leaving them to stand on their own feet because the tutor had also to activate that other part of his or her professional role, that of the researcher moving their subject on.

**Quality**

Another fundamental pressure on us was the need to raise quality. Higher Education was subject to an ever more rigorous requirement to ensure that students received the best affordable provision – not the privileged experience of universities established centuries before, with all their opulent buildings and ancient libraries, world-class laboratories and settled status at the top of the tree – but, at the very least, modern, crisp, clean and fit for purpose. What's more, it was during my time at the University that the payment of student fees shifted from the Local Education Authorities to the students themselves, so now our students became our customers, demanding high quality courses for their money. We could not afford to short-change them.

Much time and thought went into the processes of quality assurance. All our courses were subject to annual review, with reports summarising feedback from a variety of sources, including the annual External Examiners' reports, as well as from the students themselves. One of my jobs as Dean was to construct mechanisms which would allow me to sign off all our academic work for the University as being of at least a satisfactory and preferably good, or excellent, quality. It was time-consuming but necessary and sometimes exciting work to see year-on-year progress being made and to realise that, without such quality assurance processes, failings might never have come to light and so remained embedded in our work. This annual process was designed to ensure, as far as possible, that we knew the good, the bad and the indifferent in our work; that we could root out the bad; move the ordinary towards being good; and transform the good into excellent; and that we could cling on to that excellence and prevent it falling back again to being merely good. As resources came under ever more intense pressure, this was not easy.

There were outside agencies, too, which needed to be reassured of quality across the whole sector, so comparisons could be made. HEFCE undertook elaborate exercises, involving *visitations* when teams of staff from other universities would descend on us (as ours did on them in turn) to award marks for our educational provision. It was called 'peer review' because we were judged by our peers. A secondary virtue of the process was that good practice was on show during such exercises, taken back by the participants on both sides to their own institutions and thus spread through the system. The idea was that 'teaching quality' (the *portmanteau* term for the appraisal of an academic area's quality of work) could be 'marked' and the results recorded in the public domain. As members of the public looked around for courses, they could access the quality reports of institutions to which they might apply and make choices based on evidence of these reviews. The theory, at least, was comprehensible and intelligent. The reality was less than ideal, because of the work involved in preparing for such visits.

Faculty offices were filled to the ceiling with boxes of paper-work. Staff spent half their lives, or so it seemed, in preparation meetings. Nerves were raw as the first day of the week-long visitation approached. Stories abounded of appraisers demanding to see papers which someone had forgotten to include, resulting in staff staying up till the small hours searching for long-lost documentation. Knowing how much depended on the outcome, people naturally grew nervous lest they said or did anything which might be out of place. Imagine how awful it would be to sink the whole ship because of a misplaced remark, a lost piece of paper, a less-than-accomplished moment in a teaching session in front of the unblinking gaze of an assessor! How could one ever look one's colleagues in the eyes again? Many people, Vice-Chancellors included, ended up suggesting this expensive process had gone into over-kill. Was the fundamental purpose of Higher Education to teach students and do research, or to get high marks in a quality appraisal?

Those visitations were involved with the non-Teacher Education parts of our work in the Faculty. They were tough but, at least, they were 'owned' by the Higher Education professionals who sat each side of the table at a visitation. Quality appraisal for intending teachers was of a quite different order and it was owned by other people entirely. The TTA worked with the Office for Standards in Education (Ofsted) as two arms of central government, since each reported to the Secretary of State for Education. There were often times when it seemed that those two organisations, charged by government to 'raise standards in teacher training', took over ownership of the system, wresting it away from the professionals themselves. Those two words 'training' and 'standards' were highly significant. Contrast them with 'education' and 'quality' and you'll see that they are not always the same thing, the second pair being wider in their embrace, less easy to measure, including the other two but far exceeding them in significance.

The system worked like this: the TTA would fund the providers of initial (and later in-service) Teacher Education on the basis of reports from Ofsted on the quality of the courses concerned. To make this work, Ofsted inspectors would be sent to the universities to make their appraisals of quality, write their reports, and send them to the TTA. Then they did it again. And again! Faculty staff, academic and administrative, found themselves putting at least as much effort into preparing papers for inspectors as they did into teaching their students and running the Faculty machine.

The inspection regime was remorseless. There was a time when I half-seriously considered erecting a marquee on the grass outside the main entrance to the Exmouth campus as a permanent base for Ofsted inspectors, so frequently did they visit. On one occasion, two teams of inspectors met in the campus car-park, expressing surprise at seeing the other team there as well! Such was the fixation in central government with 'raising standards in teacher training' that, for a while, Ofsted became a kind of infestation. For several years during this period, it went further than that. There was a serious attempt by elements on the right in English politics to do away with teacher education based in the Universities and move it entirely into the schools. The Chief Inspector of the time was very much in that camp, his sometimes sneering distaste for HE-based teacher education being notorious. It was alleged that, at one time, he sent his inspectors back a second time to inspect Primary teacher education in the Universities (us included) in order to find faults which, it was alleged, his inspectors failed to find the first time round! For that reason alone, every inspection carried an added edge to it. We felt that Ofsted was visiting, not in an impartial, open-minded way but with a negative, fault-finding attitude and our financial regime, so intimately linked with what Ofsted had to report was thus well described as 'funding with menaces'.

Did this approach raise quality, as Ofsted claimed? It's difficult to tell (for what would it have been like without Ofsted?). Certainly, it helped to focus us on the measurable components of quality in our work and it fostered a growing sophistication in the way we kept written records, because everything we did then needed to be permanently on file for when Ofsted demanded – as they surely would – to scrutinise it. In those ways, one could make a strong argument to suggest that Ofsted enforced careful attention among us to the *minutiae* of our work as well as its overall reach and the depth of its impact on our students and (though harder to judge) on the children they taught in school. However, in my view, it became subject to the law of vanishing returns. People would say, "You can't fatten a pig by weighing it" and "You don't make a plant grow by digging it up to inspect its roots" and both those old sores were at least partly appropriate. The more Ofsted inspected, the less time we had to innovate because we were forever checking to make sure we were teaching to their criteria (set down in London). Innovation, experiment, seeking new and better ways of preparing new teachers were all risky, as all experiments are, and many commented that, had the huge sums of public money spent on Ofsted and TTA, been spent instead directly on improving facilities for students preparing for the profession, they would no doubt have done as much, or more, to raise quality.

**Research**

When I first went to Rolle College in 1989, very little research went on. By the time I left in 2004, research had become a significant part of the work of much of the Faculty. Rightly so, for what are universities for if not to work with knowledge; share what we know with those who come to learn; validate the truth of what we know by exposing it to the scrutiny of the 'disciplines' embraced by each subject taught within the academy; and to extend what we know by finding out new knowledge. We reflected, during this period, on the answer to the question: what is the difference between *research* and *scholarship* in the practice of a University lecturer? For some subjects – such as History – 'scholarship' is synonymous with research. In others, such as Education, the distinction is more marked. Certainly, those preparing people to become teachers should be scholarly in their approach: well-read in others' research so that they can bring up-to-date and reliable evidence to bear upon the practices they are seeking to instil in their students. Does this mean, though, that they, too, should be operating as researchers, undertaking research projects, publishing their results in learned journals, writing scholarly books? The answer, though never unequivocal, increasingly came to be 'yes'.

This presented difficult challenges. The first being background. The Faculty was home to many who came from a practitioner base as artists, designers and performers as well as teachers. In Exmouth, many, perhaps most, people who prepared students for work in school came to work at Rolle without extensive research experience. They were employed principally on the grounds that they had years of distinguished experience working in the classroom. The contrast was often marked between offering a new post to someone like that, and recruiting a new lecturer in, say, English, where the main criteria might be: "How many research papers have you published? What are you working on at present? Have you managed to land any valuable research grants?" For those in the first group, research often came to be defined as 'practice-based', as they inspected their own practice from the outside as well as from within: a kind of principled and detailed *mindfulness* about what they did which could then form the material from which to write research articles and books. Such an approach was widely known as 'action research'.

Such questions were asked because of the growing significance of Research Assessment Exercise (RAE). Since the whole university sector had to compete for scarce funding every few years in a peer-reviewed exercise, a team of experts was drawn together to scrutinise the written submissions made by every university department about their research in the subject concerned, grading the results. On the basis of those grades, universities received funding. There was never enough to go round. Research in some subjects (particularly the 'big sciences') was enormously expensive to sustain, needing world-class laboratories and state-of-the-art equipment while, in others, little more than a good library and plenty of time was required. Academic reputations were crucially important to success at the RAE. Rumour was rife that Vice-Chancellors would sometimes drive to clandestine meetings in motorway service-stations with research professors from other universities, offering them large sums of money to come across from their present institution in time for their research record to be 'counted' at the next RAE – a kind of transfer market on the soccer model. Perhaps they still do! Whether true or not, it is certainly the case that, by the time I left Rolle, a major shift had taken place in which 'active researchers' had moved into focus as the people on whom the university's future would depend, while the value of those who 'merely' taught students became, in the eyes of some, downgraded – the drudges who did the donkey work of teaching undergraduates, leaving their colleagues free to do research, publish books, score highly at the RAE and so bring money, praise and even glamour into the institution. In the hectic competitiveness of HE in the early years of the twenty-first century, perhaps we lost sight of the idea of a community of learning and scholarship in our quest for a high score at the next RAE.

**Students**

From my description of the machinery which made Rolle work during its last years, and some of the big issues which affected its operations for good or ill, I hope you will have more of an understanding of the work behind the scenes and the prevailing pressures to which we were subject, as indeed were all English university departments working in our range of disciplines. We were building a new institution out of the old and I sometimes felt our job was to struggle away at ground level, laying the drains, pouring on concrete, making sure foundations were in place for those who came after us to build on.

For the students, however, their experience of studying in Exmouth should have been quite different. They would have had little interest in the machinery I have described and indeed it should have been invisible to them – necessary to make everything happen properly, but itself out of sight and, I hope, largely out of mind. So I believe those who studied with us will look back and remember a place full of the energy of youth and the excitement of learning. I hope they will have made many friendships and come into contact with a talented teaching staff deeply committed to their academic, professional and personal growth. Doing the job I did, it was often all too easy to forget that everything we did, we did for them.

The great day would come at the end of each summer term when that year's graduating students met to collect their awards, their families proudly by their sides. Seagulls – those perpetual commentators on life at Rolle as they

laughed on the rooftops and swooped jeering above the campus – would have seen, looking down from a summer sky, the unusual sight of hats and mortar boards as those below made ready for the moment towards which they (or their grown-up children) had worked for so long. For many years, our Award Ceremonies took place in a large marquee erected on the games field off Douglas Avenue. Notwithstanding the air-conditioning units murmuring away throughout, I remember the heat inside as, academic gowns heavy on our shoulders, lights blazing for the cameras and sun beating down from above, the staff filed in and sat facing the thousand or so people gathered within, graduands (that rare creature once a student but about to become a graduate) on one side of the central aisle, their relatives on the other. The scene was busy with the swishing of a thousand programmes as people fanned themselves to keep cool. In those days, I used to make a closing speech to say 'well done and goodbye'. Starting with what seemed like a good way to release the tension after the solemnities of the ceremony itself and the seriousness of the Vice-Chancellor's address, I would say, "It's amazing what people get up to in tents!" When you think of everything which had led up to that moment each year, to say it was 'amazing' was no under-statement.

However, as the Faculty grew ever larger, doing anything much in tents became increasingly anomalous and so, thanks to the kindness and forbearance of the Dean at Exeter Cathedral, our Faculty Award Ceremonies moved to that ancient and wonderful building. Three separate ceremonies – one each for Education, Art & Design and the Humanities – were needed over two days to complete the handing out of the awards. So many students turned up in their gowns and mortar boards, some a little disoriented by having family members with them, others grinning to see their friends suddenly appearing smartly-dressed and ready for the world.

Be it in a tent or in a cathedral, I shall always remember the thrill of sitting each summer, looking out over the faces in front of me – the new graduates clapping, cheering, sometimes whooping in open delight as their friends were called out to collect their degrees. This was a rite of passage known only to those who had made the commitment, often over many years, to submit themselves to the rigours of their chosen degree courses and to come through successfully. For our new graduates, it was a major moment in their lives as it was, too, for their family and friends. For the staff who worked at Rolle – be they academics, administrators, technicians or support staff – Degree Days were occasions of great pride and pleasure, giving shape and meaning to everything that had happened in the past year. Afterwards, many swapped addresses so the pleasure of the occasion had about it a flavour of parting.

**An ending**

During my time at Rolle College, I witnessed a great transformation. When I arrived, it was a Teacher Training College with its main traditions in Primary Education but had begun to diversify into other purely academic areas in the Humanities (a happy spin-off from the requirement on Primary Teachers to have substantial elements of 'subject study' at undergraduate level in their courses alongside Education and professional studies and teaching practice). By the time I left, the Faculty was very large, had moved into Secondary Teacher Education as well as running courses for educators in a wide variety of other educational settings (Further Education and the Steiner method). It had also greatly extended the breadth and depth of its work in courses entirely distinct from Teacher Education and had begun to build a solid foundation in research. It had become a substantial component in a very extensive regional University, its work extending across large areas of the south west of England.

Shortly before I left in 2004, a new Vice-Chancellor, Professor Roland Levinsky, had decided to reorganise the University's academic structure so my Faculty was divided back again into the component parts which had existed when I first arrived – Education and Arts. What's more, he decided that the latter should move from Exmouth and Exeter to Plymouth, leaving Education isolated at Rolle. That decision effectively closed Rolle for there was never a chance that, left alone, Education could sustain sufficient income to keep the Exmouth operation viable. My predecessors had discovered that fact years before I arrived and it was obvious to me throughout my time there. For Rolle to flourish, sustaining student numbers in Education and the Humanities was essential. Though I do not believe the Vice-Chancellor had looked that far ahead when he carried out his reorganisation, splitting the Faculty could lead to only one conclusion. My successor stayed only a short time as Dean of Education before moving to Plymouth as Deputy Vice-Chancellor and then moving on. His successor at Rolle became Acting Dean. A year later, another Dean took up his post, though he too soon left. The inevitable decision was taken to move the whole of the Education Faculty to Plymouth and close the Exmouth campus. By 2008, the place was deserted and at the time of writing, it still lies empty.

## <u>Chapter 11</u>: ROLLE FORWARD

### 2003 – 06 & 1969 – 74: "I came, I saw, I returned" by Andrew Bailey

I had been working as a clerk in a large Insurance Office when a friend encouraged me to look at teaching as a career. Browsing the prospectuses of various Colleges, I decided that either Aberystwyth or Exmouth would fit the bill . . . Maths with Science, continuous assessment and by the sea! Thus it was that, in the summer of 1969, I came down and was interviewed by Harry Pratt, the Head of Maths. He proved to be a very nice man, very encouraging who sent me away with a book on "New Maths" to break me out of the Victorian/Grammar School mould that I had been cast in.

That autumn, my new wife, Cherrill, and I set up home in a furnished flat in Hartley Road. She immediately found a job and I became a "student" or, to be precise, my hair got longer! There was a "buddy" system in place and I was shown the ropes by my college "Father". There was no College Bar in those days but we found solace in "The Deer Leap" and "The Foresters Arms" (a great establishment demolished to make way for the Magnolia Centre).

The first week of each of the first three terms was dedicated to what we termed "Pathetic Studies" as, to me there was nothing aesthetic about it! The College had only recently taken on more students destined to teach in Secondary Schools and some aspects of the course/lecturers were deeply wedded to the Primary/Junior School tradition. So I grudgingly finger painted and tried not to "curl up into a little ball and float across the room" for the late Gordon Crone. I wanted to get on with the Maths and Science!

Harry Pratt was an inspirational teacher, very relaxed but able to impart new ideas with infectious enthusiasm. He lived in an office at the top of the brand new "Three Storey Block". It had a fabulous view that always mesmerised me when I visited him there. He led a team that included Brian Hughes (later to take his place), Tony Draper, Margaret Adams and Cynthia Mogford. I enjoyed their teaching and learned a lot of Mathematics and gradually grew to understand that being a Mathematician was not just about "sums".

Each member of the Maths staff had a different style. Tony Draper was very relaxed but a hard task master. Unfortunately, he was still a young man when he died. Margaret Adams came across as a gentle soul, whereas Cynthia

Mogford seemed, to some of us, as sometimes quite difficult to follow. She could talk for two hours without apparently drawing breath! Her specialism was Statistics and she interlaced the facts and theories with illustrations from her working life as a Government Statistician along with anecdotes from her private life. Unpicking those three threads, delivered in parallel, was an art that some students didn't manage easily but I have fond memories of her. And an eye for bogus statistics as a result!

I had used simple mechanical calculators in the Insurance business but I was fascinated by the tricks you could perform on the Husqvana rotary calculators in the College Mathematics Department [right]. Brian Hughes introduced us to Boolean Logic and a Busicom programmable electronic calculator was acquired. It was the size of a large personal computer and five times the weight but it set me off on a path to building a P.C. with fellow student Dave Carne, learning how to write computer programs and, eventually, creating and running a very large I.T. department at Exmouth Community College. I also have very fond memories of Bob White, the technician. He was a gentle fellow who lived down on the Colony initially and I spent many happy hours in his garden shed, learning the rudiments of television and television repair from him.

The Science Department was led by Ray Jones, one of the Rolle College "Taffia", for there were many Joneses! Ray was a tall, blue-eyed, cheerful man who could fire up the dullest of students. Erics Rolfe and McDowell and Harry Smith were his teaching team and all were very welcoming and willing to talk through any point one-to-one. My Science was pretty rudimentary but I enjoyed catching up under their tutelage. And I learned even more in the way of electronics, photographic processing and basic engineering workshop skills from the chief technician, Tony Rogers. The other technician, David Amos [page 36], was very skilled in the "Blue Peter" department, fabricating classroom models from cardboard and bottles but his chief claim to fame was making the lobby of the Spicer Building echo to the sound of a London Underground Train arriving at a platform, all done without artificial aids!

I blagged my way onto a Science Department expedition to Matlock, where we undertook fieldwork and paid visits to sites of industrial archaeology – the Qualcast Foundry and a working coalmine. The shock of seeing real work is still with me! I got to play with another programmable calculator to process data collected from a transect of a Derbyshire Hillside. I have remained friends with Jack Skinner, the coach driver, who whisked John Flook, Robin Bambridge and I out to country pubs where locals taught us dominoes.

Robin features in two other memories, the first being a field trip to Leigh Farm, near Ford Abbey. The farm was owned by fellow student, Sandra Dare (now Appleby)'s parents. I imagine that we went there to look at a mixed farm but Robin came back with a dead badger! As it was the end of the summer term, the corpse was quickly wrapped in a plastic bag and left in the bottom of a freezer. I spent that summer as Tony Rogers' technician runner and, when the smell became unbearable, I dragged Robin in. He skinned it and buried the carcass in the grounds. Out came the D.I.Y. tanning instructions and, much later, we had a set of clean, white bones – all good for the "Science Collection" as we were all encouraged to amass quantities of educational materials (junk) to illuminate our Teaching Practices! During that summer, Tony and I took ciné film of the destruction of the chimney of the Salterton Road brick works. I often wonder what happened to that footage or the aerial photos that Tony took of the College from a home made balloon.

On another occasion, Robin and I decided to concatenate various discrete experiments to determine the components of air. We worked late into the night stringing together U tubes full of various chemicals designed to dry a measured amount of air, extract the oxygen and $CO_2$ and leave us with nitrogen and other oddments at the far end. Each section was removed and carefully weighed then reinstalled. Unfortunately, one went in back to front and we drew acid into a tube of caustic soda, which got very hot and agitated. The entire apparatus exploded, showering us in all sorts of nasty things and shards of glass so we had to deep clean the lab. My clothes fell into holes at the next wash but somehow Robin and I remained unscathed.

My personal tutor was Miss Barbara Curry, an Historian. I used to do D.I.Y. jobs for her at her bungalow in the Rivermead area. She was the first real feminist I encountered and she frequently rose to my bait. Besides "proper" subjects we were exposed to Philosophy, Sociology, Education and Religion.

There was English, too in the gothic grandeur of *Langstone*. The weekly Education lecture was a low point for me although I enjoyed the encounters with John Ireland afterwards. He was a pleasant, dapper chap with a distinctive style of speech and was a dispenser of sound advice. Before Teaching Practice, he said: "Forget all this modern stuff and do what they do in your placement." I always looked forward to him coming into a class on Observation because he joined in rather than sitting awkwardly at the back.

I recall that we treated one lecturer very badly. Our group of heathen wannabe Secondary School teachers were rather uncooperative and rowdy to a gentle retired missionary of old-fashioned demeanour. One day a large, Clement Freudian gentleman sat in her place with an arc of chairs around him. We trooped in, sat down and he looked at us, smiling . . . And we looked at him . . . And he looked at us, and we looked at him, puzzled. Eventually, Ray Braithwaite asked when the session was to begin and our tormentor rounded on him. "Who asked you to speak?" A very lively debate ensued and some good lessons on class control were delivered. We treated Olive with more respect from then on . . . and the guy went on to become Deputy Principal.

Another area of the college I enjoyed was Audio Visual Aids. I can't for the life of me remember who ran it but he was assisted by Alan Gentle and latterly by Felicity Kirton. I still have a stop motion ciné film I made of the workings of the internal combustion engine, albeit in digitised format now.

Three characters who never taught me but came to the fore afterwards were: Ken Rockett (who taught music but I knew him for playing trad. in the town's pubs); Alan Cotton, who worked in the Art Department before he become a celebrity and Phil Tushingham, who drove interesting left-hand-drive vehicles including a Citroen DS and a VW Karman Ghia, and was a cousin to Rita.

Someone I still see is Phil Livesey. He encouraged me to join a couple of expeditions to Dartmoor. These were based at Prince Hall and one occasion stands out. He dropped a party of us off near Lydford Gorge on a very cold March day. The gorge was open to all in those days and we walked along its length marvelling at its splendour. Snow started to fall as we walked along the old railway line. I was well dressed in a brand new outfit loaned to me by a Royal Marine of my acquaintance. And so we trekked across the moor. Yes Tor was on the route, I remember. The ground was frozen solid but every so often a foot would break through the grass into a void below. It was slow and hard walking with packs on our backs. We set up our tents near one of the leats and with the sky darkening we ate our rations and most people turned in. Three of us volunteered to walk into Princetown and report our revised location. So to the Plume of Feather – yes, I had volunteered. Here we found Phil and one or two from another party. And after a glass or two we wound our way back in bright moonlight. The leat had frozen solid in our absence and that shortened our journey quite considerably. Boy was it cold that night! I kept my boots on! Those who didn't had a great deal of trouble breaking back into them. Back at Prince Hall, the others had all decamped leaving 40 or so sets of plates and cutlery. I had changed my clothes and arranged my sodden R.M. kit around a wood burning stove, leaving it steaming then, bleary eyed, set to and washed up. I sure felt virtuous until I went back into the bunkhouse and found the ashes of my borrowed kit. That cost me a bottle of whisky and a lot of grovelling!

When the College Bar opened, we soon had people who would get up and sing. Matt Cogan was the instigator and Laurie Dover and Jean Billett were two of the performers. The Bar was often manned by one of the porters, Mike Farrant, a big amiable guy with a beguiling smile and a great deal of tolerance Because the College hosted students who originated from Dartington, we had many talented musicians amongst our number. Whilst on the subject of drinking, a favourite monthly event was a Forester's Night. The little town centre pub sported two small bars, barrels of beer and cider, a lot of red-faced old men and no spirits or fancy drinks. The challenge was to arrive en masse and drink the house dry – a feat achieved on more than one occasion!

Other entertainments included regular Balls with well-known bands, and theatrical events. The staff version of "Under Milk Wood" was superb – with so many Welsh on the books it couldn't fail! But the highlight of those years was a termly Review called "And So To Bed". Poetry, music, comic sketches, dramatic readings. John Onley had a lot to do with that but I think most of the performers were students.

Then we got down to business – Teaching Practices. I was supposed to meet my mentors and choose some topics to teach during the Observation Day for my first at Kingsbridge. I noticed that a pattern soon emerged. As I entered each classroom, the teacher handed me the chalk and said "We are just doing x or y or z would you like to take over?" And off they went for a ten-minute smoke-o, I suspect. I was billeted in Stokenham and travelled in on the school bus each day. I can remember teaching a Biology Class a suspect lesson about the muscles of the arm. The best bit was when a kid at the back of the class fell off his stool whilst I was writing on the board. Without turning, I called him by name and told him to stand at the side of the class. The class were amazed and I gained a lot of respect – just for being able to read a reflection in the door!

My second Practice was at Heymoor Secondary School in Penzance. Although Maths was my main subject, that school hadn't got a Science teacher so my timetable was slightly unbalanced. Electricity and magnetism was a mainstay of my lessons and I had to dilute the acid needed for the simple cells we made. I did it backwards and everything got very hot. A great glass vat burst and I flooded the preparation room, taking all the varnish off the floor so that meant another deep clean at the end of a very tiring day.

The highlight of that Practice was finding myself with Matt Cogan and Laurie Dover in the Commercial Hotel, St. Just late one evening. The St. Just choir came in and the rafters rang until early in the morning. Magic! Matt had been a wireless operator on tankers and with the Diplomatic Service. He arranged for Ann French, Laurie and myself to visit his erstwhile workmates at Land's End Radio. It was a fairly quiet day on the airwaves when we toured the station, fired up the standby generator, discharged a great lightning spike from a giant capacitor and then, in the days of male-only operators, set Ann down to do an "All Ships". She had barely finished the first sentence when all the boards lit up and ships for miles around were calling in!

I went to a school in Torquay that was shortly afterwards merged with a neighbour to become "Westlands". Half my timetable was Science and, again, I never saw the Science teacher. He was off on the Observation Day and fell sick the day my six weeks began! But that just gave me a little more freedom. The external professor who signed me off didn't realise that I managed to fit electricity and magnetism into each class' curriculum, thereby minimising the amount of kit I needed to prepare!

And then, for the next thirty years, I taught at Exmouth Community College. I was pleased to teach many of the sons and daughters of the aforementioned lecturers and to know they supported the Comprehensive ideal. I hope I gave them as good as I got from their parents. When our family came along, we took advantage of the Saturday Morning Family Club that operated across the campus. Both the children and their parents made lasting friendships there.

Over the years, I transmogrified from Maths teacher to Computer Science Teacher – a role I loved. I wasn't so happy at being dragooned into teaching I.T. but it did lay the foundations of my next, short career. When I retired, I applied for a part-time post as an I.T. Support Assistant at Plymouth University, Rolle Campus. The interview with Noel Davis and Rosemary Smith went well but, even if it hadn't, I'd have been happy because, while waiting, I found an advert for my ideal boat! I never did get my Induction Course, but I soon found myself surrounded by properly-trained experts assisting the I.T. users of Rolle, playing with the network and fixing machines. It is amazing what daft things well-paid, highly intelligent people can do to, or with, a computer. The number of times I walked the length of the campus to switch on a monitor or extract inappropriate objects from C.D. drives is nobody's business!

Noel is probably the most politically incorrect person I know. But, with his charm and his blue eyes and his ex-Marine's bravado, he had an edge that was breathtaking. He would organise staff training "Away Days" in which the rest of us of both sexes, mostly middle-aged, would find ourselves splashing about in the Exe or being bounced around on the end of bungee straps. I have never knowingly taken exercise but this came perilously close to it.

There weren't many survivors from my earlier Rolle Days. I think Ken the gardener was the only one fully employed. A few of the old lecturers and Alan Gentle would pop their heads round the door occasionally. Besides the lecturers, I made a lot of new friends right across the various grades of staff – admin., porters, maintenance etc.

When Rolle's demise was announced, I bailed out early. Its closure was a great loss to Exmouth as it had bought young people into town, provided a cultural focus, not to mention much-needed employment. And then there was the education . . . . .

[Andrew's involvement with Rolle spans many of the changes in buildings summarised in the chart on the following page:]

## Buildings associated with Rolle Campus site:

| Date acquired | Event – emboldened buildings are still on campus in 2015 |
|---|---|
| 14 February 1946 | Exmouth Emergency Training College opened on Southlands School site, providing 1-year teacher training course in *Fairfield* (1888–1964), *Brockhurst* (1912–1957) and ***Eldin*** (from 1920) |
| 15 June 1946 | Formal opening by Ellen Wilkinson (Minister for Education) |
| September 1948 | 2-year teacher training course started and *Brockhurst*, *Coonoor Lodge* (sold *c*1962), *Ryll Court* (sold 1962 and demolished), *Ferniehurst* (sold 1996 and demolished) and *St. Hilarian* (demolished 2000) became hostels |
| 1950 | *Seacroft* (admin from 1998) + *Seacroft Lodge* (both dem. 2011) |
| 1951 | *Dunsinane* (demolished 2013) and *Hasledene* (dem. 2009) |
| 1953 | ***Langstone*** **Hall** of Residence, Sick Bay & Principal's flat |
| 1957 | *Kingsthorpe* (demolished 1997) |
| 9 July 1959 | Dean of Winchester officially opened the **Daw Building** |
| 1960–17May/Sep | *Carlton Hall* accidentally burnt down/3-year course began |
| 6 October 1961 | Dame Smieton DBE (Permanent Secretary of Ministry of Education) laid foundation stone of the new buildings |
| 1962 | Study-bedroom blocks (dem. 2010–13): Courtney + Fulford (by *Seacroft*); Clinton + Gifford (by *Dunsinane*); Cary, Edgcumbe Fortescue, Grenville, Peverell, Russell & Tracy (by *Hasledene*) Pavilion built at **Playing Fields** (acquired 1955) |
| 1965 | *Tamar* (sold 2011) – Deputy Principal's house |
| 1966/1967 | *Midway*/*Wandale* – Principal's House; *St Olan's*/*Seymour* |
| 1971 | First students awarded degrees: post-graduate training began |
| 1978 | *Kempston* Hall (dem. 1987) & *Kempston Lodge* (sold 2009) |
| 1979 | **Spicer Building** and **Memorial Garden;** also **Stork Building** |
| 1 September 1988 | Became Rolle Faculty of Education after merger with Plymouth Polytechnic & Exeter College of Art & Design |
| 1992/1995 | Rolle campus of University of Plymouth/*Kimsbury* acquired |
| 16 April 2002 | Margaret Hodge MBE, MP (Department of Education & Skills) opened the **Owen Building** |
| 31 August 2008 | Move to Rolle Building, University of Plymouth at Plymouth |

## Chapter 12: A NEW ROLLE

Having analysed the acquisition and disposal of the principal properties associated with Rolle College over its 62 years of existence as seen in the chart on page 220, we turn to the experience of someone who was involved in the conversion of office space back into a three-bed semi, three years after Rolle's move to Plymouth in 2008.

### "Converting office space back to a 3-bed semi" by Maureen White

We had lived in Exmouth for 25 years but had wanted to move nearer to the centre of the town so, when we saw that three properties were advertised for sale under the heading "1 Douglas Avenue", we decided to submit a closed bid for one of the semis – *Kimsbury*. Although our bid was under the guideline figure of £200,000, it was accepted, possibly because our's was a cash offer and not dependant on a sale. We had chosen the semi the furthest from Salterton Road as we thought it would be quieter than *Tamar* or the detached *Seymour*. Rolle College had bought *Tamar* in 1965 and *Seymour* in 1967 whereas *Kimsbury* had not been bought by the College until 1995.

Although *Kimsbury* had not been used by the University of Plymouth for three years when we bought it in 2011, we were surprised to see that filing cabinets, tables and other office furniture had been left, even with paperwork still in place, as this photo of what was originally a bathroom, shows. We found that the University were not interested in most of those items when we mentioned them to them so we found ourselves donating them to friends – Exmouth Rowing Club was particularly pleased with the filing

cabinets and 14 fire doors! The heavy curtains from the room which we assumed had been used for audio-visual studies came in useful for our daughter when her job entailed her needing to sleep during the daytime.

We were fortunate that we still had our previous house so we could give our builders free reign for the eight months they needed to convert educational offices for lecturers back to residential accommodation. By removing a

chimney (photo left) we gained a lot more space, including a laundry room. Fortunately, many of the original features, such as picture rails, remained from the days when *Kimsbury* had been a 3-bed semi built in the 1930s. Interestingly, the house has a basement. However, we found that the best points from our perspective were the fact that Rick could use the original garage for his music practice and the view from our Juliet balcony loft conversion is amazing as, not only can we see over part of the Rolle campus, but also over much of the town, including Holy Trinity Church and, even more importantly, the sea out towards Dawlish as can be seen here:

*Seymour*, *Tamar* and *Kimsbury* are shown on this 2002 Campus Plan:

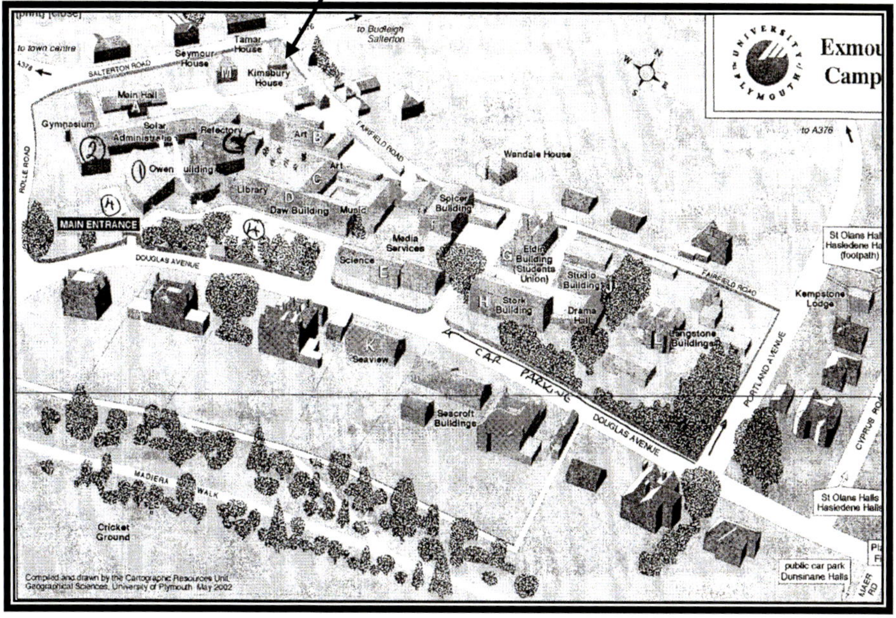


Of the original buildings on the main site, *Eldin*, *Langstone* & *Langstone Cottage* still remain, albeit requiring care and attention, as do the newer *Daw*, *Spicer*, *Stork* and *Owen* buildings. The full extent of the campus is outlined in red on this plan of 2005:

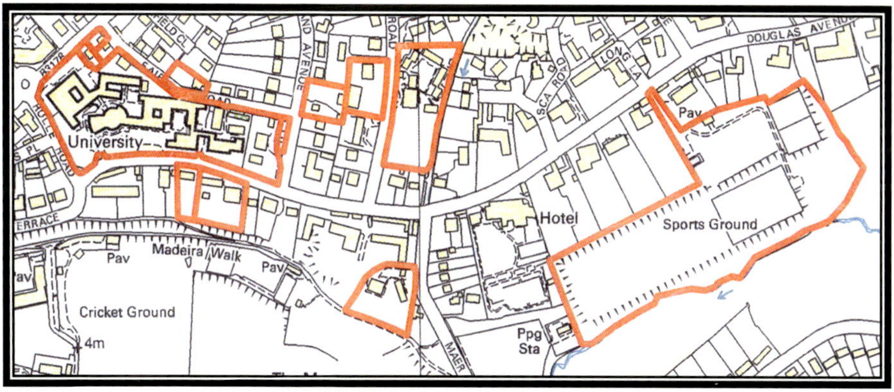


As can be seen there, by far the largest individual piece of property remaining is the Rolle Playing Fields (Sports Ground on the plan above). This was sold to Eagle One in the autumn of 2009. They in turn passed the leasehold to the

Gloucestershire Boys Brigade who held summer camps there until 2014. The site has also been the venue for many youth football and rugby matches. The future for this valuable green field site is uncertain at the time of going to press although there was talk in 2012/13 that it could be a possible new home for Exmouth Rugby Club. Whether a scene such as the one shown here from the 1983-4 Rolle College Prospectus will ever be seen again is unknown.

During the seven years since the University of Plymouth moved its Rolle Campus from Exmouth, all of the properties external to the main site have been sold. Some, such as *Wandale*, *Tamar* and *Kempston Lodge* remain as private homes while others have been demolished to make way for modern housing developments – *Hasledene* has become Cyprus Gardens (below) while *Seacroft* and *Seacroft Lodge* have made way for Roswell Court Assisted Living complex. Some names have been retained

such as happened in the case of *St. Hilarian* Hall of Residence in Portland Avenue. When that was demolished in 2000, it was replaced by a block of exclusive apartments but retained the *St. Hilarian* name. *Ferniehurst* at 19 Douglas Avenue, demolished in 1996, was replaced by a similarly-named Nursing Home.

Although, by his own admission, Andrew Bailey bailed out early on hearing of Rolle's demise, others had set to to try and save the site (or some of it) for future generations of Exmouthians.

## A ROLLER-COASTER experience for Rolle Centre Directors

It was not to be easy or straightforward to save the site as the first chairman of Rolle Exmouth Limited (REL), Roy Pryke, summarised on 20th July 2011:

> "It has been a **roller-coaster experience** and at times we have felt that we would not make it. But the University kept us fully informed and in the end we have the desired outcome. We now have three years to make it work. It is a big, exciting challenge and we shall need genuine support from the community to make it into a success story for Exmouth."

Later in the second issue of *The Rolle Centre Newsletter* (Spring 2012), he wrote on behalf of his fellow Directors of REL that the share issue in the six weeks ending 11th May 2012 had produced a remarkable response in that:

> "People bought 23,051 shares at £5 each, yielding a total of £115,255. There are now 742 shareholders in Rolle Exmouth Ltd. Additionally donations stand at £750. We believe this is already the most successful public fund-raising effort in local history. This result and the two open days at Rolle, attended by more than 700 people, demonstrate the amount of interest and goodwill there is in Exmouth and surrounding area."

At that stage, the Directors had applied to the Coastal and Communities Fund and were exploring other possible sources of funding as the plan was to bring the buildings back into use in phases, starting with the *Owen* Building. However, that funding was not forthcoming and the Newsletter of September 2012, mentioned that £350,000 was the amount needed for the whole of the first year from shares and grants. In addition, detailed surveys had shown that the likely costs of refurbishment were more then four times the anticipated sum and approximately £2.5m was required before the revenue flow could be established to make the business plan work.

Early in 2013, shareholders were told that REL had not secured European Development Funding although a forum held at Bicton had been encouraging as it had confirmed that those attending would support a project based on the three pillars of education & training, community & arts, business & enterprise.

The first scheduled shareholders' meeting was held on 26th June 2013. By November of that year, shareholders were being told that an option had been negotiated with Plymouth University for the acquisition of the whole 6.7 acre site, including the Portland Avenue end, previously designated to be sold separately for housing – an exceptionally important parcel of land for the future of Exmouth because of its history, location and size. Key objectives remained vocational training facilities, promotion of enterprise and provision of community facilities. Therefore, although the three years mentioned by Roy Pryke as being the time allocated to REL to make the project work, expired in July 2014 without his hoped for "success story for Exmouth", this new partnership with Plymouth University seems to be making better progress.

Subsequent discussions established two criteria for the partnership:

- meeting the needs of Exmouth and East Devon communities for education and vocational training; business incubation/support and community facilities.
- creating the maximum value for the University.

In their fourth Annual Report (but only the second to shareholders) published in late summer 2014, REL Directors mentioned that Stride Treglown had been appointed to devise a master plan for the whole site to meet the requirements of both Plymouth University and REL. By 1st December 2014, it was announced that REL had been awarded a grant of £99,000 by Social Investment Business (SIB) group from the Community Ownership and Management of Assets Feasibility Fund to develop plans for the future of the site. That planning and feasibility work should be completed in April 2015.

Ever since starting this book, I had been hoping that its launch might coincide with a new phase in the life of the former Rolle College site and, amazingly, on the day "Exmouth's ROLLE" goes to the printers – 26th March 2015 – a press release from the new Chairman of REL, Deborah Hallett, has announced "ROLLE CENTRE REOPENING FOR FESTIVAL PRODUCTION". Plymouth University have given permission for 18 matinée and evening performances of "Jason and the Argonauts" to be performed by the Devon-based theatre company *Four of Swords* between 25th May and 6th June during the 19th Exmouth Festival. The performances will be in the Owen building where the circular atrium with its mezzanine and skylight will be transformed into "the ancient Colchean's midsummer festival, complete with taiko drumming", according to Sarah White, co-founder of *Four of Swords*.

After standing empty for almost seven years, there is very little evidence of any vandalism to the buildings, only normal wear and tear, showing that those living in or visiting Exmouth still respect this educational site and hope for its reinstatement for future generations to enjoy. As Deborah comments:

> "most importantly the gates of the Rolle site will be open again and I hope the people of Exmouth will enjoy the productions and gain a sense for what the future Rolle Centre will offer."

# List of Principal Sources

**PRIMARY**

## Dissertation

1973: 16 December: AVF Conridge's Inservice B. Ed. Course dissertation

## Documents

1933: *The Case For The Improvement of Spelling* (p. 1, 4, 10, 20/1)

## Insight

1968: 22 January: *Bar In Sight At Last & Background Facts* (No 19 p 1)
25 October: *On last legs or just B.Ed. ridden?* (No. 33 p.1)

## Interviews

2012: 11 September: Edna Ireland

## Letters

**a) written from Southlands School, Exmouth**

1926: 11 February: Miss E.C.E.V. (Betty) Nottingham to L. Elmhirst
13 February:
27 May: On embossed Southlands School writing paper
15 June:
7 July:

**b) from other sources**

1962: 15 October: Information about interview at Rolle College

## Personal Diaries

Daphne Barnes: 1962 – 1966 inclusive:

## Planning Application

1915: 17 August: Exmouth Urban District Council re *Fairfield*
5357A-0/P/1456 1915

## Rolle Centre Reports

2012 – 2014 4 from Rolle Exmouth Ltd. (2 for shareholders)

## Rolle College Prospectuses

1966 September: *Qualifications for Admission* (page 16)
1973-4 Aerial view of campus and photographs

## Rolle College Students' Union Handbook

1967 – 1968 *Sick Bay* (page 11)

**Rolle Sportlight**
1969: 1st October: *Student Centre Offers New Amenities*
Changing Rooms yet to be completed

**Southlands School Magazines**
Number 43: 1937: *School Calendar* (p. 3), *S.S.J.B.L.N.U.* (p. 11)
*Geographical Society* (p. 12), *Mrs Quicke* (p. 25)
S.S.O.G.A. Secretary's report (p.18)
Number 44: 1938: *From yacht Equinox on June 29th in Lerwick* (p. 5–7)
*Examination Successes & School Calendar* (p. 23)
*Charles Ware, School Porter for over 31 years* (p.31)
*VALE. MISS LEIGH* (p.33)
Number 45: 1939: *CIRCLE 35 – Joan Campbell* (p. 53)
Number 46: 1940: *Mrs Percy Vinter & Miss Dorothy Bannon* (p. 21/22)
*Report of Scholarship Committee* (p. 23)
Number 47: 1941: *CIRCLE 35 – Joan Campbell* (p. 41)
Number 48: 1942: *Miss Hoyle's Letter* (p. 2)

**Tickets**
1964: 23 May: *Fancy Dress Rag Ball*
19 June: *Going Down Ball*
10 December: *Christmas Ball*

**SECONDARY**

**Books and Booklets**
Kay, Diana & Mills, Robert: (1992) *Refugees or Migrant Workers? European Volunteer Workers in Britain 1946 – 1951*
Kennerley, Alston(2000):*The Making of the University of Plymouth ch 7 Rolle*
Kimble, George H T (1938): *Geography in the Middle Ages* (p. 8 of 314)
Morris, W F (1928): *Operative Geographies; British Isles*

**Interviews and Exhibitions**
1992: 28 December: *Elisabeth Frink* by Sarah Kent at British Library
1996: 1 August: Professor Andrew Quicke on *Diana Elena Harris*
2004: May: Dr AEL Davis on *Archive of female mathematicians*
2015: February: *Secret Army Exhibition* at Beaulieu, Hampshire

**Letters**
**From University of Sussex Library Special Collection on concentric.net**
1870 – 1910 Letters 3, 19 & 103 written by William Hale White to Richard and/or Sarah Colenutt

## Newspapers

**The Devon and Exeter Gazette**

| | | |
|---|---|---|
| 1885: | 30 October: | Adverts for *Southlands* and *Fairfield Schools* (p. 7) |
| 1902: | 3 June: | *Southlands Sch. Fairfield, Exmouth* Advert (page 4) |
| 1905: | 15 December: | *Exmouth* (page 14) |
| 1915: | 8 December: | *Southlands School Exmouth Extension of Buildings*-5 |
| 1923: | 26 July: | *Shakespeare Festival. Southlands School Players* |
| 1930: | 4 March: | *Children's Home. Great Work of an Exmouth Charity* |
| 1937: | 8 January: | *Exmouth and Protection against Fire* |
| 1942: | 11 December: | Advert (page 1) re *Sale of Furnishings & equipment* |

**Exeter and Plymouth Gazette**

| | | |
|---|---|---|
| 1881: | 7 September: | Advert (page 1) |
| 1891: | 27 August: | Advert (page 1) |
| 1891: | 23 October: | Advert (Page 7) |
| 1902: | 19 December: | *Prize Distribution at Southlands School, Exmouth The Lord Bishop of Exeter present* (page 9)<br>*Prize Distributions at Exeter School* (page 9) |
| 1908: | 13 March: | *Exmouth News* |
| 1915: | 8 October: | (page 8) |
| 1931: | 3 June: | *LITLEHAM-CUM-EXMOUTH's NEW VICAR* |
| 1942: | 2 January: | Advert |
| 1946: | 15 November: | *Langstone, Exmouth* – advert page 1 |

**Exeter Flying Post**

| | | |
|---|---|---|
| 1896: | 4 April: | *Exmouth Chatter* section (page 5) |

**Exmouth Chronicle**

| | | |
|---|---|---|
| 1959: | 11 July: | *Daw Building opened at College* |

**Exmouth Herald**

| | | |
|---|---|---|
| 1988: | 17 June: | *College chiefs quit over merger plans* |
| 1988: | 24 June: | *Lecturers to retire, then return to work* |
| 1990: | 6 April: | *They're lapping it up at Rolle* |

**Exmouth and East Devon Journal**

| | | |
|---|---|---|
| 1981: | 25 September: | *Rolle College Principal off to Africa* |
| 1988: | 25 June: | *Rolle moves into a new era* |

**Exmouth Journal**

| | | |
|---|---|---|
| 1971: | 11 December: | *War hero to be Rolle College principal* |

1972: 30 September: *New principal settles in at Rolle College*
1976: 24 July: *Rolle College 'favoured' not 'victim'*
1978: 1 April: *Leaving, but he's not forgetting Rolle College*
1981: 21 February: *Keeping it in the family!*
1981: 14 November: *Dr Michael Preston new principal of Rolle*
1986: 24 May: *Boost for Rolle College*
1988: 9 July: *Rolle lecturer Les Johnston to lay down the law to Chinese*
2002: 12 November: *University shake-up*
2012: 24 May: *Remainder of Rolle campus* (page 7)

**The Independent**
1992: 7 February: *Joslyn Owen's Obituary*

**London Gazette**
1942: 23 October: Executor's Notice re ROBERT TUCKER PAIN

**Telegraph**
2009: 17 July: Elizabeth Catherine Todd's Obituary

**Times Higher Education Supplement**
1988: 24 June: Advert for *Dean of Faculty of Education*

**The Western Morning News**
1943: 1 May: *FAREWELL GIFTS (also 26 June 1943)*
1945: 27 April: *TRAINING OF TEACHERS* – p. 2
1945: 27 August: *DEVON SCHEMES – Plans to be considered by CC*
1946: 17 June: *Minister opens Devon College* (p. 3)
2002: 2 November: *School's Industry Link*
2007: 20 July: *Frink Sculptures Overwhelm Estimates to Make £1m at Sale*

**The Western Times**
1885: 20 November: Advert–*School for Girls on High School system* (p. 6)
1886: 10 February: *College of Preceptors Local Examinations Christmas 1885* (page 3)
1891: 24 April: Advert
1900: 4 May: Education advert (page 4) *Holmewood School*
1901: 27 July: *Fairfield, Exmouth* (Advert page 1)
1919: 12 December: Advert (page 5)
1920: 25 June: *Fairy Dancing. Pleasing Outdoor Entertainment at Exmouth* (page 8)
1946: 1 November: *Beware of "Body Snatching" Bewildered World*

1948: 4 June: *WOMEN ONLY When Exmouth Training College Reopens* (page 7)

**Street Directories**

1830 Pigot's Directory of Devon and Cornwall, p. 211
1850 White's History Gazetteer and Directory of Devonshire, p. 235
1857 Billing's Directory and Gazetteer of the County of Devon, p. 483
1878 Harrod's Royal County Directory of Devonshire, page 298
1897 Kelly's Directory of Devonshire, pages 276, 278
1902 Kelly's Directory of Devon – Exmouth Section & Commercial
1906 Kelly's Directory of Devonshire, pages 299, 304
1914 Kelly's Directory of Devonshire, pages 306, 311
1919 Kelly's Directory of Devonshire, page 292
1921 Smith's Directory of Reading, page 286
1923 Kelly's Directory of Devonshire & Cornwall, page 306
1926 Kelly's Directory of Devonshire
1930 Kelly's Directory of Devonshire
1939 Kelly's Directory of Devonshire
1944 Kelly's Directory of Reading, page 327
1947 Street Directory and Gazetteer for Exmouth, page 123
1948–9 Street Directory and Gazetteer for Exmouth
1951–2 Street Directory and Gazetteer for Exmouth
1952–3 Street Directory and Gazetteer for Exmouth, Littleham, Withycombe
1961 Kelly's Directory of Devonshire Commercial Directory
1970 Kelly's Directory of Devonshire Commercial Directory

**The University of Reading Calendars**

1920 – 1946 with reference to W.F. Morris and Joan Campbell

**Websites**

beauxartslondon.co.uk: Biography of Elisabeth Frink
books.google.co.uk: Alumni Cantabrigienses (Page 468)
britainfromabove.org.uk: 1928 Southlands School on Rolle Road, Exmouth
freebmd: Births, Marriages and Deaths
findmypast.co.uk: British India Office Births and Baptisms
British Newspaper Collection
genesreunited: Censuses 1841 – 1911 inclusive
havant.gov.uk: Burial records of Havant United Reformed Church
wikipedia: Definitions

## Other recent titles by author and historian Daphne Barnes-Phillips

### George Palmer School in photographs – 1907 to 2014

An updated photographic record of events in the life of George Palmer School, Reading from 1907 to 2014. NOW with COLOUR photographs.

48 pages. **Price £7.50** ISBN 978 1 897715 18 5

### The Top of Whitley revisited – 1840 to 2013

Following the success of her first book – ***The Top of Whitley*** – in 2002, Daphne Barnes-Phillips was contacted by many people with their own memories and photographs of the Spring Gardens area of Reading, Berkshire, England so, when the original print-run sold out, she decided that this updated version was a better option than a reprint.

160 pages **Price £9.95** ISBN 978 1 897715 22 2

### Taylor-Made Jackpot – sheep, horses, cats and dogs

With ancestral backgrounds as diverse as shepherding in South America and Childrey, Berkshire, Jack and Barbara developed his father's back-street bookie enterprise into a thriving Bookmakers' Business in Reading and beyond. They successfully raced and bred horses and greyhounds then relaxed at home with their cats! Includes 2 colour photo sections.

176 pages. **Price £12.95** ISBN 978 1 897715 17 8

### This is our School: Reading British School, 1811 – 2011

Built in two months in 1810; considered unsuitable for a Board School in 1902; it still stands in Southampton Street two centuries after it started life as Reading Lancasterian School on 8th January 1811. In *This is our School*, Daphne brings us tales of educational life in the 19th century, through the characters involved in it, including George Palmer MP, who was School Secretary for 50 years while running his biscuit factory.

208 pages. **Price £9.95** ISBN 978 1 897715 12 9

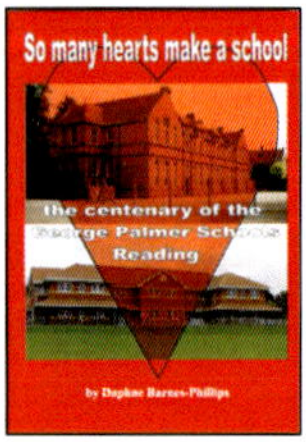


### So many hearts make a school – the centenary of GPS

Daphne, born and raised just a quarter of a mile from George Palmer Infant, Junior, Senior and Central Schools, recalls her own memories, and those of 50 other pupils and staff across the 100 years that are celebrated in this book. Hours of research at Berkshire Records Office, Reading Library and on-line showed up facts and figures previously unknown to most pupils, staff and governors throughout the century.

240 pages. **Price £12.95** ISBN 978 1 897715 07 2

**All books are fully illustrated with black & white and/or colour photographs and available from: Corridor Press, 19 Portland Avenue, Exmouth, Devon, EX8 2BS email: corridorpress@yahoo.co.uk or phone: 01395 263494.**

**All Prices include postage & packing within UK.**

**Please make cheques payable to "Corridor Press".**